The 1820 Russian Survey of the Khanate of Shirvan:

A Primary Source on the Demography and Economy of an Iranian Province prior to its Annexation by Russia

Books by George Bournoutian

Eastern Armenia in the Last Decades of Persian Rule, 1807–1828 *
The Khanate of Erevan under Qajar Rule, 1795–1828 *
A History of the Armenian People, 2 vols. three editions *
A History of Qarabagh: An Annotated Translation of Mirza Jamal Javanshir Qarabaghi's "Tarikh-e Qarabagh" *
The Chronicle of Zak`aria of K`anak`er *
Armenians and Russia, 1626–1796: A Documentary Record *
The History of Vardapet Arak`el of Tabriz, 2 vols. *
Tigranes II and Rome (Manandyan)*

Russia and the Armenians of Transcaucasia, 1797–1889: A Documentary Record
The Chronicle of Abraham of Crete
Abraham of Erevan's History of the Wars, 1721–1738
The Journal of Zak`aria of Agulis
Two Chronicles on the History of Karabagh
The Travel Accounts of Simeon of Poland
Simeon of Erevan's Jambr
Esayi Hasan Jalaleants's Brief History of the Aghuank` Region
Arak`el of Tabriz, Book of History
A Concise History of the Armenian People from the Earliest Times to the Present (currently in its sixth edition)
Spanish edition: *Historia Sucinta del Pueblo Armenio* (Buenos Aires)
Turkish edition: *Ermeni Tarihi: Ermeni Halkının Tarihine Kısa Bir Bakiş* (Istanbul)
Arabic edition: *Mawgaz Tarikh al-Sha`b al-Armani* (Cairo)
Armenian edition: *Hay Zhogovrdi Hamarod Patmut`yun* (Yerevan)
Russian edition: *Kratkaia Istoriia Armianskogo Naroda* (Yerevan-Moscow)
Japanese edition: *Arumenia-jin no Rekishi* (Tokyo)
Tarikh-e Qarahbagh: Persian translation of the introduction and the annotations of *A History of Qarabagh* (Tehran)
Tarikh-e Jangha: Persian translation of Abraham of Erevan's *History of the Wars* (Tehran)
The 1823 Russian Survey of the Karabagh Province: A Primary Source on the Demography and Economy of Karabagh in the Early 19th Century
From Tabriz to St. Petersburg: Iran's Mission of Apology to Russia in 1829
The 1819 Russian Survey of the Khanate of Sheki
The 1829–1832 Russian Surveys of the Khanate of Nakhichevan

* Out of Print.

The 1820 Russian Survey of the Khanate of Shirvan

A Primary Source on the Demography and Economy of an Iranian Province prior to its Annexation by Russia

Annotated Translation from the original 1867 Edition
with an Introduction, Explanatory Remarks and Appendix

by

George A. Bournoutian

Gibb Memorial Trust

Published by

The E. J. W. Gibb Memorial Trust

Opisanie Shirvanskoi provintsii: English
The 1820 Russian Survey of the Shirvan province: a primary source on the demography and economy of an Iranian province prior to its annexation by Russia/ annotated translation from the original 1867 edition, with an introduction, explanatory remarks and appendix by George a. Bournoutian

1. Iran—Caucasus--Shirvan (Azerbaijan)—Population—Statistics. 2. Households—Azerbaijan—Statistics. 3. Revenue—Azerbaijan—statistics. 4. Taxation—Azerbaijan—statistics. 5. Registers—Azerbaijan—statistics. 6. Economic conditions

Madatov, V. G. (Valerian Grigorevich) and Mogilevskii, P. I. (Pavel Ivanovich)

Printed in the United Kingdom by Short Run Press, Exeter

ISBN 978-1-90972-480-8

Further details of the E. J. Gibb Memorial Trust and its publications
are available at the Trust's website

www.gibbtrust.org

To:

Vadim Gomoz

Прими с улыбкою, мой друг,
Свободной музы [κλειω] приношенье

Pushkin: *The Prisoner of the Caucasus*

Contents

Transliteration, Geographical Names and Dates

Persian, Russian and Armenian terms, with minor deviations, are transliterated according to the Library of Congress tables, without the use of diacritical marks. However, commonly used terms, place names and Anglicized forms (e.g. hajji, mullah, sheikh, shah, bazaar, caravansary, khan, etc.) remain unchanged. Since Persian was the literary and administrative language of Shirvan, the Persian pronunciation will be transcribed for most proper names; hence Mostafa, Hoseyn, Mohammad, Ebrahim and Esma`il instead of Mustafa, Hussein, Muhammad/Mamad/Memet, Ibrahim, Isma`il, etc. The Russian letter "E" is transcribed as "Ye" when it appears at the beginning of a name; hence Yermolov instead of Ermolov and Yerevan instead of Erevan. Russian names such as Alexander, Nicholas and Paul appear in their westernized versions.

The Russian spelling for proper and place names listed in the survey posed a problem. The two Russian officials, who prepared the survey, tried to phonetically transcribe the place names supplied by the *mirzas* (scribes/accountants) of Mostafa Khan from the *daftars* (tax registers), which were written in Persian.

Unfortunately, the Russian alphabet lacks the Arabo-Persian letters of غ, ق, ه, ح, and ع. In addition, the phonetic values of the local Turkish dialect (*Torki*)[1] could not be reproduced in Russian. In 1922 Soviet officials and local intellectuals, living in the newly-created republic of Soviet Azerbaijan, in order to reduce the influence of Islam and Iran, as well as to instill a much-needed national identity, introduced a Latin alphabet, similar to the new Latin alphabet created in Turkey for much the same reasons.

In 1939, a new alphabet, using the Cyrillic script, was introduced on Stalin's order. Stalin wished to sever any ties between Turkey and the various Turkic people of the Soviet Union. In 1958, that alphabet was slightly modified and remained in use until the collapse of the Soviet Union. In 1991, the Republic of Azerbaijan reverted to using the former Latin alphabet, with minor changes. A year later, however, the alphabet was again modified with the removal of ä, replacing it with ə (the "schwa"), which had been used from 1929 to 1991.

The following transliteration table for the Azeri alphabet indicates the various changes and will hopefully enable readers to find their way through this maze.

---

1 According to the historian `Abbas-qoli Aqa Bakikhanov, this dialect (now referred to as Azeri) was a combination of Ottoman Turkish, Qumuq, Noghay, Jaghatai; see *Golestan-e Eram*: based on the critical text by A. Alizade, Baku, 1970 (reprinted in Tehran 1383/2004), 37; see also I. P. Petrushevskii, N. G. Bogdanova & Ya. M. Pritykin, eds., *Kolonial'naia politika rossiiskogo tsarizma v Azerbaidzhane v 20–60-kh gg. XIX v.*, part I (Moscow-Leningrad, 1936), 135. Modern linguists base the dialect spoken by the Oghuz Turks.

	Cyrillic		Latin				IPA
Persian	1939–1958	1958–1991	1922–1933	1933–1939	1991–1992	1992–	
ا	А а		**A a**				[ɑ]
ب	Б б		B ƀ	B в	**B b**		[b]
ج	Ҹ ҹ		C c	Ç ç	**C c**		[dʒ]
چ	Ч ч		Ç ç	C c	**Ç ç**		[tʃ]
د	Д д		**D d**				[d]
ی	Е е		**E e**				[e]
ع	Ә ә		Ə ə		Ä ä	**Ə ə**	[æ]

<table>
<tr><td>ف</td><td>Ф ф</td><td colspan="3">F f</td><td>[f]</td></tr>
<tr><td>گ</td><td>Ҝ ҝ</td><td>Ƣ ƣ</td><td colspan="2">G g</td><td>[ɟ]</td></tr>
<tr><td>غ</td><td>Ғ ғ</td><td>G g</td><td>Ƣ ƣ</td><td>Ğ ğ</td><td>[ɣ]</td></tr>
<tr><td>ح, ه</td><td>Һ һ</td><td colspan="3">H h</td><td>[h]</td></tr>
<tr><td>ی</td><td>Ы ы</td><td>I̦ ı̦</td><td>Ь ь</td><td>I ı</td><td>[ɯ]</td></tr>
<tr><td>ی</td><td>И и</td><td colspan="2">I i</td><td>İ i</td><td>[ɪ]</td></tr>
<tr><td>ژ</td><td>Ж ж</td><td colspan="2">Ƶ ƶ</td><td>J j</td><td>[ʒ]</td></tr>
<tr><td>ک</td><td>К к</td><td>Q q</td><td colspan="2">K k</td><td>[c], [ç],
[k]</td></tr>
<tr><td>ق</td><td>Г г</td><td>K k</td><td colspan="2">Q q</td><td>[ɡ]</td></tr>
</table>

ل	Л л	**L l**		[l]
م	М м	**M m**		[m]
ن	Н н	**N n**		[n]
ۆ	О о	**O o**		[ɔ]
و	Ө ө	Ө ө	**Ö ö**	[œ]
پ	П п	**P p**		[p]
ر	Р р	**R r**		[r]
س, ث, ص	С с	**S s**		[s]

ش	Ш ш		З з	**Ş ş**		[ʃ]
ط, ت	Т т		**T t**			[t]
و	У у		Y y	**U u**		[u]
و	Y ү		U u	Y y	**Ü ü**	[y]
ۋ, ڤ	В в		**V v**			[v]
ی	Й й	J j	J j		**Y y**	[j]
یَ	Я я	JA ja	JA ja		**YA ya**	[jɑ]
ێی	E e[1]	JE je	JE je		**YE ye**	[je]

<table>
<tr><td>عی</td><td>Э э[1]</td><td>E e</td><td colspan="3">E e</td><td>[e]</td></tr>
<tr><td>ۆی</td><td>Йо йо</td><td>JO jo</td><td colspan="2">JO jo</td><td>YO yo</td><td>[jɔ]</td></tr>
<tr><td></td><td>Ю ю</td><td>JY jy</td><td>JY jy</td><td>JU ju</td><td>YU yu</td><td>[ju]</td></tr>
<tr><td>ذ, ز, ض, ظ</td><td colspan="2">З з</td><td colspan="3">Z z</td><td>[z]</td></tr>
</table>

[1] In the beginning of a word and after vowels. The table is reproduced, with permission, from the excellent article by L. Hatcher, "Script change in Azerbaijan: acts of identity," *International Journal of the Sociology of Language*, 192 (2008), 105–116.

I have tried to find the present-day names and the current Azeri spelling (they appear in parentheses) of the villages and the nomad settlements named in the survey (see map 2). Today, the territory of the former khanate of Shirvan is situated within two administrative regions of the Republic of Azerbaijan: Aran and Dağlıq-Şirvan; the first has eighteen districts, while the second has only four. Any assistance from the readers to identify individuals or place names will be greatly appreciated.

The terms "Azerbaijan/Azerbaijani," "Persian/Iranian" and "South Caucasus" need clarification.

A) Although the overwhelming number of nineteenth-century Russian and Iranian,[2] as well as present-day European historians view the Iranian province of Azarbayjan and the present-day Republic of Azerbaijan as two separate *geographical* and *political* entities, modern Azeri historians and geographers view it a single state that has been separated into "northern" and "southern" sectors and which will be united in the future.[3] This unsubstantiated claim rests on a number of factors:

a) Although *politically* the two rarely formed one region, since the majority of the population of Iranian Azarbayjan spoke the same Turkic dialect as the overwhelming numbers of Muslim Tatars in the South Caucasus, modern Azerbaijani historians view the people and the two regions as one. One cannot argue that *linguistically* and, to a much lesser extent, *ethnically* and *religiously* (Shi`a form of Islam) the two regions are very similar and *could* be seen as one. Hence, after the rise of their national consciousness at the start of the twentieth century, it was convenient for the Muslim Tatars living in the South Caucasus to refer to themselves as Azeris and to their newly formed independent republic (1918) as Azerbaijan.[4] The objections of the weak and dying Qajar Iran were ignored.

b) The khanate of Nakhichevan and parts of southern Karabagh (the Qapanat) had been, for a short period, included in the administrative division of the Iranian province of Azarbayjan.

c) Following the Treaty of Gulistan, the khanates of Nakhichevan and Yerevan and their khans were subordinate to `Abbas Mirza, the commander-in-chief of the Iranian forces in Tabriz (Azarbayjan).

d) The *Tadhkirat Al-Muluk*,[5] an important Persian source on the administration of Iran in the last years of the Safavids, *seems* to include the three provinces of Chukhur-e Sa`d (Yerevan and Nakhichevan), Karabagh (Ganja and Karabagh) and Shirvan (Shirvan, Baku, Kuba and Sheki) as being under the governorship (*beglerbegi*) of Azarbayjan centered in Tabriz.[6]

---

[2] To be fair, one has to note that at least two nineteenth-century Russian sources occasionally confuse some of the khanates of the South Caucasus as being part of what they refer to as "Aderbaidzhan; see, P. G. Butkov, *Materialy dlia novoi istorii Kavkaza, s' 1722 po 1803* (St. Petersburg, 1869); II, 132, 139–140, 155; 176, 287, 318–320 and *Akty*, I, 93, 159, 611; III, 458, 366, 370. However, in other pages, both of these sources consider it as the Iranian province lying south of the Arax (Aras) River, see Butkov, I, 60, 109, *Akty*, III, 252, 291, 324. Iranian historians note that the region was known as "Aran" and was never referred to as Azerbaijan, for example see, *Asnadi az ravabe-te Iran ba mantaqe-ye qafqaz* (Tehran, 1993), 53–60.

[3] Stalin's unsuccessful occupation of Iran's Azarbayjan province in 1945-1946 spurred Azeri historians and politicians to accept the (earlier) Soviet notion of a "southern Azerbaijan" and "northern Azerbaijan," which had been separated by force.

[4] If *linguistic*, *ethnic* and *religious* criteria justify the union of two *politically* separate groups, then a part of Belgium belongs to France, parts of Kazakhstan and Ukraine belong to Russia, etc. In that case, the Azeris should not object that Nagorno-Karabakh is part of Armenia.

[5] Vladimir Minorsky, Trans. *Tadhkirat Al-Muluk* (London, 1943), 100–102.

[6] Upon careful examination, however, Minorsky's commentary reads: "The list starts in the north-west with the enumeration of the four governorships, those of Tabriz, Chukhur-e Sa`d, Qarabagh and Shirvan. The term Azarbayjan

As noted, in order to construct an Azerbaijani national history and identity based on the territorial definition of a nation, as well as to reduce the influence of Islam and Iran, the Azeri nationalists, prompted by Moscow devised an "Azeri" alphabet, which replaced the Arabo-Persian script. In the 1930s a number of Soviet historians, including the prominent Russian Orientalist, Ilya Petrushevskii, were instructed by the Kremlin to accept the totally unsubstantiated notion that the territory of the former Iranian khanates (except Yerevan, which had become Soviet Armenia) was part of an Azerbaijani nation.[7] Petrushevskii's two important studies dealing with the South Caucasus, therefore, use the term Azerbaijan and Azerbaijani in his works on the history of the region from the sixteenth to the nineteenth centuries.[8] Other Russian academics went even further and claimed that an Azeri nation had existed from ancient times and had continued to the present.[9] Since all the Russian surveys and almost all nineteenth-century Russian primary sources referred to the Muslims who resided in the South Caucasus as "Tatars" and not "Azerbaijanis,"[10] Soviet historians simply substituted Azerbaijani for Tatars.

Azeri historians and writers, starting in 1937, followed suit and began to view the almost three-thousand-year history of the region as that of Azerbaijan. The pre-Iranian, Iranian, and Arab eras were expunged. Anyone who lived in the territory of Soviet Azerbaijan was classified as Azeri; hence the great Iranian poet Nezami, who had written only in Persian, became the national poet of Azerbaijan.[11]

---

which stands before this enumeration refers *perhaps* (italics mine) to the whole four provinces, similarly to the "Khorasan" in the north-east, although such an *abusive use of the term* (italics mine) would be incorrect and not supported by geographical works. In fact, the province of the governor-general of Tabriz alone covered most of the historical Azarbayjan." Minorsky then lists the following districts as being under the *Beglerbegi* of Tabriz: Astara, Maragheh, Qarajedagh, Chors, Qapanat [present-day southern part of Zangezur in Armenia], Hashtrud, Mishkin, Sarab, Ardabil, Salmas, Marand, Khoy, Urmiyeh, parts of Mughan and parts of Talesh, *ibid.*,164–165.

[7] Minorsky, the other great specialist of the region, had left the country and did not follow this dictum; see his *Studies in Caucasian History* (London, 1953) and *A History of Sharvan and Darband* (Cambridge, 1958).

[8] I. P. Petrushevskii, N. G. Bogdanova & Ya. M. Pritykin, eds., *Kolonial'naia politika rossiiskogo tsarizma v Azerbaidzhane v 20-60-kh gg. XIX v.*, 2 parts (Moscow-Leningrad, 1936–1937) and I. P. Petrushevskii, *Ocherki po istorii feodal'nykh otnoshenii v Azerbaidzhane i Armenii v XVI-nachale XIX vv.* (Leningrad, 1949). Both sources wrongly include Nakhichevan (which was a part of the Armenian and Yerevan provinces from 1828 until 1920) as a part of "Azerbaijan."

[9] For example see, A. E. Krymskii, "Stranitsy iz istorii severnogo ili Kavkazskogo Azerbeidzhana (klassicheskoi Albanii). Sheki," *Sbornik statei k piatidesiatiletiiu nauchno-obshchestvennoi deiatel'nosti Sergeio Fedorovichu Ol'denburgu* (Leningrad, 1934), 369–384.

[10] See V. Grigor'ev, *Statisticheskoe opisanie Nakhichevanskoi Provintsii* (St. Petersburg, 1833); O. Evetskii, *Statisticheskoe opisanie Zakavkazskogo kraia* (St. Petersburg, 1835); I. Shopen, *Istoricheskii pamiatnik sostoianiia Armianskoi Oblasti v epokhu eia prisoedineniia k Rossiiskoi imperii* (St. Petersburg, 1852); *Opisanie Shekinskoi Provintsii sostavlennoe v 1819 g.* (Tiflis, 1866); *Opisanie Shirvanskoi Provintsii sostavlennoe v 1820 g.* (Tiflis, 1867); *Opisanie Karabagskoi Provintsii sostavlennoe v 1823 g.* (Tiflis, 1866); *Akty sobrannye Kavkazkoiu Arkheograficheskoiu Kommissieiu*, 12 vols. (Tiflis, 1866–1904); N. F. Dubrovin, *Zakavkaz'e ot 1803–1806 goda* (St. Petersburg, 1866) and his *Istoriia voiny i vladychsestva Russkikh na Kavkaze*, 6 vols. (St. Petersburg, 1871–1888); V. Potto, *Kavkazskaia voina v otdel'nykh ocherkakh, epizodakh, legendakh i biografiiakh*, 4 vols. (St. Petersburg, 1885–1888). Even the January 1897 official survey of the population of the Russian Empire, which was based on the languages spoken by the people, refers to the language of the Russian Muslims (excluding the Tajik, Ossetian, and the Daghestani languages) as "Turkic-Tatar," see N. A. Troynitskii, ed. *Pervaia vseobshchaia perepis' naseleniia Rossiiskoi Imperii* (St. Petersburg, 1905).

[11] The same policy has been adopted in Turkey; it views the Hittites as the ancestors of the Turks and ignores the Greek, Armenian and Kurdish historical presence. One can imagine the global outcry if the present-day Spanish-

Although after Stalin's death arguments rose between Azerbaijani historians and Soviet Iranologists dealing with the history of the region in ancient times (specifically the era of the Medes),[12] no Soviet historian dared to question the use of the term Azerbaijan or Azerbaijani in modern times. As late as 1991, the Institute of History of the Academy of Sciences of the USSR, published a book by an Azeri historian, in which it not only equated the "Tatars" with the present-day Azeris, but the author, discussing the population numbers in 1842, also included Nakhichevan and Ordubad in "Azerbaijan." The author, just like Petrushevskii, totally ignored the fact that between 1828 and 1921, Nakhichevan and Ordubad were first part of the Armenian Province and then part of the Yerevan guberniia and had only become part of Soviet Azerbaijan, some eight decades later.[13]

Serious historians and geographers[14] agree that after the fall of the Safavids, and especially from the mid-eighteenth century, the territory of the South Caucasus was composed of the khanates of Ganja, Kuba, Shirvan, Baku, Talesh, Sheki, Karabagh, Nakhichevan and Yerevan, all of which were under Iranian suzerainty (see map 1).[15] Following the conquest of the former Iranian khanates of Baku, Shirvan, Sheki, Karabagh and Talesh, the Russians combined them into the "Military District of Muslim Provinces," while Kuba and Derbent were made part of the "Daghestan Military District."[16] After General Yermolov formally annexed the khanates of Sheki (1819), Shirvan (1820) and Karabagh (1822),[17] they remained part of the "Military District of Muslim Provinces." Following the Second Russo-Iranian War (1826–1828), the khanates of Yerevan and Nakhichevan were combined to form the "Armenian Province." At the end of the Russo-Turkish War (1828–1829), the *pashaliks* of Akhalkalak and Akhaltsikh were added to Georgia (see map 1).[18]

In 1840, tsarist policy, which favored a more uniform system for the region, consolidated all of South Caucasus into two provinces (*guberniias*): the Georgian-Imeretian and the Caspian. Georgia, together with the Armenian, Elisavetpol (Ganja) provinces and the above *pashaliks* were made part of the Georgian-Imeretian Province, while the rest of the former Iranian khanates formed the Caspian Province.

---

speaking nations of Central and South America not only erased their pre-Columbian history, but viewed it as belonging to the heritage of Spain.

[12] See the recent article by Harun Yilmaz, "A Family Quarrel: Azerbaijani Historians against Soviet Iranologists," *Journal of the International Society for Iranian Studies*, volume 48 (no. 5, September 2015), 769–783.

[13] D. I. Ismail-Zade, *Naselenie gorodov Zakavkazskogo kraia v XIX-nachale XX v.* (Moscow, 1991), 110. It is indeed mind-boggling that the Academy of Sciences, the highest scientific body of the Soviet Union, ignored such a blatant and purposeful falsehood.

[14] The best and the most objective source of the geographical divisions is the recent atlas by Arthur Tsutsiev, *Atlas of the Ethno-Political History of the Caucasus* (New Haven, 2014).

[15] See also *ibid.*, maps 2, 3 and 5.

[16] The khanate of Ganja (renamed Elisavetpol) was made part of Georgia in 1806; see *ibid.*, maps 6 and 7.

[17] As will be noted these three khanates had, between 1805 and 1807, become Russian protectorates and, by formal treaties, had kept their internal autonomy; see Introduction.

[18] See Tsutsiev, maps 7 and 8. For a detailed report on these administrative divisions, see *Kolonial'naia politika*, I, 261–264.

In 1844, Tsar Nicholas I ordered the consolidation of the entire region of the Caucasus and the South Caucasus into a single unit called the *Kavkazskii krai* and appointed Prince Michael Vorontsov (1782-1856) as its Viceroy. In 1846, Vorontsov decided to split the South Caucasus into four *guberniias*: 1–Tiflis (the former Georgian kingdoms, the Armenian Province and the khanate of Ganja), 2–Kutais (Imeret`i, Akhalkalak and Akhaltsikh), 3–Shemakha (former Baku, Shirvan, Sheki and Karabagh khanates) and 4–Derbent (the former Kuba and Derbent khanates). In 1849, he separated the former Armenian Province (khanates of Yerevan and Nakhichevan) and the Alexandropol (Shuragel/Gyumri) district from the Tiflis *guberniia* and formed a fifth, the Yerevan guberniia.[19] In 1864, the new viceroy, Grand Duke Michael, initiated new changes. The Shemakha Province was divided into the Baku Province (the former Baku, Kuba, Karabagh, Sheki and Shirvan khanates) and the Daghestan Province (the former Derbent khanate and the lands of the various tribes of southern Daghestan), while the former *soltanates* of Jar, Belokan and Ilisu formed the small Zakatal district (*okrug*).[20] By 1868, South Caucasus experienced yet another division. It was divided into five regions: The Elisavetpol Province (created from the former Ganja, Sheki and Karabagh khanates and the *soltanates* of Kazakh and Shamshadil), and the Yerevan, Tiflis, Kutais and Baku provinces. Following the Russo-Turkish War of 1877–1878, Russia obtained additional territory in the Southwest Caucasus (the Kars and Batum *oblasts*).[21]

In 1918, after the collapse of the Russian Empire, the Tiflis and Kutais *guberniias*, together with the Batum *oblast* created the independent Georgian Republic (to 1921); the Baku and Elisavetpol guberniias, declared their independence (to 1920), and, despite Iranian protests, took the name of Azerbaijan (as noted, the same designation as the historical region in northwestern Iran), while the Yerevan *guberniia* and the Kars *oblast* formed the independent Armenian Republic (to 1920). Following the partition of the Republic of Armenia (1920) and the Sovietization of the South Caucasus (1920–1921), the Soviet Republics of Georgia, Azerbaijan and Armenia, with major border alterations, became part of the Soviet Union until 1991.[22]

Since the collapse of the Soviet Union the current Azeri historians have not only continued to use the terms "northern" and "southern" Azerbaijan, but also assert that the present-day Armenian Republic was a part of northern Azerbaijan. In their fury over what they view as the "Armenian occupation" of Nagorno-Karabakh [which incidentally was an autonomous Armenian region within Soviet Azerbaijan], Azeri politicians and historians deny any historic Armenian presence in the South Caucasus[23] and add that all Armenian architectural monuments located in the present-day Republic of Azerbaijan are not Armenian but [Caucasian] Albanian.

---

[19] *Ibid.*, maps 8 and 9.

[20] *Ibid.*, map 10.

[21] *Ibid.*, map 10.

[22] *Ibid.*, maps 22–29.

[23] For example, see the baffling volume published by the Azerbaijan National Academy of Sciences, *The Iravan Khanate: The Russian occupation and the relocation of Armenians to the lands of North Azerbaijan* (Baku, 2010).

B) All Persian sources of the time refer to their state as "Iran" and to themselves as "Irani" (Iranian). Thus, "Iran" will replace the Russian and western term "Persia" throughout the volume.

C) Russian sources of the time, refer to the territory south of the Caucasus Range as *Transcaucasia*, I have decided to forgo this biased term and to use instead the neutral term of "South Caucasus."

D) Maps of Soviet Azerbaijan, published prior to the collapse of the Soviet Union, used the Russian and Armenian designation for the main river, that is, the Arax, which separated Iran from the USSR. Iranian maps referred to it as the Aras River. Recent European, Azeri and Armenian maps, however, use the Azeri "Araz," the Turkish and Iranian "Aras," and the Armenian "Arax," depending on the country through which the river traverses. I have decided to use "Aras," the local designation used at the time.

Lastly, in this period, Russia used the Julian calendar, which, in the nineteenth century, was twelve days behind the Gregorian calendar employed in the West. In the same period, Iran used the Islamic lunar calendar of 354 days starting from the date of the Prophet Mohammad's departure from Mecca for Medina in AD 622. All dates are accom-panied in parentheses by their equivalents according to the Gregorian calendar.

Weights, Measures and Currencies

aghach: A league.
batman: A Persian weight measure, also known as *mann*. This weight varied greatly from region to region. The *batman* here refers to the Tabrizi *batman*, which equaled 3 kilos or 6.61 lbs.
chervonets: A Russian gold ruble minted during the reign of Catherine II. It contained 3.47 grams of gold and was worth 3 silver rubles or 5 Shirvani rubles.
chetvert: A Russian weight measure (literally a quarter) equal to 6 bushels or 126.41 lbs.
desiatin: A Russian measure equal to 2.7 acres.
funt: Russian weight equal to 410 grams (0.9028 lb.).
kharvar or khalvar: A Persian weight (literally an 'ass load'), weighing 100 *batmans* or 300 kilos.
mizani batman: 7 kilos or 15.69 lbs.
pud: Russian weight equal to 36 lbs.
stil: Russian weight measure of approximately a quarter of a pound of silk. There were 24 *stils* in a *batman* of silk and 48 *stils* in a *mizani batman* of silk.
taghar: A local weight measure equal to 50 *batmans* (330 lbs.) in Shirvan.

During the years 1805–1822 the khanates of Karabagh (1805–1822), Shirvan (1806–1820), and Sheki (1807–1819), in addition to Russian rubles, also used their own currency.[24] The local currency in Shirvan was the silver *abas*, from the Iranian *`abbasi*, referred to in the survey as the khan's money, Shirvani currency, or local rubles, which also equaled 100 local kopeks. Some of these coins had Russia's coat of arms overstruck on the obverse side. The survey calculates one Russian silver ruble as being equal to one ruble and 60 kopeks in local currency. The local Shirvani money continued to be used for more than a decade after the Russian annexation.

The Russian silver ruble minted from 1798 to 1885 contained 20.73 grams of silver and equaled 100 kopeks.

Note: With the exception of gold rubles, the survey lists all revenues collected in cash and kind in local rubles and equates it to the Russian currency at the last entry for each village or nomad pasture and at the end of each register.

---

[24] The khanates of Yerevan and Nakhichevan, which remained under Iranian control until late 1828, used Iranian currency.

Preface

My interest in the Caucasus began as a graduate student, when I chose to examine the social and economic history of the Khanate of Yerevan in the last years of Iranian rule as the topic for my doctoral dissertation. The work was based on the Russian survey, conducted in the Yerevan Province immediately after its annexation to Russia in 1828. It revealed unique data on the population, administration, land tenure and taxation of the khanate, and added a great deal of new information to our knowledge of the region.[25]

In order to paint a more accurate picture of Persian rule in the lands laying south of the Caucasus Mountains, I had to examine the system of land tenure and taxation of yet another Iranian khanate prior to its incorporation into the Russian Empire. Although I translated several accounts on the history of Karabagh during Iranian suzerainty, they lacked specific demographic and economic information detailed in the study on Yerevan.[26]

Years later, I discovered that the Russians had conducted four similar surveys after their annexation of Sheki (1819), Shirvan (1820), Karabagh (1823), and Nakhichevan (1829–1832). The first three suveys were produced in very small quantities and could not be found outside a handful of libraries in the Soviet Union. After a long search, I managed to find the 1823 Russian survey of Karabagh and published an annotated English translation, which was welcomed by scholars interested in the Caucasus.[27] It has taken me another four years to obtain a readable and complete 1820 survey of Shirvan, which I present here in an annotated English translation.[28]

In order to fit the 286 large (143 double) unnumbered pages and the small print into a more readable form, I have, once again, decided to reproduce the original tables in a narrative format without altering any of the data.[29] My explanations appear in brackets, and spelling variants appear in parentheses, while my comments appear

[25] See G. Bournoutian, *Eastern Armenia in the Last Decades of Persian Rule, 1807-1828: A Political and Socioeconomic Study of the Khanate of Erevan on the Eve of the Russian Conquest* (Malibu, 1982), revised and enlarged as The Khanate of Erevan Under Qajar Rule, 1795-1828 (New York, 1992).

[26] See G. Bournoutian, *A History of Qarabagh: An Annotated Translation of Mirza Jamal Javanshir Qarabaghi's "Tarikh-e Qarabagh"* (Costa Mesa, CA, 1994); *Two Chronicles on the History of Karabagh* (Costa Mesa, CA., 2009); and Esayi Hasan Jalaleants': *Brief History of the Aghuank` Region* (Costa Mesa, CA., 2009).

[27] G. Bournoutian, *The 1823 Russian Survey of the Karabagh Province: A Primary Source on the Demography and Economy of Karabagh in the early 19th Century* (Costa Mesa, CA., 2011 and 2012).

[28] I have also managed to obtain and publish annotated English translations the Russian surveys of Sheki and Nakhichevan; see *The 1819 Russian Survey of the Khanate of Sheki [Shakki]: A Primary Source on the Demography and Economy of an Iranian Province prior to its Annexation by Russia* (Costa Mesa, CA., 2016) and *The 1829–1832 Russian Surveys of the Khanate of Nakhichevan [Nakhjavan]: A Primary Source on the Demography and Economy of an Iranian Province prior to its Annexation by Russia* (Costa Mesa, CA., 2016).

[29] For an example, see a page of the original survey, which is reproduced on page 186 of this book.

immediately after my annotated English translation of the survey. I have followed the example of the survey and have used numerals instead of spelling out the numbers in the registers; hence "2 rubles" instead of "two rubles", "3 mullahs" instead of "three mullahs." The survey refers to the local currency used in Shirvan as the "Khan's money;" I have translated it as "local currency." The survey, as noted, calculates each Russian silver ruble as being equal to 1 ruble and 60 kopeks of local currency. I have also numbered the registers in order to identify them in the notes and comments. Finally, I apologize for the lack of an index, which was not possible to compile from material, which, after all, is a census.

I realize that some individuals may object to the notion that eastern Georgia and the khanates of the South Caucasus were within the Iranian realm prior to the Russian conquest. In response, I direct their attention to Article III of the 1813 Treaty of Gulistan (Golestan), which clearly states: "His Majesty, the Shah … acknowledges in his own name and that of his heirs, the sovereignty of Russia over the khanates of Ganja, now called Elisavetpol Province, as well as the khanates of Sheki, Shirvan, Derbent, Kuba, Baku, and Karabagh[30] and such parts of Talesh as is now possessed by the Russian Empire; in addition, Dagestan and Georgia, from the Province of Shuragel to Imereti, Guria, Mingrelia and Abkhazia, an all the lands and inhabitants that lie between them and the Caucasian Line and that of the Caspian Sea."[31] Moreover, Article I of the treaty between Russia and Mostafa Khan of Shirvan, states: "I, Mostafa Khan of Shirvan, in my name and that of my heirs, remove myself forever from the vassalage or honors of Persia (Iran) or any other state."[32] Article IV of the said treaty reads: "We shall not accept any letters from across the Arax (Aras)[33] River, from the sardars (commanders) of Baba Khan [Fath `Ali Shah], from Baba Khan himself, or from anyone else." Obviously, Russia considered the above khanates as part of the Iranian realm.

Furthermore, the letters from Fath `Ali Shah and `Abbas Mirza to the khans of the region and especially the response of the latter, also indicate their vassal status. In addition, the fiscal year, as indicated in the tax records of Shirvan, ended on March 21, the start of the Iranian New Year. In addition, many of the khans (including Mostafa Khan) and high-ranking officials sought refuge in Iran following the Russian takeover. Finally, much of the terminology used by the local officials, as well as the tax records, is in Persian, which remained the main literary language of the region until the twentieth century. It has to be remembered, however, that although the treaties between Russia and the three aforementioned khanates gave the khans control over the courts, administration and revenues, Russia viewed them as "protectorates" and not independent entities.

In conclusion, it is important to note that in the absence of similar data on demography

---

[30] Parts of the southern and western regions of Karabagh were disputed pending the final demarcation of the borders.

[31] T. Yuzefovich, *Dogovory Rossii s Vostokom* (St. Petersburg, 1869), 210.

[32] See number 1 in the appendix.

[33] Arax is in the original.

and revenues on the Iranian provinces south of the Aras River, the information on population, land tenure, taxation and administration of yet another Caucasian khanate can not only serve as primary material for historians of the early Qajar period, but also for scholars interested in the South Caucasus prior to its annexation by Russia.

Acknowledgments

I wish to express my sincere gratitude to Vadim Gomoz of Moscow, who provided me with a perfect scanned copy of the original survey of the Shirvan Province printed in Tiflis in 1867. Special thanks are due to Arsène Saparov for apprising me of the existence of a 1913 Russian gazetteer of the Caucasus. I am grateful to Professor Charles Melville for introducing the manuscript to the Gibb Memorial Series. The staff at the libraries of Columbia University and University of California at Berkeley and especially Edward Helmrich of the Inter-library Loan Services at Iona's Ryan Library located a number of primary sources. Joseph Rabb prepared the maps based on my sketches and my wife, Ani, read the final draft of the work. The Committee on Rank and Tenure at Iona approved my sabbatical and Iona's Committee on Faculty Development and Travel provided the needed travel funds. I thank them all. I am, of course, responsible for any shortcomings or inconsistencies, which is inevitable in a work abundant with figures and names.

Introduction

The lands lying south of the Caucasus Mountains, between the Caspian and the Black seas, had been a bone of contention between the Iranian Safavid shahs and Ottoman sultans throughout most of the sixteenth century. Following the 1639 Treaty of Qasr-e Shirin (Zohab), Iran gained suzerainty over much of the region north of the Aras (Arax) River, which, apart from eastern Georgia,[1] was included in the following three *beglarbegis*, or provinces: 1) Chukhur-e Sa`d, composed of the regions of Yerevan and Nakhichevan; 2) Qarabagh (Karabagh) and Ganja; 3) Shirvan, composed of the regions of Shirvan, Sheki, Kuba, Derbent and Baku.[2] Although the *beglarbeg*, or governor-general, of Azarbayjan in Tabriz may, at times, have had some loose jurisdiction over these three provinces, hereditary khans or trusted local tribal chiefs, appointed by the center, were placed in charge of these northern borders.

Throughout the seventeenth and the early part of the eighteenth centuries Shirvan, together with the above borderlands, remained under Iranian suzerainty. The region was home to various Turcoman and Kurdish tribes, Georgians, Armenians, a small number of ethnic Iranian groups and Jews. The Georgians were concentrated primarily in the K`art`li and Kakhet`i (eastern Georgia), or in Megrelia, Guria and Imeretia (western Georgia) and were ruled by their princes, albeit as vassals of the Iranian shahs or Ottoman sultans. The Armenians were scattered throughout the region, but had sizable numbers in what had been part of historical eastern Armenia, especially around their religious center in Echmiadzin in the Yerevan region and in the five mountainous districts of Karabagh.[3] The Muslims, a large part of whom was nomads, were divided into Shi'is and Sunnis. They spoke Turkish and Kurdish dialects and formed the dominant part of the population in much of the region.

The fall of the Safavid dynasty, in 1722, cast the former Caucasian provinces adrift and prompted Peter the Great to advance into the Caspian littoral. A year later, the Ottomans also took advantage of the disorder and sent their troops into Azarbayjan, eastern Georgia, and the rest of the South Caucasus. The two belligerents almost went to war, but, after the mediation by the French, agreed, in 1724, to divide the region. Russia obtained the coastal strip from Derbent to Lenkoran, while the Ottomans occupied the remaining territory.[4]

---

[1] The Safavids named the kings/princes of eastern Georgian as their *valis* (viceroys).

[2] V. Minorsky, *Tadhkirat al-Muluk* (London, 1943), 44.

[3] For details, see V. Minorsky, "Caucasica IV: Sahl ibn Sunbat of Shakki and Arran. The Caucasian Vassals of Marzuban in 344/955," in *The Turks, Iran and the Caucasus in the Middle Ages* (London, 1978), 504–529.

[4] The mountainous districts of Karabagh, ruled by local Armenian *meliks* (petty princes) resisted the Ottomans and managed to maintain their autonomy.

By 1736, however, Iran, under the leadership of Nader (shah after 1736) restored the borders of the former Safavid realm.[5] Following Nader's assassination in 1747, Iran experienced what some historians refer to as a fifty-year period of internal anarchy. This was especially evident in the borderlands of the South Caucasus, where local khans fought for territorial gains. In the absence of a central authority in Iran, these khans and district *soltans*[6] tried to maintain their rule by making alliances with King Erekle II of eastern Georgia or with their neighbors. The region was soon divided into the khanates[7] of Ganja, Yerevan, Nakhichevan, Karabagh, Sheki, Derbent-Kuba, Talesh, and Baku,[8] as well as semi-autonomous districts, such as Qazzaq (Kazakh) and Shams od-Dinlu (Shamshadil), Javad, Salyan, Shuragel, Ilisu, Jar and Belokan (see map 1).

Russia's defeat of the Ottomans in 1774 prompted a number of Russian statesmen, led by Gregory Potemkin, to urge Catherine II to agree to a bilateral treaty of friendship (the Georgievsk treaty of 1783) with King Erekle II.[9] In exchange for Russian protection, Erekle abjured his loyalty to Iran. Russia guaranteed Georgia's territorial integrity and the continuation of the Bagrationi dynasty in return for having a voice in the conduct of Georgian foreign affairs.

Despite pressures from a number of her advisors, Catherine refused to get involved in the rivalry of the numerous khans in the South Caucasus, who, taking advantage of the chaos in Iran, sought to consolidate their positions by coming to terms with Russia. Thus, during the next decade, the khans of that region, especially those of Derbent-Kuba, and Shirvan, encroached upon the territory of their neighbors, forcibly removed peasants to work on their private domains and formed various short-lived alliances against their rivals.

The situation changed dramatically after 1791, when Aqa Mohammad Khan Qajar consolidated his position as the new ruler of Iran. Angered by Erekle's "betrayal" and learning of the independent actions of the khans of the South Caucasus, he invaded the region in 1795. Most of the khanates either submitted or were looted. Aqa Mohammad then proceeded to Tiflis, the capital of Erekle. After intense fighting, Erekle fled and Aqa Mohammad Khan's army plundered the city for two weeks, killing many and taking some 15,000 women and children as slaves.

Catherine, who viewed the attack as a direct insult to Russia, ordered Valerian Zubov, the brother of her then favorite, Platon Zubov, to invade the South Caucasus, march into

---

[5] For an excellent map of the 1722–1736 period, see A. Tsutsiev, *Atlas of the Ethno-Political History of the Caucasus* (New Haven, 2014), map. 2.

[6] The term *soltan* should not be confused with the Ottoman sultan. The term in Iran implied a military commander in charge of a district.

[7] It is important to note that the term "khanate," does not exist in Persian. It is derived from the Anglicized version of *khanstvo* in Russian and *khanut`iun* in Armenian. The Persian term for these provinces was *ulka* or *tuman*, which was administered by a *hakem* or governor, who could either have been elevated to the rank of khan by the shah or had assumed the title. Hence the proper name for a khanate in Persian is *hakem-neshin*.

[8] Since the survey uses the Russian version for the names of the khanates, I have followed suit. The Persian names are Ganjeh, Iravan, Nakhjavan, Shakki, Qarabagh, Qobbeh-Darband, Talesh and Badkubeh.

[9] For the text of the treaty, see *Polnoe Sobranie Zakonov*, Vol. XXI, No. 15835.

Iran, depose Aqa Mohammad Khan and replace him with Aqa Mohammad's brother, Morteza Qoli Khan, who had sought refuge in Russia. Aqa Mohammad Khan's absence from the South Caucasus and Zubov's promise to keep any khan who submitted to Russia in his post, soon brought all the khans, except that of Yerevan, into the Russian orbit. Catherine's death, in November 1796, however, ended the Russian campaign. Her son, Tsar Paul (1796–1801), recalled the Russian army and dismissed her favorite commanders and courtiers. Aqa Mohammad Khan, now crowned Aqa Mohammad Shah, returned to the South Caucasus in the spring of 1797. All the khans either submitted, fled, or were ousted. However, the shah's assassination in June 1797, once again, plunged the region into uncertainty and started a renewed struggle between rivals for the Iranian throne.

Meanwhile, following King Erekle's death, some Russian officials intentionally exaggerated the potential of Georgia's resources and the size of her army in order to convince Tsar Paul to reconsider his policy of backing away from the South Caucasus and went so far as to advocate the annexation of Georgia. In fact, prior to his assassination, Paul, in January of 1801, did issue a manifesto to that effect. Although some of the advisors of his son and heir, Tsar Alexander I (1801–1825), were against the annexation, others, led by General Karl Knorring,[10] argued in favor of it.

In September of 1801, Tsar Alexander I officially annexed Georgia to the Russian Empire. Knorring and Peter Kovalenskii[11] were put in charge of its administration, but their abuses soon brought forth numerous complaints from the local population. In September 1802, the tsar appointed General Paul Tsitsianov[12] as the Commander-in-Chief and Civilian Governor of Georgia, Inspector of the Caucasian Line, and Military Governor of Astrakhan. Having been given such unprecedented authority, Tsitsianov, himself a Russianized Georgian prince, decided to prove himself to the tsar by completely subjugating the kingdom of eastern Georgia (K`art`li and Kakhet`i) and by bringing the various khanates located south of the Caucasus Mountains, which, as noted, had been nominally under Iranian suzerainty for some three centuries, under Russian authority.

After arresting and exiling most of the Georgian royal family to Russia, Tsitsianov began to threaten the Muslim khans of Ganja, Yerevan, Nakhichevan, Sheki, Shirvan, Karabagh, Talesh, Kuba, Derbent and Baku. Tsitsianov's intention was to frighten the khans to such an extent that they would turn away from Iran—which, by now had resolved its internal problems and had accepted Fath `Ali Shah Qajar (the nephew of Aqa Mohammad Khan), as the new shah—and seek Russian protection.

After writing numerous threatening letters, Tsitsianov, at the start of 1804, decided to demonstrate the might of the Russian army by laying siege to Ganja. His destruction of Ganja (which he renamed Elisavetpol in honor of Tsar Alexander's wife), where a large number of Muslims, including Javad Khan of Ganja, his son and some of his relatives

---

10 General Karl Fedorovich Knorring.

11 Peter Ivanovich Kovalenskii, Russian envoy to Georgia, died in 1827.

12 General Prince Paul Dmitrievich Tsitsianov (1754–1806).

were killed, triggered the First Russo-Iranian War (1804–1813). Having failed to take Yerevan in 1804, Tsitsianov then tried to intimidate or entice the khans of Karabagh, Kuba, Sheki, Shirvan and Baku to submit to Russia.

On December 25, 1805 [January 6, 1806], Tsitsianov and Mostafa Khan of Shirvan signed a treaty by which the khanate of Shirvan also became a Russian protectorate. Mostafa Khan promised to be a loyal subject of the Russian emperor, to pay an annual tribute of 8,000 gold rubles to the treasury in Tiflis, and to send hostages to Tiflis. In exchange, Russia gave Mostafa Khan a military rank and promised that he and his sons would continue as the khans of Shirvan and that local rule, including the courts and administration, as well as tax collection, would remain under his jurisdiction.[13]

Unable to come to a similar agreement with Sheikh `Ali Khan of Kuba and Derbent and Hoseyn `Ali Khan of Baku, Tsitsianov threatened to destroy Derbent in the same manner as Ganja. Instead, the inhabitants of the town drove out their khan and surrendered the city to the Russians. Emboldened, Tsitsianov marched on Baku. Hoseyn Qoli Khan of Baku feigned submission and asked to meet Tsitsianov outside the city gates. The Russian general, not suspecting a trap, rode with only one officer to meet the khan and his entourage on February 20, 1806, and was shot to death by one of the khan's attendants.

Tsitsianov's death, for a time, removed the Russian threat from the region. Taking advantage of the confusion caused by the Russian general's demise, Fath `Ali Shah now tried, through threats and rewards, to convince the khans of Karabagh, Sheki and Shirvan to once again swear allegiance to Iran. In the summer of 1806, Ebrahim Khan of Karabagh again submitted to the shah and, together with some members of his family, left his capital of Shushi. The commander of the Russian garrison in Shushi pursued them and killed most of the entourage, including the khan, one of his wives and a son. However, General Ivan Gudovich, Tsitsianov's successor, wisely honored the 1805 Russo-Karabaghi treaty and appointed Ebrahim's second son, Mahdi Qoli, as the new khan of Karabagh.

Meanwhile, that same summer, Salim Khan of Sheki expelled the Russian garrison from Nukha, the center of his khanate. By October of 1806, however, the Russians, who by then had recovered from the shock of Tsitsianov's death, took Sheki by force. Salim Khan fled the khanate, but soon after asked the tsar's pardon. Gudovich, although wishing to honor the 1805 Russo-Sheki treaty, refused to accept Salim Khan and replaced him with Ja`far Qoli Khan of Khoy, an anti-Qajar chief, as the new khan of Sheki. Although Mostafa Khan of Shirvan vacillated, he, too, eventually threw his lot with the Russians and continued to rule his khanate according to the 1806 Russo-Shirvani treaty. The remaining two khanates, that is, Baku and Derbent-Kuba were annexed by force.

The First Russo-Iranian War, as noted, ended with the Treaty of Gulistan (1813), by which Iran acknowledged Russia's sovereignty over Daghestan, Georgia, Imeret`i,

---

[13] See the number 1 in the appendix for the full text of the treaty. A similar treaty was signed earlier with Ebrahim Khan of Karabagh. Negotiations with Salim Khan of Sheki were not finalized until his successor, Ja`far Qoli Khan, signed a final treaty with Tsitsianov's successor, General Ivan Gudovich, in January of 1807.

Guria, Mingrelia, Abkhazia, and the khanates of Karabagh (minus the Qapanat),[14] Sheki, Shirvan, Baku, Ganja, Kuba, Derbent and the part of Talesh that was already in Russian hands (see map 1).[15] Although the exact demarcation of the new borders was to be decided later, Russia, for all intents and purposes, became the master of all the lands and inhabitants between the so-called Caucasian Line by the Terek River and the Caspian Sea.

Russia, however, continued to honor the treaties with Sheki, Karabagh and Shirvan and these provinces—as the khanates were now called by Russia—and the khans were left to administer their own territories. These three former khanates continued to send their annual tribute in gold rubles, as well as hostages to Tiflis, and provide food and lodging for the Russian garrisons. More importantly, the khans and their administration remained in charge of appointing officials, collecting taxes or granting tax-exemption, and farming out revenues.

The state of affairs changed drastically at the end of 1816 with the appointment of General Alexei Yermolov,[16] as the new commander-in-chief of Georgia with jurisdiction over the whole of the Caucasus, as well as ambassador-extraordinary to the Court of Iran. Yermolov felt that the entire Caucasus and the region south of the Caucasus Mountains must become an integral part of the Russian Empire. He was not only against the continuation of independent or semi-independent khanates or enclaves, but also felt that Russian security in the region depended on the conquest of the khanates of Yerevan and Nakhichevan, with the Aras River forming the new boundary between Russia and Iran.

During his mission to Iran in 1817, Yermolov purposely ignored his government's instructions. He insulted his hosts, especially `Abbas Mirza, by ignoring the latter's status as Prince Regent and by paying his respect to his rival, Mohammad `Ali Mirza, instead. Yermolov's boorish manners and impossible demands not only failed to resolve the border disputes, but also actually worsened relations between the two states. Unsatisfied with the Gulistan treaty, and ambitious to make a name for himself, Yermolov did everything in his power to start a new war with Iran.

First on his agenda was to absorb the self-ruling khanates of Sheki, Shirvan and Karabagh. He began by sending disparaging reports to St. Petersburg, interfered with the collection of their revenues and questioned their tax rolls. When Esma`il Khan of Sheki died in 1819 without any male heirs, Yermolov brought the province under direct Russian rule and immediately ordered a detailed survey of the revenues of that khanate, which would now belong to Russia.[17] His next move was to send a critical

[14] The present-day districts of Meghri, Goris and Kapan (which made up the Qapanat), located in the southern part of Zangezur (Republic of Armenia) were not part of the Karabagh khanate but were under the supervision of the *beglarbeg* of Tabriz, see, *Tadhkirat al-Muluk*, 164.

[15] Since the Khan of Talesh was at odds with the Iranian court, the Russians accepted that khanate's limited autonomy until the conclusion of the Second Russo-Iranian War.

[16] General Alexei Petrovich Yermolov (1777–1861).

[17] *Opisanie Shekinskoi Provintsii, sostavlennoe v' 1819 godu* (Tiflis, 1866). For an annotated English translation with explanatory notes, see G. Bournoutian, *The 1819 Russian Survey of the Khanate of Sheki [Shakki]: A Primary Source on the Demography and Economy of an Iranian Province prior to its Annexation by Russia* (Costa Mesa, CA, 2016).

report on the conditions in Shirvan to the tsar[18] and to increase the number of Russian officials in the administration of that khanate.[19] Reading the writing on the wall, Mostafa Khan of Shirvan fled to Iran on September 1, 1820.[20] Calling the khan a traitor, Yermolov informed St. Petersburg that he had now brought Shirvan under the direct rule of Russia and ordered the detailed survey, which is the subject of this monograph. Finally, taking advantage of the rivalry between the khan of Karabagh, Mahdi Qoli, and a pretender, as well as the economic instability and the complaints by the Armenian population of Karabagh, who felt that they paid more than their fair share of taxes, Yermolov instructed the Russian commander at the fort of Shushi, Prince Madatov, to put pressure on the khan. In December of 1822, Mahdi Qoli Khan also abandoned his domain and fled to Iran. Yermolov then proclaimed Karabagh a Russian province and ordered a similar survey.[21]

Ignoring directives from St. Petersburg, Yermolov continued to send inflammatory reports and goad the Iranians by sending sorties into disputed territories. Meanwhile, the complaints of the fugitive khans about the treatment of Muslims in the South Caucasus by Christian Russians inflamed the Shi`a religious hierarchy. They called a *jihad* and forced Fath `Ali Shah, in 1826, to invade Russia and to initiate the Second Russo-Iranian War. Yermolov was caught unprepared, and the Iranian army, which was welcomed by the local Muslims, gained a number of victories. In 1827, Tsar Nicholas I finally replaced Yermolov with General Ivan Paskevich,[22] who roundly defeated the Iranians and forced them, in 1828, to sign the Treaty of Turkmanchay (Torkmanchay), by which the last two remaining Iranian khanates of Yerevan and Nakhichevan, as well as the disputed districts of Talesh, Mughan and Qapanat were annexed to Russia. A year later, Paskevich defeated the Ottomans, who not only conceded the Russian possessions on the eastern coast of the Black Sea, but also surrendered Akhalkalak and Akhaltsikh (see map 1).

Russia thus became the master of the entire region south of the Caucasus Mountains between the Caspian and the Black seas and retained it until 1918. Russian historians portrayed the Russian conquest as the liberation of the region from tyranny and backwardness and the start of its cultural transformation under the guidance of the enlightened Russian people.[23] Except for a short-lived period of independence (1918–

---

[18] Archives of the Viceroyalty of the Caucasus: *Akty sobrannye kavkazskoiu arkheograficheskoiu kommissieiu*, VI/1 (Tiflis, 1874), doc. no. 1211.

[19] See number 2 in the appendix.

[20] See number 3 in the appendix.

[21] *Opisanie Karabagskoi Provintsii, sostavlennoe v' 1823 godu* (Tiflis, 1866). For an annotated English translation with commentary, see G. Bournoutian, *The 1823 Russian Survey of the Karabagh Province: A Primary Source on the Demography and Economy of Karabagh in the Early 19th Century* (Costa Mesa, CA, 2011 and 2012).

[22] Field Marshal Ivan Fedorovich Paskevich, Count of Yerevan, Prince of Warsaw (1782–1856).

[23] See P. G. Butkov, *Materialy dlia novoi istorii Kavkaza s' 1722 po 1803*, 3 vols. (St. Petersburg, 1869); N. F. Dubrovin, *Zakavkaz'e ot 1803–1806* (St. Petersburg, 1866) and his *Istoriia voiny i vladychestva russkikh na Kavkaze*, 6 vols. (St. Petersburg, 1871–1888); and V. A. Potto, *Kavkazskaia voina*, 4 vols. (St. Petersburg, 1885–1888). The Russian conquest of the South Caucasus has been the subject of a number of books in English: John Baddeley's *The Russian Conquest of the Caucasus* (London, 1908) is not only extremely pro-Russian in its outlook but concentrates largely on the Russian conquest of Daghestan and the Muslim tribes living in the high Caucasus. Muriel Atkin's excellent study,

1921), most of the terriory south of the Caucasus Mountains then became part of the Soviet Union. Russian and local historians were directed to ignore the more than three centuries of Iranian cultural and linguistic heritage and to focus instead on the "national formation" and "the historical friendship" of the local Georgians, Armenians and Turkish-speaking Muslims (called Azeris after 1918).[24] After the fall of the USSR in 1991, the three independent republics of Azerbaijan, Georgia and Armenia had to face the realities of past differences and conflicts, which unfortunately continue to plague the region to this day.

Russia and Iran, 1780–1828 (Minneapolis, 1980) presents a more balanced point of view, while my *The Khanate of Erevan Under Qajar Rule, 1795–1828* (New York, 1992) concentrates on the history of the last years of Iranian rule in the Khanate of Yerevan.

[24] See L. Tillet, *The Great Friendship: Soviet Historians on the Non-Russian Nationalities* (Chapel Hill, 1969).

Map 1: South Caucasus ca. 1800–1921

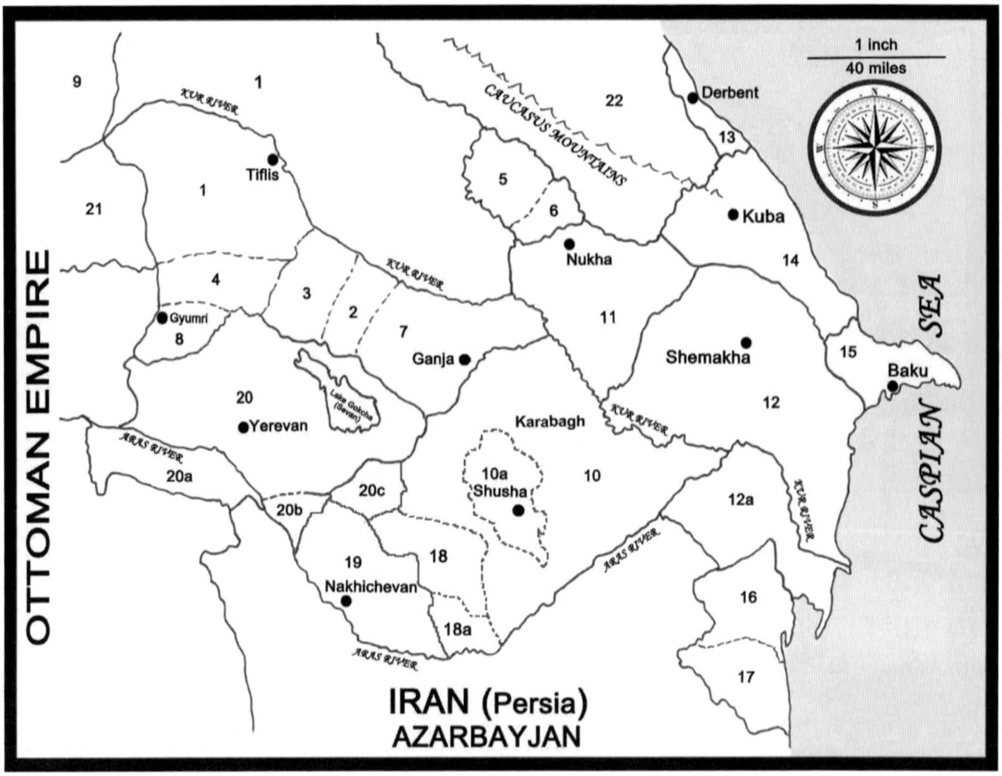

1. Kingdom of K`art`li and Kakhet`i (1801), today part of Georgia.
2. Soltanate of Shamshadil (Shamsh oddin) (1801), today part of Azerbaijan.
3. Soltanate of Kazakh (Qazzaq) (1801), today part of Azerbaijan.
4. Pambak, Lori, Borchalu districts (1801), claimed by Armenia and Georgia, today part of Armenia.
5. Districts of Jar and Belokan (1803), today part of Azerbaijan.
6. Soltanate of Ilisu (1804), today part of Azerbaijan.
7. Khanate of Ganja [Elisavetpol] (1804), today part of Azerbaijan.
8. Region of Gyumri [Alexandropol] (1805), became part of the Armenian Province, today part of Armenia.

9. Kingdom of Imeret`i (1809), Kutais province of Georgia, today part of Georgia.
10. Khanate of Karabagh (submitted in 1805, annexed in 1822), today part of Azerbaijan.
10a. Region of Mountainous Karabagh (Nagorno-Karabakh), claimed by both Armenia and Azerbaijan awarded to Soviet Azerbaijan in 1923, broke away in 1994 as an independent republic.
11. Khanate of Sheki (submitted in 1805, annexed in 1819), today part of Azerbaijan.
12. Khanate of Shirvan (submitted in 1806, annexed in 1820), today part of Azerbaijan.
12a. Mughan (1806), today part of Azerbaijan.
13. Khanate of Derbent (1806), today part of Russia.
14. Khanate of Kuba (1806), today part of Azerbaijan.
15. Khanate of Baku (1806), now part of Azerbaijan.
16. Khanate of Talesh (1813), today part of Azerbaijan.
17. Khanate of Talesh (1828), today part of Azerbaijan.
18. Region of Zangezur, claimed by the khanate of Karabagh, disputed between Russia and Iran from 1813 to 1826, annexed by Russia in 1828, claimed by both Armenia and Azerbaijan, today part of Armenia.
18a. Qapanat, claimed by the khanates of Nakhichevan and Karabagh and occasionally under the control of Tabriz, today part of Armenia.
19. Khanate of Nakhichevan (1828)—became part of the Armenian Province and Armenia, today part of Azerbaijan.
20. Khanate of Yerevan (1828)—became part of the Armenian Province, today part of Armenia.
20a. District of Surmalu (part of the khanate of Yerevan, became part of the Armenian Province and Armenia), today part of Turkey.
20b. District of Sharur (part of the Yerevan khanate, Armenian Province and Armenia), today part of Nakhichevan (Azerbaijan).
20c. Daralagez (part of Nakhichevan, but under the jurisdiction of the last khan of Yerevan), today part of Armenia.
21. Pashalik of Akhalkalak and Akhaltsikh (1829), became the Kutais province of Russia, today part of Georgia.
22. Daghestan, today part of Russia.

Note: 1–16—renounced by Iran in the Gulistan treaty, 1813; 17–20—renounced by Iran in the Turkmanchay treaty, 1828; 21—renounced by the Ottoman Empire in the Adrianople treaty, 1829; 19, 20a–20b—renounced by Armenia in the Moscow and Kars treaties, 1921.

ОПИСАНІЕ ШИРВАНСКОЙ ПРОВИНЦІИ,

СОСТАВЛЕННОЕ

въ 1820 году,

по распоряженію главноуправлявшаго въ Грузіи Ермолова,

ГЕНЕРАЛЪ-МАІОРОМЪ КНЯЗЕМЪ МАДАТОВЫМЪ

и

ДѢЙСТВИТЕЛЬНЫМЪ СТАТСКИМЪ СОВѢТНИКОМЪ МОГИЛЕВСКИМЪ.

ТИФЛИСЪ.

ВЪ ТИПОГРАФІИ ГЛАВНАГО УПРАВЛЕНІЯ НАМѢСТНИКА КАВКАЗСКАГО.

1867.

The Descriptive Survey of the Shirvan Province

Compiled in the year 1820

On the Order of the Commander-in-Chief of Georgia,
[General Alexei] Yermolov

by
Major-General Prince [Valerian Grigorevich] Madatov
and
Active State Counselor [Paul Ivanovich] Mogilevskii

Tiflis

The Press of the Central Administration of
the Viceroy of the Caucasus

1867

To His Excellency, Cavalier and General-of-Infantry, the Commander-in-Chief of
Georgia, Governor of Astrakhan and the Caucasus,
Alexei Petrovich Yermolov

REPORT

We have carried out Your Excellency's order number 184,[1] which instructed us to record in situ all the revenues of the Shirvan Province. We have examined and judged their accuracy and have now the honor to present for Your Excellency's consideration, the information from the 17 *mahals*, [districts] together with the survey of the city of Fitdagh (İsmayıllı).[2] In addition, we have included one register, containing five lists of farmed out [leased] properties in Shirvan, which continued to remain in effect until Mostafa Khan's flight from the province. Furthermore, there are two other registers: the first lists the khan's belongings and flocks, which we have sold.[3] The second is a brief register regarding the general income from the various *mahals* of the Shirvan Province. In total, together with the farmed out lists, we have compiled 26 registers [19 of which are included herein[*]].

Among the most important revenues we have included the large landholdings of Mostafa Khan and his family, who have fled to Iran. In order to maintain all the large grain-producing lands, as well as the income from the numerous silk farms, we have left the same assessments set by the khan. These [taxes] have not provoked the population [to rebel] and require only careful control over the grain harvest and the silk farms to continue to produce revenues. In addition, the revenues we have recorded herein depend upon the harvest and are impossible to predict. We have, therefore, recorded the average yield of a large and small harvest.

Major-General Prince Madatov
Active State Councilor Mogilevskii
December 1820
Tiflis

[1] The order is in *Akty*, VI/I (Tiflis, 1874), no. 1217, dated August 27 (September 7, 1820). See no. 4 in the appendix.

[2] The city of Shamakhi was the capital of Shirvan until Nader Shah destroyed most of it in 1742. Nader then ordered the building of the town of New Shamakhi, some 16 miles to the west of the former capital. Following Nader's death in 1747, the inhabitants abandoned the new town; some returned to rebuild and settle in Old Shemakhi, others settled elsewhere. After Mostafa Khan decided to make Fitdagh his headquarters, he encouraged, through reduced taxes, some of the former inhabitants of Shamakhi to settle in his new capital.

[3] See number 5 in the appendix.

[*] (Included in the original text). The following registers are not published here: The five registers of the farmed out [leased] properties [the information appears in Register 1]; and two other registers: one on the khan's private property and flocks sold by Major-General Prince Madatov and Active State Councilor Mogilevskii and the second a brief account of the total revenue from the *mahals* of Shirvan. The first has nothing to do with the total revenue from the province and the second can be ascertained by adding the total revenues from each *mahal*.

To the Commandant of Fitdagh (İsmayıllı), Captain Prince Makaev[1]

No. 41. November, 27 (December 9), 1820, Fitdagh

We submit to the attention of Your Excellency, the 17 registers of all the *mahals* of the Shirvan province with the detailed information on the revenues from each *mahal* and village which we have obtained by questioning the *beg* of the *mahal*, the *yüzbaşi*[2] or the elder of each village;[3] we also include a register for the city of Fitdagh, which includes the revenue from the Jewish village of Magele,[4] located at the foot of the mountain. All said revenues are, from now on, forwarded to the treasury[5] of His Majesty the Emperor. Another register enumerates the revenues in the Shirvan province that were farmed out; 19 registers altogether.

We have recorded the revenues from the private holdings of Mostafa Khan and members of his family, which were collected in wheat, barley or silk, prior to his flight, those which were forgiven by the khan or gifted by him to his near associates. We cannot be certain, however, what was collected and what remains to be gathered. We cannot ascertain the exact amount of grain, due to the drought and invasion of locusts this year, as well as the flight of Mostafa Khan, which has left the khanate in chaos. Our report will be forwarded to the Commander-in-Chief. Meanwhile, from Your Excellency's reports, prepared and submitted to us by Mirza Hoseyn and Mirza Mohammad Hoseyn,[6] it is clear that the *mal-o-jehat*[7] dues in grain was not collected from all locations and that some of the *mahals* have not yet sent the required amount; this applies also to dues

[1] He was the commander of the Russian garrison in Fitdagh.

[2] The Turkish term, *yüzbaşi,* means head of 100 men; it is equal to the rank of captain. Some of *yüzbaşis* in Shirvan acted as the head of a village or nomadic settlements.

[3] The survey refers to the elders as *kevkha*. However, such elders were called *kadkhoda* or *kedkhuda* in Muslim villages and *kevkha* in Armenian villages

[4] The text later refers to this town as Migele. It was most probably near the present-day town of Mican.

[5] The text uses the same term to identify the treasury in the khan's chancery and that of the Russian administration. To avoid confusion, the term *divan* will be used for the khan's chancery. The term "treasury" will refer to the treasury of the Russian administration in Shirvan, as well as the Central Treasury of the Caucasus in Tiflis. See Explanatory Remarks.

[6] The above two individuals were the *mirzas* (accountants/secretaries) in the *divan* of Shirvan.

[7] The term *mal-o-jehat* is composed of two words, *mal* refers to the tax on property (houses, animals, wells, looms, mills, oil-presses and orchards) and *jehat* refers to the tax on cultivated fields. These two taxes were generally estimated together and, for the most part, paid in kind by the *ra'iyats* (peasants) and nomads to the khan, landowner, or local administrator. The amount of this tax varied in different khanates. In Shirvan it equaled one-tenth of the grain harvest and one-fifth of the silk, cotton, and rice harvest. Moreover, the tax from the orchards was not included in the *mal-o-jehat*, but was collected separately in cash and was called the *bagh-bashi*. The *mal-o-jehat* could belong entirely to the khan, the landowner, or could be divided in defined agreed proportions, between the peasants/nomads and the khan, landowner, or administrator.

in silk, not all of which were collected by the khan prior to his flight abroad. We, therefore, assign this duty on you, as the local official and the commandant of this province, to reconcile these two records as much as possible, so that the Commander-in-Chief can determine the revenues and act in a way that would benefit the local population, prevent evil men to take advantage of the people and collect what was supposed to go to the treasury. We ask that Your Excellency immediately carry out the order of the higher officials.

The record of the revenues from the mahals as listed in our registers, will serve to inform you as to how much in grain[8] and *mal-o-jehat*, both in cash or kind, was collected this year (which according to the Muslim calendar ends on March 10 (22) 1821);[9] what part belonged to the khan and his family, which will now go to the treasury. Another short account from the *mirzas* will apprise you of how much grain and *mal-o-jehat* was collected prior to the khan's flight. The numbers in these accounts will assist you to examine and ascertain their accuracy.

The harvest of rice and cotton, belonging to Mostafa Khan, his family and the *begs* who fled with him has not yet been determined, because it has not yet been harvested everywhere. [The entire harvest now belongs to the treasury.] It is imperative that the correct amount be recorded and sent to the treasury of His Imperial Majesty. The registers of our *mahals* indicate the harvests during normal and prosperous times. Your Excellency and your staff have to determine what is the amount to be collected in this fiscal year; which *mahals* have suffered blight or other difficulties and reconcile them with the official reports and records. As far as rice and cotton is concerned, you can collect the dues in cash if the inhabitants so wish. You can also sell the crop as long as you do not sell it below the average price indicated in our registers: rice for 8 rubles and 10 kopeks a *taghar*,[10] cotton for 5 rubles and 4 kopeks a *taghar* in local money. Your efforts will benefit the interests of the treasury and you shall serve His Imperial Majesty.

We are also submitting 80 *barats*[11] given to us by Mirza Hoseyn and Mirza Mohammad Hoseyn, which indicate the amount of butter and cheese already collected by the khan from the *mahals* populated by nomads, prior to his flight. In addition, our registers indicate the exact numbers to be collected from such *mahals*, in the form of floor mats,[12] small rugs,[13] cords,[14] and straw,[15] as well as various cash dues under the

[8] The registers list this tax under the *sursat*, see page 19 note 1.

[9] The fiscal year in Shirvan began the day after the start of the Iranian New Year (Nowruz), which begins on the first day of the spring equinox (March 20–21). As noted, the Russian Julian calendar, in the 19th century, was 12 days behind the Gregorian calendar used in the West.

[10] A *taghar* equaled 50 *batmans*, or half a *khavar* or *khalvar* (half an ass-load). A *batman* or *mann* equaled 3 kilos (6.61 lbs.); hence 50 *batmans* weighed approximately 350 lbs.

[11] A *barat* signifies a bill of exchange, quittance or a receipt.

[12] The Russian text reads 'floor covering,' which probably refers to the coarsely woven floor mats called *palas*.

[13] The Russian text reads 'small rugs.' These were coarsely woven colorful rugs, resembling small kilims.

[14] The Russian term *veryovki* can be translated as ropes, cords or nooses. The nomads wove them from wool and not jute.

[15] Chaff, or the husks separated from the grain by threshing, was used to feed livestock and to be mixed with clay to make sunbaked bricks.

names of *kharaj*,[16] *bagh-bashi*[17] and dues for madder[18] from the village of Muratkhana (Muradxan) and other items for which there are no receipts and could not have been collected by Mostafa Khan prior to his flight. You have to come to an agreement with the local people and collect all the dues from the villages and nomad settlements and submit them to the treasury, either in cash or kind, according to the prices indicated by us in the registers.

You will need two sewn notebooks, one to record the revenues that have already been collected, and the other for the revenues that have yet to be collected in the Shirvan Province. You should also record all administrative expenses. You are required to send a register for the monthly income and expenses to the Military Commander of Georgia, Lt.-General Veliaminov, The First.[19] You should also keep a copy at the City Court.

Finally, we have the pleasure to inform you that the more accurate and detailed your reports are, the more they shall bring honor for Your Excellency and the gratitude of your superiors.

Major-General Prince Madatov
State Councilor Mogilevskii

[16] The *kharaj* tax in Shirvan was similar to the *bash-puli*, *saraneh* or the *jizya* tax. It was collected only from the Armenian villages.

[17] A tax collected from an orchard belonging to a village or an individual.

[18] The root of the madder plant produces a red dye that is used to dye wool used in carpets.

[19] Text refers to Ivan Aleksandrovich Veliaminov (1771–1837), a close confidant of Yermolov and a member of the Georgian administration.

***Memorandum** compiled from documents supplied by Mirza Hoseyn and Mirza Mohammad Hoseyn on the revenue collected [and to be collected] from the mahals of Shirvan prior to the flight of Mostafa Khan; the mal-o-jehat which has already been collected; and the various other revenues that have yet to be collected for the fiscal year 1820, which corresponds to the Muslim year ending on March 10 (22), 1821. The said revenues will now be transferred to the treasury.*

Karasubasar (Qarasubasar) Mahal

Excluding the *sursat*[1] and the harvest from the private landholdings of the khan and his family, that is, the villages of Leki 1 (Upper Ləki) and Leki 2 (Lower Ləki) and Muradxan, as well as the income from the plows, which the inhabitants utilized for farming, and the income from silk production, all of which, according to the above mirzas, belonged to the khan, or was given by him to various indi-viduals prior to his flight, we have determined from the register for the Qarasubasar *Mahal* that the villages of this *mahal* had to provide 63 *taghars* of wheat, 25 *taghars* of barley and 50 *batmans* of cleaned cotton in taxes to the khan's *divan*. However, according to the same *mirzas*, due to a terrible blight caused by locusts, Mostafa Khan exempted them from this tax. The inhabitants of the Muradxan village had to pay 225 local rubles this year to Esma`il Beg, Mustafa Khan's brother, as dues for the madder produced in that village, as well as 150 local rubles in *toujih*[2] taxes. Moreover, the aforementioned *mirzas* stated that they had no information on the amount of cotton harvested in the *mahal*. The commandant of the province has to be instructed to ascertain the correct amount and tax it accordingly.

Biulket (Boluket) Mahal

In the village of Akhsu (Ağsu), aside from the private property of the khan and his family, the dues of which were collected by them even prior to their flight, there are two mills, each with two mill-stones, which belonged to the khan. They have now been repaired but have not been rented out as of yet. The commandant has to note that even

[1] The *sursat* (also *surusat* and *soyursat*) best translates as 'purveyance'. In this case, they were provisions and fodder for the troops and their horses collected during wartime. The peasants had to haul such provisions on their own to the camps. However, by the 19th century, the *sursat* collected in Shirvan went to maintain the khan, his family, his tribal cavalry, his household servants and the various officials in the khanate. It also provided the food for the Russian garrison at Fitdagh. The *sursat* resembled the *salianeh* dues collected from peasants and the *kira-khana-kharji* dues collected from the nomads in the Karabagh Province in this period. It was collected from the peasants, mainly from the wheat and barley harvests, and from the nomads, mainly in form of butter cheese, meat, floor mats, and small rugs.

[2] This levy was originally part of the *ekhrajat* dues, which went to support civilian and military officials. From the second half of the 18th century to the start of the 19th century, the *toujih* in the khanates of Sheki and Shirvan was collected from the peasants by the *kadkhoda* or *yüzbaşi* of a village as part of the *sursat* dues and was paid in cash.

without rent, the mills can yield an income of 5 *taghars* of grain to the treasury by March 10 (22), 1821. There is a large orchard in the same village, which belonged to Ja`far Qoli Aqa, the son of Mostafa Khan, and half of another orchard, which belonged to the khan's wife Kichkin. The first is listed in the register as providing an income of 200 rubles, the second 150 rubles in local money. The income from these, prior to the khan's flight, have to be ascertained and the commandant has to demand the revenue from the overseers of these orchards for the treasury.

From the village of Karasakalli (Qarasaqqal), the treasury has to collect the revenue from the vineyard, which belonged to the Shirvan treasury. According to Mirza Hoseyn, the overseers of the vineyard have already amassed dues of 65 rubles in local money. The income from this vineyard has to be recorded in the tax-rolls.

From the village of Samuilli (Ismuili), aside from the revenues in wheat, barley and silk from lands belonging to the khan and his family, there was also income from cotton and rice, as well as from the Esrafil hollow. The harvest from these has only been gathered a month ago and could not have been collected by the khan. It must all be diverted to the treasury. We have not determined the amount, which has to be ascertained by the commandant. The village also has 3 orchards belonging to the treasury. According to the register of this *mahal*, the income from these orchards is 250 local rubles, but Mirza Hoseyn states that they received only 110 rubles. This discrepancy has to be examined and the correct sum has to be listed in the tax-rolls.

From the village of Shakhmezit (Şixmizid), we have farmed out 5 mills belonging to the treasury for 29 *taghars* of wheat a year. The commandant has to verify this income at the conclusion of the lease. The 3 orchards in this village produce an income of 7 rubles, which belonged to Mostafa Khan's brother, Esma`il Beg, but now belong to the treasury. We will have to check for any irregularities and ascertain the correct amount. The same is true regarding the 95 rubles income from the 4 orchards in this village, which belonged to Zeyveh Khanum, the khan's sister. Two of the older orchards have been farmed out for 200 rubles, the other two are abandoned and bring no income to the treasury. Their condition must be examined. Finally, according to Mirza Hoseyn, the entire grain revenue from the *mal-o-jehat* of this village was forgiven due to damage by locusts.

Karabaghlar Mahal

Aside from all the revenues in grain and silk from this *mahal*, which, according to the above *mirza*, were collected by the Mostafa Khan prior to his flight, only the *mal-o-jehat* from the rice harvest remains, and now has to go to the treasury. The commandant has to verify the exact amount of revenue from each village so that the private landowners will not shortchange the treasury.

Khozourt (Khazarud) Mahal

The village of Gialage (Qalagah) has been assessed 200 rubles in local money as part of their *kharaj*. Mirza Hoseyn has attested that 170 rubles have already been paid. In addition, 7 rubles were collected by the *mohassels* (tax-collectors) for their services. Thus, 23 rubles remain to be paid to the treasury. The above amounts should be recorded in the tax-rolls.

The village of Ushtal (Uştal) had to pay 90 rubles in local money as their *kharaj*, but according to the *mirza*, they have paid only 80 rubles in local money. The above amounts should be recorded and the remaining 10 rubles must be collected.

The revenue in butter, cheese, small rugs and cords, from the villages of this *mahal*, indicated by us in the register, should be paid in cash or kind to the treasury. The remaining *mal-o-jehat* dues in grain listed in the register is 54½ *taghars* of wheat and 23 *taghars* of barley. However, according to Mirza Hoseyn, Mostafa Khan, prior to his flight, gave a *talaqa* (*ta`liqeh*)[3] stating that no *mal-o-jehat* was to be collected from this mahal and if it had already been collected, one was not to collect the *gullukhi*[4] dues for this year. The said *ta`liqeh* has to be examined carefully.

Akerat (Ekeret) Mahal

Aside from the *sursat* in grain and income from silk, which, according to the inhabitants, had already been collected by the khan prior to his flight, the entire *mal-o-jehat* from rice has to go to the treasury. Both the commandant and local overseers have to ascertain precisely if the khan actually collected the *mal-o-jehat* in grain, which according to the register, was to have been 6 *taghars* and 15 *batmans* of wheat and 1 *taghar* of barley; for Mirza Hoseyn has no knowledge of its having been collected.

Elat Mahal

All the butter and cheese dues from the nomads of this mahal are listed in the register and, according to Mirza Hoseyn, were already collected by the khan prior to his flight. However, there are no *barats* indicating this. The commandant has to examine this carefully. The small rugs and floor mats and everything else due to the treasury, as listed in the register, have to be paid in cash or in kind. In addition, the commandant must pay special attention to the amount of rice planted for the khan by the *ranjbars*[5] in the nomad settlements of Arab-`Abdol-Karim, and Udzharly (Ucar) for the khan's adjutant

---

[3] The term is from the Arabo-Persian *ta`liqeh*, which refers to a marginal note or addendum. In this case, it was a note attached to the general ledger of revenues, or a document given to the private owner of a fief-holder, exempting then from certain taxes.

[4] The text refers to the *qullugh-puli*, dues collected for the salary of the tax collectors.

[5] The *ranjbars* were landless peasants who were hired as sharecroppers, paying from one-third to one-fifth of the harvest to the landowner. See Explanatory Remarks for more details.

Aqa Beg, who has fled with him, which is to be collected for the treasury. According to our register the first village owed 800 *taghars* and the second 130 *taghars*.

As far as the *mal-o-jehat* dues are concerned, our register indicates that the inhabitants had to pay 7 *taghars* and 7 *batmans* of wheat and 4 *taghars* and 4 *batmans* of barley. However, according to Mirza Hoseyn, the khan, prior to his flight, only received 2 *taghars* and 33 *batmans* of wheat and 1 *taghar* and 16 *batmans* of barley. Thus they owe the treasury 4 *taghars* and 24 *batmans* of wheat and 2 *taghars* and 28 *batmans* of barley, which the commandant has to collect.

Koshun Mahal

According to Mirza Hoseyn and a number of *barats*, the khan had already collected the 15 *batmans* of butter and 7 *batmans* of cheese from this *mahal*. Thus 15 *batmans* of butter and 8 *batmans* of cheese still remain to be collected. The number of small rugs and floor mats listed in the register that are still due after the khan's flight, have to be sent to the treasury. The commandant has to see to this. As far as the *mal-o-jehat* is concerned, our register indicates that the *mahal* owed 47 *taghars* and 20 *batmans* of wheat and 19 *taghars* and 5 *batmans* of barley. According to Mirza Hoseyn, the khan, prior to his flight, had collected 25 *taghars* and 25 *batmans* of wheat and 11 *taghars* and 3 *batmans* of barley. There are *barats* certifying to the above. The *mahal*, thus, still owes 21 *taghars* and 45 *batmans* of wheat and 8 *taghars* and 2 *batmans* of barley to the treasury. The commandant has to ascertain the harvest and to collect the remaining grain.

Lagich (Lahıc) Mahal

According to Mirza Hoseyn, Mostafa Khan had collected the entire *mal-o-jehat* from this mahal prior to his flight and he has barats to prove this. The commandant has to examine these *barats* and ascertain their validity. Mirza Hoseyn has no records for the grain *sursat*, for dues in straw and firewood, as well as for the *darughegy* dues listed in the register. The commandant has to carefully search the records, question the inhabitants and determine the total revenues due to the treasury.

Gouz (Howz) Mahal

According to Mirza Hoseyn, the khan, prior to his flight, did not collect dues from the *kharaj* and *bagh-bashi* from the villages of this *mahal*. Thus, the commandant has to collect these revenues and send them to the treasury. As far as the *mal-o-jehat* is concerned, the villages of this *mahal*, according to our register, had to provide 18 *taghars* and 35 *batmans* of wheat and 14 *taghars* and 31 *batmans* of barley, minus a third part—or 6 *taghars* and 4 *batmans* of wheat and 4 *taghars* and 8 *batmans* of barley—for the *mahal*'s superintendent. The commandant has to ascertain not only the above amount, but also the entire amount of grain collected in the Shirvan khanate.

Kasan (Kessan) Mahal

The village of Genza (Kənzə) has to pay 70 local rubles a year in *kharaj*. The commandant has to ascertain if the landowner [Naft `Ali Beg] has, indeed fled with the khan to Iran and has, according to Mirza Hoseyn, already collected this revenue.

Sadarin (Sedenrud) Mahal

The entire *mal-o-jehat* collected in rice and listed in our register, has to be collected for the treasury. The commandant has to pay special attention to this. In addition, the *mahal* produces silk in abundance and the *begs*, prior to their flight did not manage to collect all the *mal-o-jehat* dues from the production of silk. The commandant has to make sure that the treasury collects this revenue. Furthermore, there are 2 mills in the village of Arab, which according to the register, each of which has to provide 5 *taghars* of wheat a year to the treasury. There is also half the income from a mill in Bazavent (Bozavand), which is 2½ *taghars* of wheat, a mill in the village of Kazian (Qazyan), which provides an income of 60 local rubles a year, and a mill in the village of Shah-Arkhi (Ṣaharxi), which is farmed out for 4 *taghars* of wheat a year. The commandant has to inquire from Mirza Hoseyn if the treasury has received anything from these mills this year. We also have to find out if the nomad settlements of Türkmen and Gurt paid their taxes: 250 local rubles from the first, and 120 local rubles from the second, prior to the khan's flight to Iran or if they owe something to the treasury. There is also the matter of the 500 local rubles due from the 3 orchards in the village of Alkhasova (Alxasava) belonging to the treasury, which we have farmed out for that sum plus one gold ruble. The amount has to be recorded in the tax-rolls. According to Mirza Hoseyn, there are 4 large vineyards in the village of Arab, which belong to the children of `Omar Soltan and their mother, and which, according to the register, bring an income of 190 local rubles. The commandant has to diligently examine these types of income. From a similar orchard in the village of Kiuche-Gedi (Küçekənd) the treasury receives only 30 local rubles and the income of 100 local rubles listed in our register from the 4 orchards in the village of Ṣaharxi, which belonged to the khan's father-in-law Qasem Beg, now belongs to the treasury. Finally from the 50 rubles of the *kharaj* assessed on the village of Kelbende (Kəlbənd), the residents have paid only 24 rubles so far; the rest has to be collected. The commandant has to realize that the rice harvest from the villages of Qazyan and Chigni (Çiyni) listed in our register, which belonged to Qasem Beg, now belongs to the treasury.

Khanchoban (Xançoban) Mahal

Our register for this *mahal* will enable the commandant to ascertain how much butter and cheese, and how many floor mats and small rugs are due from each nomad settlement to the treasury. Mirza Hoseyn has *barats*, which indicate that the khan, prior to his flight, had received 33¼ *batmans* of butter and 14 *batmans* of cheese. These amounts have to be deducted from the total dues, but the commandant has to collect the remainder.

Kabristan (Qobustan) Mahal

Aside from the 73¾ *batmans* of butter and 14½ *batmans* of cheese, which according to the *barats* in the possession of Mirza Hoseyn, Mostafa Khan received prior to his flight, the remainder of the dues for this fiscal year, including floor mats and small rugs have to be collected by the treasury. Furthermore the accuracy of these *barats* has to be ascertained. In addition, the commandant has to note that the harvest of rice from village of Siyazanlu (Siyəzən), which belonged to the fugitive Malek Bagam Beg and now to the treasury, was, according to our register, 80 *taghars*, after the share of the *ranjbars* and other expenses. However, according to the *mirza*, the treasury has received only 4 *taghars* and 20 *batmans* of rice. As to the *mal-o-jehat* in grain from this *mahal*, it has to be ascertained if Mostafa Khan had assessed such dues from this *mahal* or if he had exempted it due to locust attacks.

Salyan Mahal

Aside from the wheat and barley, which Mostafa Khan collected prior to his flight, there remains the harvest of rice, which has been always plentiful in Salyan. According to `Abdollah Beg, the *nayeb*[6] of Salyan, 153 *taghars* of rice was planted on lands belonging to the *divan*, which, as our register lists, has to yield 1,377 *taghars* of rice to the treasury. Although we do not have an accurate amount of this harvest, the commandant has to note that the yield has to be not less than 2,000 *taghars*, to cover the share of the *ranjbars* and other expenses. `Abdollah Beg, the *nayeb* of Salyan, has our instructions regarding this matter.

Major-General Prince Madatov
State Councilor Mogilevskii

[6] The *nayeb* acted as the lieutenant of the khan. The khan viewed this *mahal* as his private fief and, as noted below, farmed out its revenues for large sums.

Register [1]

List of Leases Farmed Out by the Khan Indicating the Amount and the Duration

The farmed out revenues of the Salyan *Mahal*, which are also listed in its own register [see Register 3] are as follows:[1]

1) The fugitive Mostafa Khan had leased a fishing contract for 10 years to state councilor Ivanov,[2] valid until the *nowruz*, that is, March 10 (22), 1824, for which the latter has agreed to pay 15,500 gold rubles a year.

2) Lt.-Colonel Bulgakov[3] gave the right to catch red fish,[4] to the Iranian Aqamir of Gilan for six months, in exchange for 2,000 gold rubles. It will terminate on March 10 (22), 1821.

3) Mostafa Khan handed the right to collect the *rahdar* (road toll) dues; dues from the slaughter house; *darughegy*; soap-making; sale of *naft* (crude oil); dye-works; *mizan* (weighing scales in the bazaar); and dues from the shops in Salyan, to Hajji Hajji[5] Allahverdi Oghli, a resident of Salyan for one year in exchange for 2,400 gold rubles. It will terminate on March 10 (22), 1821. We have examined and confirmed the validity of this contract.

4) We have appointed Hajji Allahverdi Oghli the *Gemi-begi*[6] of Salyan, which will permit him to collect dues from boats for one year ending on October 23, 1821, in exchange for paying 450 gold rubles.

5) Mostafa Khan farmed out the tolls for the passage between Salyan and the Kur River for 100 gold rubles. We have been advised by the *nayeb* of Salyan, `Abdollah Beg, that by hiring experienced men, the treasury could receive considerable more sums than by farming it out.[7]

---

[1] The farmed out revenues are listed in gold rubles; each gold ruble equaled 5 rubles in local currency.

[2] Such contracts were handed to various Russian officials, including Ivanov, who resided in Astrakhan.

[3] He was the commander of the Russian troops in northern Talesh.

[4] The red fish, known as *kizil-kutum*, is actually a white fish found in the brackish waters of the Caspian Sea and its tributaries. It averages 20 inches long and weighs around 10 lbs. It is called *mahi-sefid* in Iran and is usually smoked, acquiring a reddish color, and eaten with rice.

[5] Appears as such in the text.

[6] The term is derived from the Turkish *gemi* (boat), which indicates that the above-mentioned person was in charge of collecting dues from boats.

[7] The total five farmed out revenues from the Salyan *Mahal* (mentioned in the report to Yermolov), some ending in

The khan sold the following contracts sold as well:

1. The fugitive Mostafa Khan gave Aqa Mirza, a resident of Fitdagh, the right to collect for one year the *rahdar* dues in exchange for 16,000 rubles in local money; the right to collect dues from the weighing scales (*mizan*) in exchange for 10,000 rubles in local money; and the right to collect the *darughegy* dues, including dues from the slaughter house, in exchange for 7,000 rubles in local money. The contract terminates on March 10 (22), 1821.

Total: 33,000 rubles in local money or 6,600 gold rubles.

2. Mostafa Khan farmed out the dues from the caravansary in the city of Fitdagh; customs dues; dues from placing seals on documents; dues from washing and re-fluffing cotton or woolen mattress-stuffing to a Shirvani resident, `Abdol-Rahim, son of Hajji Aqa-`Ali, for one year, in exchange for the sum of 800 local rubles (160 gold rubles). The contract terminates on March 10 (22) of 1821.
3. Mostafa Khan farmed out the dues from the dye works, soap works, and baths to an Armenian resident of Shirvan, Ariutin (Harut`iwn), son of Vartan the tanner, for one year, in exchange for 4,500 local rubles (900 gold rubles). The contract ends on March 10 (22) of 1821.
4. Since Mostafa Khan of Shirvan has fled, we have farmed out the *bazari*, *ekhrajat* and *mal-o-jehat* dues of the city of Fitdagh to Esma`il Allahverdi for six months, ending on March 10 (22), 1821, in exchange for 200 gold rubles, which equals to 400 gold rubles a year.[8]
5. We have farmed out the dues from the sale of madder, which belonged to khan's nephew, Qader Beg, to Shirvani residents, Esma`il Allahverdi and the Armenian Mikayel Danielov for one year, ending on 14 (26) September, 1821, in exchange for 550 gold rubles.[9]
6. The right to cross the Kur River at Zardob (Zərdab), Əlvənd and Javad (Sabirabad), which belonged to Esma`il Beg, the bother of Mostafa Khan, who has fled with him to Iran, has been farmed out by us to the Shirvani resident Ebrahim `Abdi-Oghli for six months, ending on March 10 (22),[10] 1821 in exchange for 620 gold rubles, which equals to 1,240 gold rubles a year.

---

the fiscal year 1821, others earlier or later, came to 20,450 gold rubles, which are included in the total revenues of the Salyan *Mahal* (Register 3).

[8] In an earlier report, dated October 3, 1820, the above is described as the lease of the shops in Fitdagh ending on March 14; see *Akty*, VI/1, doc. No. 1225.

[9] An earlier report, dated October 3, 1820, states that the tax-farmer could only benefit from this lease during the months of April, May and June, when the madder root was available; *ibid.*

[10] An earlier report, dated October 3, 1820, reads March 14, *ibid.*

7. Although we had individuals who wished to purchase the dues called *sharban*,[11] or the cash received from the workshops that weave silk, in exchange for 105 gold rubles, our research concluded that it was customary to collect 1 ruble and 40 kopeks in Shirvani currency from each workshop per year. In addition, each workshop paid 20 kopeks in *giullek* (*qullugh*)[12] and *julfet*,[13] or custom duties, for each batch and the fee of 10 kopeks per batch for the customs official. After consulting with the master weavers and sellers we concluded that it would be better if they collectively pay the treasury 600 local rubles or 120 gold rubles for this fiscal year, which ends on March 10 (22), 1821.

8. Mostafa Khan sold the right to affix metal plates to the heels and toes of shoes to the Shirvani residents Hoseyn `Ali and Hoseyn `Ali[14], in exchange for 250 local rubles or 50 gold rubles for one year, ending on March 10 (22), 1821.
   Note: Due to the odd nature of this fee, as well as the fact that the tax-farmers oppressed the residents, most of who are poor, we think that the Russian government should end this practice. The decision is left to the higher authority.

9. The dues for the manufacture and sale of candles in the city of Fitdagh was farmed out to Shirvani residents Hoseyn and Hasan in exchange for 180 local rubles or 36 gold rubles for one year, ending on March 10 (22), 1821.
   Note: Mostafa Khan granted this right was originally to the Shirvani resident Mirza Ja`far. He enjoyed the income for twenty years, as did other high-ranking *begs* and *mirzas* who had served the khan in the past. However, the fugitive khan did not give any written document or *ta`liqeh* to Mirza Ja`far regarding this right.

10. The khan collected 53 rubles a month from the 9 shops in the city of Fitdagh belonging to the *divan*, which amounted to an annual income of 636 rubles, or 127 gold rubles and 1 Shirvani ruble.
   Note: There are a total of 20 *divani* shops in the city, but the income from one of them belongs to Mostafa Khan's sister, Zeyveh Khanum, who donated it as a perpetual gift[15] to the [main] mosque.

11. The weighing machines (*mizan*) in the city of Fitdagh, which weigh grain for sale, have been farmed out for many years at various prices. Last year it was decided to fix the fee at 200 *taghars* of barley a year. This year, however, Mostafa Khan, prior to his flight, and at the request of the citizens who complained that, as a result of the locusts, the harvest had been extremely poor, forgave the tax. Since in this region, as well as in all of Russia, city taxes are

---

[11] The term is probably from the Turkish *şar* (hair) and the Persian *band* (cord), that is, silken hair woven into cord.
[12] Text refers to *qullughi-puli*, noted above.
[13] Text refers to a tax on weavers (from the Persian *julah*, weaver/knitter).
[14] Appears as such in the original text.
[15] Text refers to the Muslim practice of *waqf* or *vaqf*, that is, an endowment to support a religious institution.

recorded for the future, we have included the 200 *taghars* of barley at 8 local rubles a *taghar*, for a total of 1,600 rubles or 320 gold rubles a year.

12. The revenue from the sale of tobacco for many years has been farmed out in the Shirvan Province in exchange for 1,000 local rubles. Last year Mostafa Khan abolished this tax at the request of the citizens, who felt the tax-farmers were demanding too much. Most of the citizens use tobacco and we shall farm out this revenue for the same amount, which comes to 200 gold rubles.

13. The post of *sarkar*[16] belonged to Mostafa Khan's brother, Esma`il Beg, who, together with him, has fled to Iran. Last year he received no less than 1,000 sheep from the *qeshlaqs*[17] or winter camps of the nomads, and 1,000 rubles in Shirvani money. The average price of a sheep is 1 ruble and 60 kopeks in Shirvani currency, which brings the total of this revenue to be farmed out at 2,600 local rubles or 520 gold rubles.

    Note: This revenue could be collected this year, for 10,000 sheep were sold in Karabagh and the terrible drought in the pasturelands, as well as the absence of the Lezgis, who brought their sheep to winter in Shirvan.

Total revenue: 11,223 gold rubles and 1 Shirvani ruble.

Major-General Prince Madatov
State Councilor Mogilevskii

[16] The *sarkar* was the main overseer of the khanate.

[17] The nomads moved to winter and summer grazing pastures in different seasons.

[Register 2]

Survey of the City of Fitdagh (İsmayıllı) in the Shirvan Province

Prior to the time when the Shirvan Province became subordinate to Russia [1805], its main city, located by the Ağsu River, was called New Shamakhi, which today is abandoned and left in ruins by its inhabitants. Mostafa Khan collected 30,000 Shirvani rubles or 6,000 gold rubles—counting 5 Shirvani rubles to one gold ruble—in *toujih* dues a year from the entire province for his household expenses. Seven parts of this revenue came from the entire Shirvan Province, while the eighth part came from the city [New Shamakhi]. When, according to the treaty he promised to pay 8,000 gold rubles a year tribute to Russia, the above *toujih* was abolished and the residents of all the *mahals* had to collectively contribute toward the annual tribute. Meanwhile, Mostafa Khan moved his residence to Fitdagh and wishing to populate the new city, he exempted the citizens from all taxes, including the annual tribute in gold rubles. Instead the citizens were required to provide as many laborers as required by the khan and to pay the expenses of the Russian officials and host guests who visited the khan in Fitdagh. The city has an estimated 2,000 families who had come from different places. The true city residents and those who came from New Shemakhi and previously paid taxes number some 1,000 families. The craftsmen and other masters who live in the city pay their taxes in the *mahals* from where they came. There are also individuals, although few in number, who by the khan's *ta`liqeh* are exempt from all taxes, even providing labor or hosting guests.

In order to take care of the law and order of the city and take care of any complaints, Mostafa Khan appointed two *nayebs*, Ahmad Aqa and Aqa Sadeq, together with the *qal`eh-beg*,[1] or chief of police, Aqa Rahim. The first two served in the city court, presided by the Russian commandant. Their posts are now abolished. The last official is essential for the court and if the government does not wish to appoint a Russian official as the new chief of police, they should appoint an assistant to the commandant, with the rank of major, who would serve as the chief of police.

The city of Fitdagh is located between the slopes of two high mountains, with picturesque ravines, and is locked from one side by mountains. Frequent fog and the constant change in weather make this place unhealthy. The tightly stacked homes on steep streets are constantly washed away during heavy downpours. The lack of a stable source of water and mountainous terrain cuts the city off during rainy and winter months. The difficulty of obtaining provisions and the high cost of food make the location unsuitable for a city. Few of the residents will remain in the city if the Russian government permits

[1] The *qaleh-beg* was actually the person in charge of guarding a city or a fort.

them to leave. Most wish that the Old or New Shemakhi be restored. In our opinion the former place is better due to its climate and better living conditions, for New Shamakhi, due to its terrible heat in the summer and the poor quality of its water, is a place to perish. Thus if the government agrees we shall demolish the city of Fitdagh and move the population to Old Shemakhi, where we can appoint officials and begin to collect revenues.

Finally, at the base of the mountains of Fitdagh, there is the Jewish village of Migele, consisting of 60 households. They came to the city from New Shamakhi. The residents of this village are the only citizens, who, in addition to providing laborers and hosting guests, have to pay a [lump sum] tax of 600 local rubles, which Mostafa Khan gave to his wife, Kichkin, in addition to the 120 rubles in *darughegy* dues, for a total of 720 rubles or 144 gold rubles.

Major-General Prince Madatov
State Councilor Mogilevskii

[Register 3]

Salyan Mahal[1]

Revenues from the Salyan Mahal, which were the private property of Mostafa Khan of Shirvan, indicating the total number of villages and families, as well as the revenues from the various leases, all of which now belong to the treasury

Villages of Salyan, which belonged of the khan and now belong to the treasury

1. Arbatan, the main village of the *mahal.*
2. Surra (Aşaği Surra).
3. Karamanni (Aşaği Qaramanlı), which belonged to Mirza `Abdollah, who fled with Mostafa Khan and now belongs to the treasury.
4. Gezekenargi.
5. Marishliu (Marışlı).
6. Shilly; the inhabitants of this village are all engaged in catching red fish.
7. Salyani (Salyan); formerly the main village of this *mahal.*
8. Boyat.
9. Ahmad-Begli; belonged to Mohammad `Ali Aqa, who fled with Mostafa Khan and now belongs to the treasury.
10. Ballydzha (Balıcallı).
11. Sarvan.
12. Khodzha-Chobany (Hoca-Çobani).
13. Chereja (Çerece).
14. Nowruz `Ali-Begli.
15. Mohammad `Ali-Begli; Aqa Sadeq, the *qal`eh-beg* of Fitdagh, was annually given 4 *ranjbars* from this village.
16. Kazminni (Kazmin).
17. Ardabilli (Ardabilia).
18. Meshtali (Meştala); Mostafa Khan assigned 4 *ranjbars* from this village to Jebi-Aqa.
19. Khadzha-Chobanly (Khoşçobanlı).

[1] The term Salyan or Seylan most probably derives from the Arabo-Persian *seyl* (flood) and *seylan* (overflow), which, as will be noted in the text below, was a common occurrence in the southeastern part of the *mahal*. It could also be derived from the Turkish term, *sal* (raft). Such rafts were used on the Kur River as it flowed into the Caspian Sea.

20. Minadali Aqa.
21. Kapali.
22. Shorsuli (Şorsulu) and Khilly (Xıllı), considered one village, from which 6 *ranjbars* were given to `Abdollah Beg (the *nayeb*) of Shirvan.
23. Seydanny (Seidan).
24. Kardash-Begli.
25. Pirat Manny (Piratman).

In addition, there are 62 families who have come to Salyan from different places and who reside in the main village of Arbatan; they bear the same obligations as other villagers.

The following villages are private property (*molk*): 1) Kizil-Agach (Qızılağac) belongs to Mohammad Beg of Talesh and his brothers. They, together with 30 families, left the Khanate of Talesh some ten years ago. Later, 150 families, who were originally from Salyan and who had sought refuge in the Khanate of Talesh and other places, returned. Mostafa Khan placed them all under the supervision of Mohammad Beg. The village, which now has some 200 households, did not pay any dues to the treasury, since its inhabitants were all immigrants; the villagers paid the revenues to the beg. The authorities now have to determine the number of families and the revenues to be collected. 2) The village of Karaghachly (Karakashly) belongs to the children of Sheikh `Ali Beg. The village never paid any dues to the khan, but gave them to the owner (*molkdar*). The authorities now have to determine the exact revenues from this and all other similar villages of this *mahal*.

Finally, the total families of this *mahal* are 1,400, but, according to the *nayeb* of Salyan, `Abdollah Beg, a detailed survey would result in a higher number.

1. The fishing rights of the *mahal* were leased to councilor Ivanov for 10 years, ending on the *nowruz*, or March 10 (22), 1824, for 15,500 gold rubles.[2]

2. The right for the catching and selling of the red fish, which originally belonged to the khan's wife Kichkin, was leased in September for 6 months and nine days to the Iranian Aqamir of Gilan in exchange for 2,000 gold rubles. The lease will terminate on March 10 (22), 1821.
   Note: The catching of red fish is abundant only in the autumn and declines by the end of winter. That is why the right is only farmed out from September to March.

3. Mostafa Khan leased the right to collect the *rahdar* tolls, dues from the slaughter house, *darughegy*, soap-making, sale of *naft* (crude oil), dye-works, *mizan*

[2] Salyan was known for its riverfront fisheries even in the 18th century, when its khan, leased them to a merchant from Astrakhan for 5,000 gold coins. The fisheries expanded after 1820 and later on were generally leased for 3 years.

(weighing scales in the bazaar), and dues from the shops in Salyan, to Hajji[3] Hajji Allahverdi Oghli, a resident of Salyan for one year in exchange for 2,400 gold rubles. It will terminate on March 10 (22), 1821. We have examined and confirmed this contract.
Note: While looking over the revenues from Salyan, Lt.-Colonel Bulgakov, realized that the above buyer was insolvent and would not be able to abide by the entire agreement, which would result in a loss to the treasury. He has decided that farming out the *rahdar* and *darughegy* dues, the sale of crude oil and the income from the weighing scales would depend on establishing a customs house in Baku. He, therefore, has made a new contract, with the same Hajji Allahverdi Oghli, together with Kazarov, an Armenian from Baku, for the dues from the slaughter house, soap-making, dye-works and dues from the shops, in exchange for 250 gold rubles, for 4 months, from September to January 1821. The *nayeb* of Salyan, `Abdollah Beg, interceded on behalf of Hajji Allahverdi Oghli and stated that he was one of the premier capital owners in Salyan and guaranteed that he would be now able to pay the above four lapsed dues. A new agreement was signed for the remaining three months for 338 gold rubles and 1 ruble and 80 kopeks of Russian silver rubles for the *rahdar* and *darughegy* dues, sale of crude oil and the weighing scales. In the future, a customs post has to be set on the land route from the Kur River to Baku.

4. Mostafa Khan farmed out the custom dues from the *gemi-begi*, that is, payment for transferring the fishermen's catch from small boats to large seagoing vessels—for large vessels cannot approach the shore, together with the right to catch the red fish, for 400 gold rubles a year. However, after our arrival in Salyan, we have leased this right to Hajji Allahverdi Oghli for one year, from October 23 of this year to October 23, 1821, in exchange for the sum of 450 gold rubles.

5. The khan had farmed out the dues for crossing the Kur River in exchange for 100 gold rubles.
Note: We have not been able to find anyone to purchase this right. The *nayeb* of Salyan, `Abdollah Beg, has informed us that since the Shahsevan and other nomads have to cross the river every winter, the treasury can collect more than 100 gold rubles in such dues.[4]

6. Salyan has three main salty lakes, which always produce salt. During heavy rainfall other salty lakes appear, which produce very good salt. The khan gave the dues from the salt of these lakes to his wife, Nakhay, the daughter of Sorkhay Khan, who fled with the khan to Iran. It now belongs to the treasury.

---

[3] Text repeats Hajji.

[4] The above five leases have been noted in Register 1 and have been deducted from the totals revenue from this *mahal*.

All the inhabitants of the villages of Salyan have to work and collect the salt. Their pay consists of a small amount of salt. They perform this labor in August for two weeks, or more if needed. When Russia forbade Mostafa Khan to sell the salt from Salyan and gave it to the Baku treasury, the salt was sold on small boats from 3000 to 4,000 gold rubles or more. In fact, after the prohibition, the income from salt declined, for it was sold illegally. Now that the lakes of Salyan belong to the treasury, the inhabitants state that the revenues can reach 5,000 gold rubles.
Note: The amount of salt gathered from the Salyan lakes, especially after a major rainfall can approach 10,000 gold rubles.

7. At present there are 32 plows in the various fields in Salyan, which belonged to the khan and now to the treasury. They use 70 oxen, belonging to the treasury. In addition, 38 *ranjbar* families, from various villages of Salyan, are obliged to work on these fields. The amount sown was sometimes high, other times low, but on average, it came to 200 *taghars* of wheat and, sometimes, included barley. After deducting one-fourth for the *ranjbars*, the khan, and now the treasury, received 2,000 *taghars*, valued at 20 rubles per *taghar* in Shirvani currency, for a total of 40,000 rubles in local money or 8,000 gold rubles.
Note: This year the treasury only received 100 *taghars*, because there were irregularities in the accounts after the khan fled abroad. If we receive rainfall this year, we shall sow another 100 *taghars*.

8. The khan planted 200 *taghars* of rice in Salyan. There is no need to work on these lands. When the winds blow the water from the sea, the level of the Kur River rises and overflows its banks and covers the rice fields. After that, it recedes. This occurs regularly every year. There are no regular *ranjbars* to plant the rice, but there are always volunteers, for they receive half of the harvest as their share. Those *ranjbars* who came only to harvest the rice received one-tenth. The average yield of rice is 20 to 1, hence, after all labor and expenses, the khan and now the treasury collect 1,800 *taghars*—4000 minus 2000 minus 200. Since a *taghar* of rice is worth 8 rubles and 10 kopeks in Shirvani currency, the total collected is 14,580 rubles in local money, or 2,916 gold rubles.

9. Above Salyan, in the marsh of Seidan, where the Kura flows over, two large ponds are formed almost every year. The overflow from these ponds forms a third pond. Canals are dug and water covers the rice fields of the khan, now belong to the treasury, where up to 100 *taghars* of rice is planted. The harvest yield is the same as described in no. 8 above and after all expenses amounts to 900 *taghars*, or 7,290 rubles in local money, which equals 1,458 gold rubles.

10. In addition, in the marsh of Diulbardzhan (Dülbarcan), the *ranjbars* and inhabitants of Salyan sow 50 *taghars* of wheat every year. The harvest yield is the same as mentioned in the Navahi and Qobustan *mahals*, that is, after all

expenses, 30 *taghars* of wheat is left from every *taghar* sown, which amounts to 1,500 *taghars*, or 30,000 rubles in local money, which equals 6,000 gold rubles.

11. The *ranjbars*, as well as local inhabitants of Salyan plant some 1,000 *batmans* of cotton on the khan's, now the treasury's, land. The yield, after all expenses, which includes cleaning and the payment of one-fourth to the laborers, produces 1,000 *batmans* of clean cotton, which at 5.40 rubles a *batman* in local money, bring 5,040 rubles, or 1008 gold rubles.

12. The orchards[5] in the Salyan *Mahal*, which belonged to the khan and now to the treasury, are famed for their watermelons and especially their superb melons. They can be farmed out in exchange for 100 gold rubles.

13. Those inhabitants of Salyan, who grew grain on their own private properties, excluding the *begs*, *seyyeds*, mullahs and other exempt individuals, had to pay the khan, and now the treasury one-tenth (*bahreh*) of the grain in *mal-o-jehat*, which comes to 200 *taghars* of wheat and 15 *taghars* of barley, totaling 4,120 local rubles, or 824 gold rubles.
    Note: According to the report of Salyan's *nayeb*, this year, due to a poor harvest, Lt.-Colonel Bulgakov forgave 90 *taghars* from the *mal-o-jehat* and the treasury received only 125 *taghars* of grain altogether.

14. The *mal-o-jehat* from cotton this year yielded only 30 *batmans*, but in the coming year, depending on the harvest, the yield should be more. The total revenue was 151 rubles and 20 kopeks in local money, or 30 gold rubles and 1.20 silver ruble.

15. The *mal-o-jehat* from rice, depending on the harvest, is 130 *taghars*, which comes to 1,053 rubles in local money, or 210 gold rubles and 3 silver rubles.

16. The *mal-o-jehat* from beans[6] was 78 *batmans* this year, which at 40 kopeks per *batman*, came to 31.20 local rubles, or 6 gold rubles and 1.20 silver rubles.
    Note: It is better to cancel this revenue in the future.

17. The inhabitants of Salyan had to pay 1,000 gold rubles for the tribute and 40 gold rubles in *qullughi* dues.
    Note: The *nayeb* of Salyan, `Abdollah Beg, states that the khan, each year, forgave 200 gold rubles and only collected 800 gold rubles.

18. Finally, The tax-farmer from Baku, Tarumov, during his visit to New Shemakhi and meeting with us, stated that there is some crude oil in Salyan and when it bubbles up, the residents collect it without paying any dues to the treasury. He offered to set up an oil well and claims that at least 2 *kharvars* of crude oil, each *kharvar* being some 20 *puds*, sold in Baku for 5 Russian silver rubles per *pud*. If the

[5] Text uses *bostan*, a variation of the Persian *bustan*.
[6] Text uses *lobii*, a variation of the Persian *lubiya*.

treasury puts up a well and farms the revenue it could collect some 3,650 Russian silver rubles, or 1,216 gold rubles and 67 kopeks.[7]

Total revenues from the Salyan *Mahal*: 48,259 gold rubles and 1 ruble and 4 kopeks in Russian currency.[8]

Note: Lt. Colonel Bulgakov in his register of Salyan states that the revenues from Salyan in the future will be some 45,300 gold rubles. However, according to Councilor Ivanov, if we farm out the 15,500 gold rubles in revenues, which the inhabitants gave to the khan, the income from the Salyan *Mahal* will be 48,960 gold rubles a year. The reasons are: 1) Bulgakov has cut the khan's part of the revenue almost in half. 2) The sowing of barley, which is always very small, and only some 100 *taghars*, is sown in case of need. If we sow wheat instead, the treasury and the troops will collect more money, since a *taghar* of wheat sells for an average of 20 local rubles, while a *taghar* of barley is worth only 8 rubles. The amount of time and labor for the harvest is the same. 3) The yield from the marshes of Dülbarcan and Seidan are not estimated in full. 4) The losses from farming out the *rahdar* dues, sale of crude oil and revenues from the weighing scales were 1,650 gold rubles and, after new regulations, should now yield a better income. 5) The 1,040 gold rubles in tribute paid by the Salyan inhabitants is not listed in his register. 6) Finally, the crude oil deposit is totally ignored. Bulgakov has also indicated that we should not give a share to the laborers and consider it as compulsory dues. This can be very dangerous, for if we take away their traditional rights, which were assured by the Russian Government, they, at the urging of the former khan, who lives close to the border of Salyan, could flee abroad. It will not only be difficult to stop them, but it will also require funds and personnel. If we ask the inhabitants to work for the treasury without giving them a part of the harvest, they will then request that we abolish their corvée, to Mostafa Khan, which required them to thresh the un-husked rice into hulled rice, which sells for three times as much. However, they will voluntarily surrender the customary half of the rice harvest, for the remainder feeds their families. In this manner we shall increase the production of rice and make up for the loss by selling hulled rice. As a result, our government will not lose any revenue and will gain the loyalty of the population, which was promised relief; this will, of course, depend on the decision of the higher authority.

Major-General Prince Madatov
State Councilor Mogilevskii

---

[7] Text refers to the present-day Neftçala, see map 2.

[8] If we deduct the first five leases already listed in register 1, the total comes to 27,809 gold rubles and 1 ruble and 4 kopeks in Russian currency.

[Register 4]

Gouz (Howz) Mahal[1]

Revenues from the villages of the Howz Mahal, indicating the number of tax-paying and tax-exempt families, as well as the portion [of the harvest] from each village that was assessed as the taxes paid directly to the khan, which will now go to the treasury;[2] *which villages are under the supervision of the beg of the mahal, who collected the revenue for the khan [which will now go to the treasury] and who kept a part as his salary. Also what other revenues are collected from the grain harvest, silk production and other produce, and what are the revenues for the upkeep of the darugheh.*[3]

Note: This entire *mahal* was the hereditary property of the cousins of Mostafa Khan: Khanjan Beg and Mardan Beg, who owned it jointly with the khan's nephew, Mehdi Beg. Khanjan Beg, the former superintendent, and Mehdi Beg have fled to Iran, but Mardan Beg has remained here and serves as the superintendent (*darugheh*) of the *mahal*. He is loyal to the Russian State. He collects one-third of the *mal-o-jehat* and *darughegy*[4] dues as his salary and patrimony. The other two-thirds, as well as the *sursat* belongs now to the treasury.[5]

Note: The average price of wheat in Shirvan is around 20 rubles a *taghar* or 40 kopeks a *batman*, while a *taghar* of barley is 8 rubles or 20 kopeks[6] a *batman*.

Note: One Russian silver ruble is worth 1 ruble and 60 kopeks in local currency.

---

[1] Most of the villages listed in this *mahal* are currently within the boundaries of the Ismayıllı and Ağsu district of the Azerbaijan Republic. Some are included in map 2.

[2] As noted, the term "treasury" refers either to the Shirvan treasury controlled by the new Russian administration or to the central treasury of the Caucasus in Tiflis, which may or may not have sent a percentage of the revenues to the Imperial Treasury in St. Petersburg The revenues collected by the khan went to his treasury administered by his *divan* or chancery. Thus the term divan will replace "the khan's treasury" or "the treasury" when it clearly refers to the former treasury.

[3] The post of the *darugheh* was originally that of police official in charge of a ward. In Shirvan, during the Qajar period, the *darugheh* was the overseer of a village or a group of villages and served as a prefect and tax collector

[4] The *darughegy* or *darughalik* was the dues collected for the maintenance of *darugheh* of each *mahal*.

[5] Mardan Beg did not collect a third of the *mal-o-jehat* or *darughegy* from all the villages. In some cases the treasury took it all and in others he collected the entire dues.

[6] According to the above, the price of barley per *batman* should have been 16 kopeks and not 20, for 16 times 50 equals 8 rubles. Thus, it seems that the market price of barley was higher if purchased by *batman*.

Note: Most of the villages had to provide the khan (now the treasury) with as many laborers,[7] as needed from 1 to 3 days a year.

Note: The *mal-o-jehat* refers to one-tenth (*dah-yek*) of the grain harvest and one-fifth (*dah-nim*) of the silk and cotton yield.

1. Baskal (Basqal):[8] A Tatar village.

Tax-paying families: 115. Tax-exempt families: 20.
(The 4 immigrant[9] families from Karabagh; 3 immigrant families from Kuba; 4 Shirvani families resettled from the village of Lahic; and 9 families from the khan's village of Khnisi are exempt).

Annual tribute: 190 *chervonets* (gold rubles) sent to the Central Treasury of the Russian administration of the Caucasus in Tiflis (hereinafter: Annual tribute).[10]

Sursat: 2 *taghars*[11] of wheat worth 40 [local][12] rubles.

The khan farmed out the bazaar or marketplace of this village in exchange for 720 rubles in local currency a year. Each vendor paid one *abazi* (*`abbasi*)[13] a month, which annually totaled 36 rubles in local currency. The khan collected 120 rubles in local currency from the dye works of this *mahal*, which will now belong to the treasury and will be included in the total from the farmed out dye works of the khanate. In addition, the local *beg* and his relatives, receive 33 rubles every month from the dye works, 60 rubles a year from silk production, 9 rubles a month from the baths, as well as 6 *taghars* of barley from the farms and 5 rubles from the fruit orchards.

---

[7] The text uses the term *medzhi*, which is probably from the Arabo-Persian *mejburi* (compulsory, obligatory, or forced service), or *mejjani* (free, gratis). It is also referred to as bigar, or the unpaid forced labor demanded by the khan, *beg* or landowner. The monetary value or the total number of days of such forced labor is not mentioned in the survey.

[8] The current or later name, if known, appears in parenthesis.

[9] Most khanates exempted immigrant families for a number of years from all dues, see the Explanatory Remarks for details.

[10] This sum was collected in order to pay the annual 8,000 *chervonets* (hereinafter gold rubles) tribute as specified in Article VIII of the Russo-Shirvani treaty (see appendix). The *chervonets* was a Russian gold ruble minted during the reign of Catherine II. It contained 3.47 grams of gold and was worth 3 silver rubles. In the absence of Russian gold rubles, the khan could send the equivalent amount in local rubles.

[11] A *taghar* was a large measure of grain, equal to half a *kharvar* or 50 *batmans* in Shirvan.

[12] As noted, 1.6 rubles in Shirvani silver coins equaled 1 Russian silver ruble. Except for the gold rubles and the total revenue from each village or nomad settlement, the survey lists all dues in local Shirvani money. Therefore, for the sake of simplification, the term local/Shirvani/khan's money will not be repeated after each of the various dues collected from every village or nomad settlement. It will appear only in the total revenue from each village or nomad settlement and will be followed by its equivalent in Russian currency, which, after all, was the primary concern of the Russian officials (see the facsimile of a page from the original text).

[13] *Abazi* silver coins, derived from the Iranian *`abbasi* coins, were used in Transcaucasia from the 17th to the 19th centuries. Georgia and the various khanates struck their own *abazi* coins, or stamped Russian coins, which varied in their silver content.

Mal-o-jehat: None is collected from this village since all the inhabitants are laborers and not farmers.

The *darughegy* dues belong to Mardan Beg.[14]

Total revenue:[15] 190 gold rubles,[16] 811 rubles and 33 kopeks in local money, which equals 507 rubles and 8 kopeks in Russian currency.

2. Zargeran (Zərgəran): An Armenian village.

Note: The village belonged to the khan and now to the treasury.

Tax-paying families: 30. Tax-exempt families: 1.
(An immigrant family from Karabagh is exempt).

Annual Tribute: None collected.

Sursat: One *taghar* of wheat, worth 20 rubles.

Kharaj: 50 rubles.[17]

Bagh-bashi: 3 rubles.

Mal-o-jehat: 6 *taghar* of wheat and 2 *taghar* of barley valued at 136 rubles.

Darughegy: 2 *taghar* of wheat and 2 *taghar* of barley, valued at 59 [56][18] rubles.

In addition, the village had to supply the khan with firewood and straw, and had to provide free labor, which consisted of plowing the khan's field one day a year and mowing the hay for one other day a year. These services now belong to the treasury.

Total revenue: 265 rubles in local money, or 165 rubles and 6½ kopeks in Russian currency.

---

14 Unless the village was exempt, the *darugheh* collected all or some (generally one-third) of the *daughegy* dues from each village. The *darughegy* dues in the registers only record the amount collected by the khan's *divan* (unless the *darugheh* was entitled to all the dues); see Explanatory Remarks for more details.

15 The taxes were assessed and paid each year, starting with the Iranian New Year in March. As noted, the registers indicate the revenues listed in the *divan* tax-rolls (*daftars*), that is, from March 1820 to March 1821.

16 There is an error in one column; it reads 140 instead of 190.

17 A poll tax paid solely by Armenian villages.

18 Should read 56.

3. Tirdzhan (Tircan): A Tatar Village.

Tax-paying families: 25. Tax-exempt families: 3.
(3 immigrant families from Kuba are exempt).

Annual tribute: 45 gold rubles.

Sursat: ½ *taghar* of wheat and two *taghars* of barley, valued at 26 rubles.

Bagh-bashi: 5 rubles, two-thirds of which will now go to the treasury.

Mal-o-jehat: 8 *taghars* of wheat, two thirds of which now belong to the treasury and one third to Mardan Beg. It is valued at 106 rubles and 67 kopeks.

Darughegy: 1½ *taghars* of wheat and 2 *taghars* of barley, two thirds of which belongs to the treasury and one third to Mardan Beg. It is valued at 30 rubles and 66½ kopeks.

Total revenue: 45 gold rubles, 232 rubles in local money, or 145 rubles in Russian currency.

4. Pir-Abul-Kasym [Pir-Abiul-Kasum][19] (Pirəbülaqasım): A Tatar village.

Tax-paying families: 8.

Annual tribute: 15 gold rubles.

Sursat: 12 *batmans* of wheat and 1 *taghar* of barley, worth 12 rubles and 80 kopeks.

Mal-o-jehat: 3 *taghars* of wheat and 2 *taghars* of barley, worth 50 rubles and 67 kopeks.

Darughegy: ¾ *taghar* of wheat and ¾ *taghar* of barley, two thirds of which belong to the treasury and one third to Mardan Beg, valued at 14 rubles.

Total revenue: 15 gold rubles, 77 rubles and 40 kopeks in local money, or 48 rubles and 37½ kopeks in Russian currency.

[19] The names in brackets are listed in D. D. Pagirev's gazetteer, *Alfavitny ukazatel' k'piativertsnoi karte Kavkazskogo kraia* (Tiflis, 1913). This valuable survey lists some 34,000 settlements in the South Caucasus in the final days of the Russian Empire. At the beginning of the 20th century, all the place names mentioned in the survey were in the Baku *guberniia*.

5. Keivendy (Keyvəndi): An Armenian village.

Tax-paying families: 25.

Annual tribute: 60 gold rubles.

Sursat: 40 *batmans* of wheat, valued at 16 rubles.

Kharaj: 60 rubles. Two-thirds of which belongs to the treasury.

Bagh-bashi or taxes from orchards: 50 rubles—two-thirds of which belongs now to the treasury, the two are valued together at 73 rubles and 34 kopeks in cash.

Mal-o-jehat: 6 *taghars* of wheat and 2 *taghars* of barley, two-thirds of which belongs to the treasury, valued at 90 rubles and 67 kopeks.

Darughegy: 2 *taghars* of wheat and 4 *taghars* of barley, two-thirds of which belongs to the treasury, valued at 48 rubles.

Total revenue: 60 gold rubles, 228 rubles and 1 kopek in local money, or 142 rubles and 50½ kopeks in Russian currency.

6. Miudzhiuli [Miudzhi] (Mücü): A Tatar Village.

Tax-paying families: 14.

Annual tribute: 30 gold rubles.

Sursat: 20 *batmans* of wheat and 1 *taghar* of barley, valued at 16 rubles.

Bagh-bashi: 10 rubles, two-thirds of which now belong to the treasury, valued at 6 rubles and 67 kopeks.

Mal-o-jehat: None is collected, since the village has no peasants but is populated with artisans and craftsmen.

Darughegy: None collected.

Note: The village had to give the khan 14 loads (*kharvar*) of firewood, as well as sowing his fields for one day a year and mowing the hay for one day a year, free of charge. Total revenue: 30 gold rubles, 22 rubles and 67 kopeks in local money, or 14 rubles and 16⅓ kopeks in Russian currency.

7. Sardagar [Sardakhar] (Sərdahar): A Tatar village.

Tax-paying families: 9. Tax-exempt families: 1.
(The family of 1 immigrant from Kuba is exempt).

Annual tribute: 12 gold rubles.

Sursat: 8 *batmans* of wheat valued at 3 rubles and 20 kopeks.

Bagh-bashi: 4 rubles, two-thirds of which now belongs to the treasury, valued at 2 rubles and 67 kopeks.

Mal-o-jehat: 1 *taghar* of wheat, two-thirds of which now belongs to the treasury, valued at 13 rubles and 34 kopeks.

Darughegy: ½ *taghar* of wheat, two-thirds of which now belongs to the treasury, and ½ *taghar* of barley for Mardan Beg's personal use,[20] altogether valued at 9 rubles and 34 kopeks.[21]

Note: The village is poor and is located on steep, rocky terrain.

Total revenue: 12 gold rubles, 28 rubles and 55 kopeks in local money, or 17 rubles and 84⅓ kopeks in Russian currency.

8. Zarnava [Zarnova] (Zərnava): A Tatar village.

Tax-paying families: 8.

Annual tribute: 12 gold rubles.

Sursat: 8 *batmans* of wheat valued at 3 rubles and 20 kopeks.

---

[20] This tax was called *at-arpasi* in Karabagh and Shirvan and *`alufe* in Yerevan and Nakhichevan. It was collected for fodder for the horses of the khan or the local *beg*.

[21] The total indicates that the *divan* took two-thirds from the *at-arpasi* dues as well. The *divan* sometimes took all the *darughegy* fees from some of the villages in this *mahal*.

Bagh-bashi: 3 rubles, two-thirds of which now belongs to the treasury, valued at 2 rubles.

Mal-o-jehat: none collected, since the village has no farmers.

Darughegy belongs entirely to Mardan Beg.

Note: The village has to provide labor for 2 days a year on Mardan Beg's land, one day for cutting the wheat, another day for mowing the straw.

Total revenue: 12 gold rubles, 5 rubles and 20 kopeks in local money, or 3 rubles and 25 kopeks in Russian currency.

9. Gendakhany [Gendobilu]: A Tatar village

Tax-paying families: 3. Tax-exempt families: 1.
(The family of the *nokar* is exempt).

Annual tribute to Russia: 8 gold rubles.

Sursat: 6 *batmans* of wheat, worth 2 rubles and 40 kopeks.

Bagh-bashi: 1 ruble and 20 kopeks, two parts of which went to the khan and now belongs to the treasury, worth 80 kopeks.

Mal-o-jehat: 1 *taghar* of wheat and ½ *taghar* of barley, two-thirds of which belongs to the treasury, valued at 16 rubles.

Darughegy: 15 *batmans* of wheat and 12 *batmans* of barley, two-thirds of which will go to the treasury. In addition, [two-thirds of the] ½ *taghar* of barley for the *beg*'s horses, all worth, 8 rubles and 27 kopeks.

Total revenue: 8 gold rubles, 27 rubles and 47 kopeks in local money, or 17 rubles and 16¾ kopeks in Russian currency.

10. Biznan (Bizlan): A Tatar village.

Tax-paying families: 5.

Annual tribute: 9 gold rubles.

Sursat: 6 *batmans* of wheat, worth 2 rubles and 40 kopeks.

Bagh-bashi: 3 rubles, two parts of which now belongs to the treasury.

Mal-o-jehat: 1 *taghar* of wheat and ½ *taghar* of barley, two-thirds of which belongs the treasury, valued at 16 rubles.

Darughegy: 20 *batmans* of wheat and 16 *batmans* of barley, two-thirds of which now belongs to the treasury. In addition, [two-thirds of the] ½ *taghar* of barley for the *beg*'s horses, all worth, 10 rubles and 13½ kopeks.

Total revenue: 9 gold rubles, 30 rubles and 53½ kopeks in local money, or 19 rubles and 8 kopeks in Russian currency.

11. Kiurdyvan [Kiurdevan] (Kürdüvan): A Tatar village.

Tax-paying families: 10.

Annual tribute: 15 gold rubles.

Sursat: 10 *batmans* of wheat, worth 4 rubles.

Bagh-bashi: 1 ruble, two-thirds, or 67 kopeks, of which will go to the treasury.

Mal-o-jehat: 1 *taghar* of wheat and 36 *batmans* of barley, two-thirds of which belongs to the treasury, valued at 18 rubles and 13½ kopeks.

Darughegy: None is collected, however, the village has to also supply 1 *taghar* of barley for the *beg*'s horses (*at-arpasi*), [two-thirds of which will go to the treasury] valued at 5 rubles and 34 kopeks.

Total revenue: 15 gold rubles, 18 rubles and 14½ kopeks in local money, or 11 rubles and 33¾ kopeks in Russian currency.

12. Taglibian [Taglabian] (Tağlabiyan): a Tatar village.

Tax-paying families: 12. Tax-exempt families: 3.
(The 3 tax-exempt families are immigrants from Kuba.)
In addition, there are 4 families who reside privately in this village. Almost all the residents of the village are members of the khan's family and pay little or no taxes.

Annual tribute: 7 gold rubles.

Mal-o-jehat: 30 *batmans* of wheat, two-thirds of which goes to the treasury, valued at 8 rubles.

No *Bagh-bashi, sursat, darughegy* or free labor is required from this village.

Total revenue: 7 gold rubles, 8 rubles in local money, or 5 rubles in Russian currency.

13. Zeiva (Zeyvə): A Tatar village.

Tax-paying families: 10.

Annual tribute: 15 gold rubles.

Sursat: 10 *batmans* of wheat, worth 4 rubles.

Bagh-bashi: 5 rubles, two-thirds of which, worth 3 rubles and 33 kopeks will go to the treasury.

Mal-o-jehat: 1 *taghar* of wheat and 16 *batmans* of barley, two-thirds of which goes to the treasury, valued at 15 rubles and 47 kopeks.

Darughegy: None is collected, but the village supplies 1[4][22] *taghars* of barley for the *beg*'s horses (*at-arpasi*), [two-thirds of which belongs to the treasury] valued at 13 rubles and 34 kopeks.

In addition, the village has to perform 3 days labor on the *beg*'s fields.

Total revenue: 15 gold rubles, 36 rubles and 14 kopeks in local money, or 22 rubles and 58¾ kopeks in Russian currency.

[22] Should read 4 *taghars* to equal the value of 13 rubles and 34 kopeks.

14. Ingar [Gngar] (Hinqar): An Armenian village.

Tax-paying families: 24. Tax-exempt families: 1.
(An immigrant family from Karabagh is exempt).

Annual tribute: 60 gold rubles.

Sursat: 40 *batmans* of wheat, worth 16 rubles, all of which goes to the treasury.

Kharaj: 60 rubles.

Mal-o-jehat, and the *bagh-bashi*, which is worth 50 rubles belongs to *Kevkha*[23] Mikayel.

Darughegy is not collected, but the village provides 2 *taghars* of barley for the horses of *Kevkha* Mikayel.

The village was the property of the khan and now belongs to the treasury under the supervision of *Kevkha* Mikayel.

Total revenue: 60 gold rubles, 76 rubles in local money, or 47 rubles and 50 kopeks in Russian currency.

15. Bilistan: An Armenian village.

Tax-exempt families: 20.

The village pays no taxes to the treasury. It is the personal property of Mardan Beg, who collects the dues.

16. Niuidi [Niugdy] (Nüydü): A Tatar village.

Tax-exempt families: 6.
(The families are all immigrants from Kuba).

The village does not pay any taxes to the treasury. It belongs to Mardan Beg, who collects the dues.

[23] Text refers to the Armenian version of *kadkhoda*, or village elder.

17. Alpaut [Alpaut-Mardan Bek]: A nomad settlement.

Tax-exempt families: 30.

The nomads pay no dues to the treasury. The settlement belongs to Mardan Beg.

18. Kelparach [Kel-Faradzh] (Kəlfərəc): A Tatar village.

Tax-paying families: 3.

The village pays only 4 gold rubles toward the annual tribute. The village is located in the mountains and the villagers are poor.

19. Sulut: A Tatar village

Tax-paying families: 15.

Annual tribute: 45 gold rubles

Sursat: 30 *batmans* of wheat worth 12 rubles.

Mal-o-jehat: 1 *taghar* of wheat and ½ *taghar* of barley, worth 24 rubles.

Darughegy: ½ *taghar* of wheat and ½ *taghar* of barley. In addition, 1½ *taghars* of barley (*at-arpasi*) for Aqa Beg's horses, all of which is worth 26 rubles. Since Aqa Kishi Beg has fled to Iran, that sum [that is, even the one-third] now belongs to the treasury.

Total revenue: 45 gold rubles, 62 rubles in local money, which equals 38 rubles and 75 kopeks in Russian currency.

20. Kalva: A Tatar village.

Tax-paying families: 30. Tax-exempt families: 18.
(13 immigrant families from Kuba, 5 other families, and the mullah[24] are exempt).

Annual tribute: 89 gold rubles.

Sursat: 60 *batmans* of wheat, worth 24 rubles.

Bagh-bashi: 50 rubles

Mal-o-jehat: 2½ *taghars* of wheat and 2½ *taghars* of barley.

Darughegy: 1½ *taghars* of wheat and 1 *taghar* of barley and 4 *taghars* of barley (*at-arpasi*) for the horses of the Beg.

The *mal-o-jehat*, *bagh-bashi* and *darughegy* belong to Eskandar Beg the owner of this village.

Total revenue: 89 gold rubles, 24 rubles in local money, which equals 15 rubles in Russian currency.

21. Sarusa (Sərusə): A Tatar village.

Tax-paying families: 5. Tax-exempt families: 5.
(The 5 immigrant families from Kuba are exempt).

Annual tribute: 15 gold rubles.

Sursat: 10 *batmans* of wheat, worth 4 rubles.

The *mal-o-jehat* and *darughegy* belong to Eskandar Beg the owner of this village.

Total revenue: 15 gold rubles and 4 rubles in local money, or 2 rubles and 50 kopeks in Russian currency.

[24] Christian and Muslim religious authorities were exempt from taxes in all the khanates; see Explanatory Remarks for more details.

22. Kachatan (Qıçatan): A Tatar village.

Tax-paying families: 9. Tax-exempt families: 1.
(An immigrant family from Kuba is exempt).

Annual tribute: 22 gold rubles and 2 rubles 50 kopeks in local money.

Sursat: 12 *batmans* of wheat and 5 *batmans* of barley, worth 5 rubles and 80 kopeks.

Bagh-bashi: 5 rubles.

Mal-o-jehat: 1½ *taghars* of wheat and ½ *taghar* of barley, worth 34 rubles.

Darughegy: 35 *batmans* of wheat and 28 *batmans* of barley, as well as 30 *batmans* of barley (*at-arpasi*) for the *beg*'s horses, all valued at 25 rubles and 60 kopeks.

Total revenue: 22 gold rubles, 72 rubles and 90 kopeks in local money, which corresponds to 45 rubles and 56¼ kopeks in Russian currency.

23. Muganlo [Muganly] (Muğanlı): A Tatar village.

Tax-paying families: 9. Tax-exempt families: 5.
(The families of 4 *nokars* and 1 mullah are exempt).

Annual tribute: 15 gold rubles.

Sursat: 12 *batmans* of wheat, worth 4 rubles and 80 kopeks.

The *mal-o-jehat* and *darughegy* belong to Eskandar Beg.

Total revenue: 15 gold rubles, 4 rubles and 80 kopeks in local money, or 3 rubles of Russian money.

24. Varna: A Tatar village.

Tax-paying families: 3. Tax-exempt families: 1.
(The family of the mullah is exempt).

Annual tribute: 7 gold rubles and 2 rubles and 50 kopeks in local money.

Mal-o-jehat: 20 *batmans* of wheat and 8 *batmans* of barley, valued at 9 rubles and 60 kopeks.

Darughegy: 10 *batmans* of wheat and 8 *batmans* of barley, worth 5 rubles and 60 kopeks.

The *mal-o-jehat* and *darughegy* belonged to `Ali Beg, but since he has fled to Iran, they now belong to the treasury.

Total revenue: 7 gold rubles, 19 rubles and 70 kopeks in local money, or 12 rubles and 31¼ kopeks in Russian currency.

25. Kalazeiva (Kələzeyvə): A Tatar village.

Tax-paying families: 2.

Annual tribute: 4 gold rubles.

Sursat: 5 *batmans* of wheat, worth 2 rubles.

Bagh-bashi: 5 rubles.

Mal-o-jehat: None was collected in this year.

Darughegy: None was collected. *At-arpasi*: 8 batmans of barley, worth 1 ruble and 60 kopeks.

Note: The village belonged to `Ali Beg, but since he has fled to Iran, it now belongs to the treasury.

Total revenue: 4 gold rubles, 8 rubles and 60 kopeks in local money, or 5 rubles and 37½ kopeks in Russian currency.

26. Kouluch (Kövlüc): A Tatar village.

Tax-paying families: 3.

Annual tribute: 5 gold rubles.

Sursat: 5 *batmans* of wheat, worth 2 rubles.

Mal-o-jehat: 30 *batmans* of wheat and 12 *batmans* of barley, valued at 14 rubles and 40 kopeks

Darughegy: 15 *batmans* of wheat and 12 *batmans* of barley, worth 8 rubles and 40 kopeks, plus *at-arpasi* of 10 *batmans* of barley, worth 2 rubles, for a total of 10 rubles and 40 kopeks.

Note: The village belonged to `Ali Beg, but since he has fled to Iran, it now belongs to the treasury.

Total revenue: 5 gold rubles, 26 rubles and 80 kopeks in local money, or 16 rubles and 75 kopeks in Russian currency.

27. Shamdalan: A Tatar village.

Tax-paying families: 1.

The population of this village has moved to other places and only one family has remained.

Annual tribute: 1 gold ruble.

Sursat: 2 *batmans* of wheat, valued at 80 kopeks.

Mal-o-jehat: 10 *batmans* of wheat and 4 *batmans* of barley, worth 4 rubles and 80 kopeks.

Darughegy: 5 *batmans* of wheat and 4 *batmans* of barley, worth 2 rubles and 80 kopeks, plus *at-arpasi*: 5 *batmans* of barley, worth 1 ruble, for a total of 3 rubles and 80 kopeks.

Note: The village belonged to `Ali, but since he has fled to Iran, the revenues will now go to the treasury.

Total revenue: 1 gold ruble, 9 rubles and 40 kopeks in local money, or 5 rubles and 87½ kopeks of Russian currency.

28. Pir-Kara-Chukha: A Tatar village.

Tax-exempt families: 10.
(All the families are immigrants from Kuba).

Since Mohammad Aqa brought the inhabitants to Shirvan, the last khan gave the village to him as his personal property and exempted it from all dues. The chancery (*divan*) of Shirvan has to examine the yield and assess the revenues to be collected in the future.

29. Begliian (Bəhliyan): An Armenian village.

Tax-paying families: 12.

Annual tribute: 22 gold rubles.

Sursat: 10 *batmans* of wheat and 5 *batmans* of barley, worth 5 rubles.

Note: The village belongs to Eskandar Beg and pays its *mal-o-jehat* and *darughegy* to him and not the treasury.

Total revenue: 22 gold rubles, 5 rubles in local money, or 3 rubles and 12½ kopeks in Russian currency.

30. Kirde [Kirda] (Girdə): An Armenian village.

Tax-paying families: 6

Annual tribute: 15 gold rubles.

Sursat: 8 *batmans* of wheat, worth 3 rubles and 20 kopeks.

Note: The village belongs to Bala Beg and pays its *mal-o-jehat* and *darughegy* to him and not the treasury.

Total revenue: 15 gold rubles, 3 rubles and 20 kopeks in local money, or 2 rubles in Russian currency.

31. Gurdzhevan (Gürcüvan): An Armenian village.

Tax-paying families: 40. Tax-exempt families: 1.
(An immigrant family from Karabagh is exempt).

Annual tribute: 105 gold rubles.

Sursat: 1 *taghar* of wheat and 20 *batmans* of barley, which comes to 24 rubles.

Note: The village belongs to Hajji `Ali Beg and pays its *mal-o-jehat* and *darughegy* dues to him and not the treasury.

Total revenue: 105 gold rubles, 24 rubles in local money, or 15 rubles in Russian currency.

32. Engikent (Yenikənd): An Armenian village.

Tax-paying families: 6.

Annual tribute: 15 gold rubles.

Sursat: 5 *batmans* of wheat and 4 *batmans* of barley, worth 2 rubles and 80 kopeks.

Kharaj: 12 rubles.

Mal-o-jehat: 1½ *taghars* of wheat and 1½ *taghars* of barley, worth 42 rubles.

Darughegy: 35 *batmans* of wheat and 24 *batmans* of barley, worth 18 rubles and 80 kopeks, plus *at-arpasi* of 1 *taghar* of barley, worth 8 rubles for the horses of Mardan Beg, who administers this *mahal*, for a total of 26 rubles and 80 kopeks.

Note: The village belonged to Aqa Kishi Beg, who fled to Iran; the revenues now belong to the treasury.

Total revenue: 15 gold rubles, 83 rubles and 60 kopeks in local money, or 52 rubles and 25 kopeks in Russian currency.

33. Nuran: A Tatar village.

Tax-paying families: 8.

Annual tribute: 20 gold rubles.

Sursat: 8 *batmans* of wheat and 4 *batmans* of barley, worth 4 rubles.

Mal-o-jehat: 1 *taghar* of wheat and ½ *taghar* of barley, worth 24 rubles.

Darughegy: 20 *batmans* of wheat and 16 *batmans* of barley, plus *at-arpasi* of ½ *taghar* of barley for the horses of Mardan Beg, for a total of 15 rubles and 20 kopeks.

Note: Following the flight of the khan and Aqa Kishi Beg, the revenues of this village belong to the treasury.

Total revenue: 20 gold rubles, 43 rubles and 20 kopeks in local money, or 27 rubles in Russian currency.

34. Zargava [Zargova] (Zərqava): A Tatar village.

Tax-paying families: 10.

Annual tribute: 20 gold rubles.

Sursat: 8 *batmans* of wheat and 4 *batmans* of barley, worth 4 rubles.

Mal-o-jehat: 1½ *taghars* of wheat and ½ *taghar* of barley, worth 34 rubles.

Darughegy: 25 *batmans* of wheat and 20 *batmans* of barley, plus *at-arpasi* of 32 *batmans* of barley for Mardan Beg's horses, for a total of 20 rubles and 40 kopeks.

Note: Following the flight of the khan and Aqa Kishi Beg, the revenues of this village belong to the treasury.

Total revenue: 20 gold rubles, 58 rubles and 40 kopeks in local money, or 36 rubles and 50 kopeks in Russian currency.

35. Khasy (Xası): A Tatar village.

Tax-exempt families: 7.
(The inhabitants are all immigrants from Kuba).

Note: The inhabitants of this village are all ranjbars. They pay no taxes to the treasury. The village was the private property of Aqa Kishi Beg. Since his flight, it now belongs to the treasury and will have to be assessed its dues in the future.

36. Shabian (Şəbiyan): A Tatar village.

Tax-paying families: 20.

Note: Ten families from the above were nomads brought by Hajji Aqa Begli. The village pays only 15 gold rubles in tribute and nothing else to the treasury. All other dues belong to Mahmud Beg, who owns the village.

37. Surkhana (Suraxani): A Tatar village.

Tax-exempt families: 4.
(The families of 2 *nokars* and 2 immigrants from Kuba are exempt).

The village pays no taxes and is administered by Mardan Beg.

38. Chiginny [Chigni]: A Tatar village.

Tax-exempt families: 8.

Note: The village pays no taxes to the treasury. It is populated solely by *ranjbars*, who work on rice fields. It belongs to Hajji `Ali Beg, Eskandar Beg and Bala Beg.

39. Adzhi-Dari [Adzhi-Dara]: A Tatar village.

Tax-exempt families: 15.

Note: The village is the private property of Osman Aqa. It pays no taxes to the treasury.

Totals for the Howz Mahal:

Tax-paying families: 480.
Tax-exempt families: 161.
Annual tribute: 897 gold rubles and 5 silver rubles.
Sursat in kind: valued at 1,017 rubles and 73 kopeks.
Sursat in cash: 229 rubles and 81 kopeks.
Mal-o-jehat in kind: valued at 657 rubles and 75½ kopeks.
Darughegy in kind: valued at 330 rubles and 49 kopeks.

Total revenues in cash and kind: 897 gold rubles and 5 silver rubles; 2,240 rubles and 68½ kopeks in local money, which equals to 1,400 rubles and 42¾ kopeks in Russian currency.

Note: One of the gold rubles was paid in silver rubles, which increases the annual tribute to 898 [897 plus 1] gold rubles and reduces the total in cash and kind to 1,397 [1400 minus 3] rubles and 42¾ kopeks.

Major-General Prince Madatov
Active State Councilor Mogilevskii

[Register 5]

Sadarin (Sedenrud) Mahal

Revenues from the villages[1] of the Sedernrud Mahal, indicating the number of tax-paying and tax-exempt families, as well as the portion [of the harvest] from each village that was assessed as taxes paid directly to the khan, which will now go to the treasury; which villages are under the supervision of the beg of the mahal, who collected the revenue for the khan [which will now go to the treasury] and who kept a part as his salary. Also, what other revenues are collected from the grain harvest, silk production and other produce, and what are the revenues for the upkeep of the darugheh.

Note: The price of 1 *taghar* of wheat is 20 rubles, a *batman* 40 kopeks, barley is 8 rubles a *taghar*, 20 kopeks per *batman*, rice is 8 rubles per *taghar* or 20 kopeks a *batman*, and silk is 70 rubles per *batman* and 2 rubles and 91¾ kopeks a *stil*.[2] There are 24 *stils* in a *batman* of silk.

1. Bargushet (Bərgüşad): A Tatar village.

Tax-paying families: 80. Tax-exempt families: 10.
(The families of the *yüzbaşi*, his 5 brothers and 4 mullahs are exempt).

Annual tribute: 91 gold rubles.

Sursat: 1 *taghar* and 15 *batmans* of wheat. In addition, the villagers have to plant rice and provide 120 *taghars* of rice,[3] 3 parts of which is the landowner's share and 2 parts of which belongs to the peasants. The *ranjbars* receive one-tenth of the produce. Every *taghar* of planted rice yields ten *taghars*. After deducting the share of the peasants, the *ranjbars* and other expenses, the landowner receives 648 *taghars* of rice. The village also has three silk-producing sheds, which, after deducting the cost of labor, yield 1 *batman* of silk per shed. The total *sursat* is 5,484 rubles and 8 kopeks.

[1] Most of the villages are located in the present-day districts of Göychay and Ucar of the Republic of Azerbaijan, see map 2.

[2] It refers to a Russian weight measure, around a quarter of a pound.

[3] Text reads *chaltik*, a Turkish term for rice in the husk (*çeltik*) and not husked rice.

Mal-o-jehat: No grain is collected. Instead the village has to provide 1 *batman* and 34 *stils* of silk, worth 169 rubles and 19½ kopeks.

Darughegy: ½ *batman* of silk, 32 *taghars* of rice and 12 rubles from the silk weaving machines, for a total of 306 rubles and 20 kopeks.

Note: The village does not pay its *mal-o-jehat* in wheat or barley, since it produces just enough grain for its own consumption. The village belonged to the sons of `Omar Soltan, who have fled with Mostafa Khan to Iran and is, therefore, now the property of the treasury. We have not determined if we should now take part of the harvest for the salary of the government officials who will supervise and record the harvest. The past landowners could also demand free laborers, as many as needed.

Total revenue: 91 gold rubles, 5,960 rubles and 19½ kopeks in local money, or 3,725 rubles and 12 kopeks in Russian currency.

2. Karadzhaly (Qaracallı): A Tatar village.

Tax-paying families: 32. Tax-exempt families: 11.
(The families of the *yüzbaşi*, and his 5 brothers, all of who are *nokars*, as well as their 5 *ranjbars* are exempt.)

Annual tribute: 62 gold rubles and 2 rubles and 50 kopeks in local money.

Sursat: 45 *batmans* of wheat, worth 18 rubles.

Mal-o-jehat: 2 *batmans* and 28 *stils* of silk, and 6 *taghars* of rice, worth 270 rubles and 29 kopeks.

Darughegy: 20 *stils* of silk, 4 *taghars* of rice, and 10 rubles from the silk workshops, worth 100 rubles and 75 kopeks.

Note: The village does not pay its *mal-o-jehat* in wheat or barley, since it produces just enough grain for its own consumption. The village belonged to `Omar Soltan's sons, who have fled to Iran. It now belongs to the treasury. We have not determined if we should now take part of the harvest for the salary of the government officials who will supervise and record the harvest. The past landowners could also demand free laborers, as many as needed.

Total revenue: 62 gold rubles, 391 rubles and 54 kopeks in local money, or 244 rubles and 71¼ kopeks in Russian currency.

3. Shikhamir (Şıxəmir): A Tatar village.

Tax-paying families: 8. Tax-exempt families: 2.
(The families of the *yüzbaşi* and a *ranjbar* belonging to the *beg* are exempt).

Annual tribute: 11 gold rubles and 3 rubles and 60 kopeks in local money.

Sursat: 5 *batmans* of wheat, one *batman* of silk (from 1 silk farm and its silk workshops) and fruit from one vineyard, worth 72 rubles.

Mal-o-jehat: 10 *stils* of silk, 1 *taghar* of rice, worth 37 rubles and 27½ kopeks.

Darughegy: 2 *stils* of silk, 10 *batmans* of rice and 2 rubles from the silk-weaving shed, worth 10 rubles and 53½ kopeks.

Note: The village does not pay its *mal-o-jehat* in wheat or barley, since it produces just enough grain for its own consumption. The village belonged to `Omar Soltan's sons, who have fled to Iran. It now belongs to the treasury. We have not determined if we should now take part of the harvest for the salary of the government officials who will supervise and record the harvest. The past landowners could also demand free laborers, as many as needed.

Total revenue: 11 gold rubles, 123 rubles and 41 kopeks in local money, or 77 rubles and 13¾ kopeks in Russian currency.

4. Gadzhi-Ali [Gadzhi-Ali-Kend] (Hacallı): A Tatar village.

Tax-paying families: 5. Tax-exempt families: 2.
(The families of the *yüzbaşi* and one *ranjbar* are tax-exempt.

Annual tribute: 11 gold rubles and 3 rubles and 60 kopeks in local money.

Sursat: 8 *batmans* of wheat, worth 3 rubles and 20 kopeks.

Mal-o-jehat: 10 *stils* of silk, 1 *taghar* of rice, worth 37 rubles and 27½ kopeks.

Darughegy: 3 *stils* of silk and 20 *batmans* of rice, worth 14 rubles and 15¼ kopeks.

Note: The village does not pay its *mal-o-jehat* in wheat or barley, since it produces just enough grain for its own consumption. The village belonged to `Omar Soltan's sons, who have fled to Iran. It now belongs to the treasury. We have not determined if we should now take part of the harvest for the salary of the government officials who will supervise and record the harvest. The past landowners could also demand free laborers, as many as needed.

Total revenue: 11 gold rubles, 58 rubles and 22¾ kopeks in local money, or 36 rubles and 39¼ kopeks in Russian currency.

5. Shekili (Şıxılı): A Tatar village.

Tax-paying families: 5. Tax-exempt families: 5.
(The families of 3 *nokars* and 2 *ranjbars* belonging to the *beg* are exempt.)

Annual tribute: 7 gold rubles and 2 rubles and 50 kopeks in local money.

Sursat: 5 *batmans* of wheat, 1 *batman* of silk (from one silk farm and a silk-weaving shed), for a total of 72 rubles. In addition there is a newly established silk farm.

Mal-o-jehat: 8 *stils* of silk, 1 *taghar* of rice, worth 31 rubles and 44 kopeks.

Darughegy: 2 *stils* of silk, 10 *batmans* of rice and 2 rubles from the silk-weaving shed, worth 10 rubles and 53½ kopeks.

Note: The village does not pay its *mal-o-jehat* in wheat or barley, since it produces just enough grain for its own consumption. The village belonged to `Omar Soltan's sons, who have fled to Iran. It now belongs to the treasury. We have not determined if we should now take part of the harvest for the salary of the government officials who will supervise and record the harvest. The past landowners could also demand free laborers, as many as needed.

Total revenue: 7 gold rubles, 116 rubles and 47½ kopeks in local money, or 72 rubles and 79½ kopeks in Russian currency.

6. Iagma: A Tatar village.

Tax-paying families: 4.

Annual tribute: 7 gold rubles and 2 rubles and 50 kopeks in local money.

Sursat: 5 *batmans* of wheat, worth 2 rubles.

Mal-o-jehat: 8 *stils* of silk and 1 *taghar* of rice, for a total of 31 rubles and 44 kopeks.

Darughegy: 2 *stils* of silk and 10 *batmans* of rice, worth 8 rubles and 53½ kopeks.

Note: The village belonged to the sons of `Omar Soltan and now belongs to the treasury. Two families have fled the village for Sheki and have to be returned.

Total revenue: 7 gold rubles, 44 rubles and 47½ kopeks in local money, or 27 rubles and 79½ kopeks in Russian currency.

7. Engikent (Yenikənd): A Tatar village.

Tax-exempt families: 11.[4]

All 11 families were *ranjbars* and belong to Malek Rafi`. They pay no dues to the treasury.

8. Arab: A Tatar village.[5]

Tax-paying families: 17. Tax-exempt families: 3.
(The families of 3 *ranjbars* belonging to Mirza Ahmad are exempt).

The 17 other families are also *ranjbars* who belonged to the sons of `Omar Soltan. These *ranjbars* are only responsible for taking care of the silk farms and orchards, which belonged to `Omar Soltan's family. Since `Omar Soltan and his family have fled to Iran, the following services now belong to the treasury.

[4] The text lists them as tax-paying families.

[5] There are a number of villages and nomad settlements in the Shamakhi and Göychay region: Arab-Jabirly, Arab-qadim, Arab-Mehdi Beg, Arab-Sarvan, Arab-khana, Arab-Shahverdi.

Yield from the 9 silk farms (7 belonging to the sons of `Omar Soltan and 2 to his mother), 9 *batmans* of silk and from the 3 vineyards of `Omar Soltan's children, bring an income of 150 rubles in total. From the 2 vineyards belonging to his mother, 40 rubles from one, and nothing from the other, for it is a *vaqf*. In addition, there are 2 mills in this village, each one capable of paying dues of 5 *taghars* of wheat.

No *mal-o-jehat* or *darughegy* is collected.

Total revenue: 920 rubles in local money, or 575 rubles in Russian currency.

9. Muganly (Muğanlı): A Tatar village.

Tax-paying families: 14.

These families are all immigrants from various other places. They are all nomads, whose duty was to take care of the flocks belonging to the sons of `Omar Soltan. They paid no taxes. They have to be assessed in the future and be included in the tax-rolls.

10. Turkmen (Türkmen): A nomad settlement.

Tax-paying families: 30.

The nomads are gypsies, who pay 250 rubles to the sons of `Omar Soltan. They wander around and tell fortunes.

Total revenue: 250 rubles in local money, or 156 rubles and 25 kopeks in Russian currency. It now belongs to the treasury.

11. Bozavant [Bozavand] (Bozavand): An Armenian village.

Tax-paying families: 21. Tax-exempt families: 1.
(The family of the *kevkha* is exempt).

Since the inhabitants have emigrated from various places they pay nothing towards the annual tribute and no *sursat*.

The villagers, however, pay 60 kopeks for each of the 18 plows they use to cultivate the fields. In addition they have to sow the landowner's field, using 2 *taghars* of seed provided by him, which, after all expenses, yields 5 *taghars* of wheat from each field. Furthermore, the mill, half of which belongs to the landowner, pays 2½ *taghars* of wheat; all of which is worth 260 rubles and 80 kopeks.

Mal-o-jehat: 5 *taghars* of wheat, 2 *taghars* of barley, worth 116 rubles.

Darughegy: 1 *taghar* and 40 *batmans* of wheat and 1 *taghar* and 40 *batmans* of barley, all worth 52 rubles.

Total revenue: 428 rubles and 80 kopeks in local money, or 268 rubles in Russian currency.

12. Kazyan [Kazian] (Qazyan): A Tatar village.

Tax-paying families: 70. Tax-exempt families: 18.
(The families of the 17 *nokars* and *mo`afs* and the mullah are exempt).

The village belonged to Qasem Beg and now to the treasury.[6]

Annual tribute: 38 gold rubles.

Sursat: 27 *batmans* of wheat. The village has also to plant 70 *taghars* of rice in the same manner as listed in village number 1 (Bargushet). The landowner thus received 378 *taghars* of rice. In addition, the village has a mill, which pays 60 rubles a year, for a total of 3,132 rubles and 60 kopeks.

Mal-o-jehat: 2 *batmans* of silk and 4 *taghars* of rice, for a total of 172 rubles and 40 kopeks.

Darughegy: ½ *batman* of silk, 20 *taghars* of rice and 12 rubles from the silk-workshops, worth 209 rubles.

Total revenue: 3,514 rubles in local money, or 2,196 rubles and 25 kopeks in Russian currency.

[6] In a short survey, conducted between January and May 1831, the revenues from the 15 villages listed below, which had belonged to Qasem Beg and were confiscated by provincial treasury after his flight to Iran in 1820 are enumerated; see no. 7 in the appendix. It is interesting to note the change in population and the taxes ten years after the Russian annexation.

13. Bygir (Bığır): A Tatar village.

Tax-paying families: 42. Tax-exempt families: 4.
(The families of the 3 *nokars* and 1 mullah are exempt).

The village belonged to Qasem Beg and now to the treasury.

Annual tribute: 75 gold rubles and 3 rubles in local money.

Sursat: 1 *taghar* of wheat, worth 20 rubles.

Mal-o-jehat: 2 *batmans* of silk and 5 *taghars* of rice, worth 180 rubles and 50 kopeks.

Darughegy: ½ *batman* of silk, 3 *taghars* of rice, and 12 rubles from the silk workshops, worth 71 rubles and 30 kopeks.

Total revenue: 274 rubles and 80 kopeks in local currency or 171 rubles and 75 kopeks in Russian currency.

14. Chigni (Çiyni): A Tatar village.

Tax-paying families: 19. Tax-exempt families: 9.
(The families of the *yüzbaşi*, his 5 *ranjbars* and his 3 brothers are exempt).

The village belonged to Qasem Beg and now to the treasury. The inhabitants are all *ranjbars*.

The villagers have to work in the 19 silk farms and 19 silk workshops, producing 19 *batmans* of silk. There is also a large vineyard and 5 small ones paying 100 rubles a year. In addition, the villagers have to plant 19 *taghars* of rice, in the same manner mentioned above, all of which is worth 2,260 rubles and 6 kopeks.

No *mal-o-jehat* is collected.

Darughegy: 10 *stils* of silk and 5 *taghars* of rice, worth 95 rubles and 93¼ kopeks.

Total revenue: 2,355 rubles and 99¼ kopeks in local money, or 1,472 rubles and 49¼ kopeks in Russian currency.

15. Chakhirly (Çaxırlı): A Tatar village.

Tax-paying families: 15. Tax-exempt families: 4.
(The families of the *yüzbaşi*, his uncle and 2 mullahs are exempt).

The village belonged to Qasem Beg and now to the treasury. The inhabitants are all *ranjbars*.

Annual tribute: 17 gold rubles and 4 rubles in local money.

Sursat: 12 *batmans* of wheat. There are 15 silk farms with their own silk workshops producing 15 *batmans* of silk. There is also a new vineyard, which has not produced any revenues yet. The total income is 1,054 rubles and 80 kopeks.

Mal-o-jehat: 10 *stils* of silk and 2 *taghars* of rice, worth 45 rubles and 37½ kopeks.

Darughegy: 5 *stils* of silk and 1 *taghar* of rice and 2 rubles from the silk weaving machines, worth 24 rubles and 68¾ kopeks.

Total revenue: 1,128 rubles and 86¼ kopeks in local money, or 705 rubles and 33¼ kopeks in Russian currency.

16. Alikendi [Alikend] (Êlikənd): A Tatar village.

Tax-paying families: 10. Tax-exempt families: 2.
(The families of the mullah and *kadkhoda* are exempt).

The village belonged to Qasem Beg and now to the treasury.

Annual tribute: 12 gold rubles.

Sursat: 8 *batmans* of wheat, worth 3 rubles and 20 kopeks.

Mal-o-jehat: 6 *stils* of silk, 1½ *taghars* of rice, worth 29 rubles and 65½ kopeks.

Darughegy: 5 *stils* of silk and 1 *taghar* of rice, worth 22 rubles and 68¾ kopeks.

Total revenue: 55 rubles and 54¼ kopeks in local money, or 34 rubles and 71¼ kopeks in Russian currency.

17. Shikhi-Bek [Shikh-bei] (Şıxbəy): A Tatar village.

Tax-paying families: 7. Tax-exempt families: 2
(The families of the *yüzbaşi* and the mullah are exempt).

The village belonged to Qasem Beg and now to the treasury.

Annual tribute: 6 gold rubles and 1 ruble and 60 kopeks in local money.

Sursat: 4½ *batmans* of wheat, worth 1 ruble and 80 kopeks.

Mal-o-jehat: 4 *stils* of silk and 20 *batmans* of rice, worth 17 rubles and 7 kopeks.

Darughegy: 2 *stils* of silk and ½ *taghar* of rice, worth 9 rubles and 88½ kopeks.

Total revenue: 6 gold rubles, 30 rubles and 35½ kopeks in local money, or 18 rubles and 97 kopeks in Russian currency.

18. Molla Gadzhali [Molla-Gadzhili] (Mollahacılı): A Tatar village.

Tax-paying families: 13. Tax-exempt families: 2.
(The families of the *kadkhoda* and mullah are exempt).

The village belonged to Qasem Beg and now to the treasury.

The village is populated entirely by *ranjbars*. They do not contribute to the annual tribute or pay the *sursat*.

The village has 12 silk farms, with their own sheds, which produce 12 *batmans* of silk. An old vineyard pays 25 rubles. A new vineyard has not produced any income as yet. The mill gives 6 *taghars* of wheat, for a total of 985 rubles.

Mal-o-jehat: 2 *taghars* of rice, worth 16 rubles and 20 kopeks.

Darughegy: 2 *taghars* of rice, worth 16 rubles and 20 kopeks.

Total revenue: 1,017 rubles and 40 kopeks in local money, or 635 rubles and 87½ kopeks in Russian currency.

19. Karakhadyr [Karakhydir] (Qaraxıdır): A Tatar village.

Tax-paying families: 10. Tax-exempt families: 3.
(The families of the *kadkhoda*, the mullah and one *ranjbar* are exempt).

The village belonged to Qasem Beg and now to the treasury.

Annual tribute: 8 gold rubles and 2 rubles in local money.

Sursat: 7 *batmans* of wheat and one vineyard producing an income of 50 rubles a year, for a total of 52 rubles and 80 kopeks.

Mal-o-jehat: 6 *stils* of silk, 1½ *taghars* of rice, for a total of 29 rubles and 65½ kopeks.

Darughegy: 5 *stils* of silk, 1 *taghar* of rice and 2 rubles from the silk workshops, for a total of 24 rubles and 68¾ kopeks.

Total revenue: 8 gold rubles, 109 rubles and 14¼ kopeks in local money, or 68 rubles and 21¼ kopeks in Russian currency.

20. Danibasan-Turkedzhi [Turkedzhi]: A Tatar village.

Tax-paying families: 10. Tax-exempt families: 3.
(The families of the mullah and 2 *kadkhodas* are exempt).

The village belonged to Qasem Beg and now to the treasury.

Annual tribute: 12 gold rubles and 3 rubles in local money.

Sursat: 9 *batmans* of wheat, worth 3 rubles and 60 kopeks.

Mal-o-jehat: 5 *stils* of silk and 1 *taghar* and 10 *batmans* of rice, worth 25 rubles and 38¾ kopeks.

Darughegy: 2 *stils* of silk and 20 *batmans* of rice, worth 11 rubles and 23½ kopeks.

Total revenue: 12 gold rubles, 43 rubles and 22¼ kopeks in local money, or 27 rubles and 1¼ kopek in Russian currency.

21. Melik-Kendi [Melik-kend] (Məlikkənd) and Alpi [Alpy] (Alpı): Tatar villages.

Tax-paying families: 4. Tax-exempt families: 35.
(The 35 *ranjbar* families belong to Malek Esma`il and Ahmad Aqa).

The villages belonged to Qasem Beg and now the treasury.

Annual tribute: 6 gold rubles and 1 ruble and 60 kopeks in local money.

Sursat: 4½ *batmans* of wheat, worth 1 ruble and 80 kopeks.

Mal-o-jehat: 5 *stils* of silk, 15 *batmans* of rice, for a total of 18 rubles and 63¾ kopeks.

Darughegy: 2 *stils* of silk and 10 *batmans* of rice, worth 8 rubles and 53½ kopeks.

Total revenue: 6 gold rubles, 30 rubles and 57¼ kopeks in local money, or 19 rubles and 10¼ kopeks in Russian currency.

22. Kelbende [Kelbend] (Kelbend): An Armenian village.

Tax-paying families: 22. Tax-exempt families: 2.
(The families of the *kevkha* and the priest are exempt).

Note: The inhabitants are all immigrants from Karabagh.
The village belonged to Qasem Beg and now the treasury.

Kharaj: 50 rubles.

A ruble from each of the 16 plows; in addition, the landowner [Qasem Beg] has 3 plows and 6 oxen with which the villagers have to till and sow 2 *taghars* of wheat, using the 3 plows. The yield, after all expenses, is 5-fold, bringing an income of 666 rubles.

Mal-o-jehat: 4 *taghars* of wheat and 1 *taghar* of barley, worth 88 rubles.

Darughegy: 1 *taghar* and 30 *batmans* of wheat and 1 *taghar* and 24 *batmans* of barley, worth 44 rubles and 80 kopeks.

Total revenue: 798 rubles and 80 kopeks in local money, or 499 rubles and 25 kopeks in Russian currency.

23. Gurt: A nomad settlement.

Tax-paying families: 20.

The nomads are gypsies; they pay 120 rubles to the sons of `Omar Soltan. They wander around and tell fortunes.

Total revenue: 120 rubles in local money, or 75 rubles in Russian currency. It now belongs to the treasury.

24. Kiurt [Kurdany] (Kürd): A nomad settlement.

Tax-paying families: 20.

The settlement belonged to Qasem Beg and now the treasury.

The nomads are all immigrants from Sheki. They are very poor and pay no dues. They served as shepherds for Qasem Beg's flocks. If they are to remain in Shirvan, they must be assessed accordingly.

25. Khalilly [Khalilu] (Xalillı): A nomad settlement.

Tax-paying families: 45.

The settlement belonged to Qasem Beg and now the treasury.

The nomads are all immigrants from Kuba and pay no dues. They served as shepherds for Qasem Beg's flocks. They have lived in Shirvan for 25 years and it is time to assess them accordingly.

26. Marty [Murty] (Mırtı): A nomad settlement.

Tax-paying families: 30.

The settlement belonged to Qasem Beg and now the treasury.

These nomads were in charge of Qasem Beg's horse herds and pay no dues. They must be now assessed accordingly.

27. Shagaarkhi (Şah-arxi): A Tatar village.

Tax-paying families: 24. Tax-exempt families: 1.
(The family of the barber is exempt).

The rest of the village is composed of *ranjbars*, who do not pay the tribute, the *sursat* or the *mal-o-jehat*.

The village belonged to Qasem Beg and now the treasury.

There are, however, 19 silk farms with sheds producing 19 *batmans* of silk. Five *ranjbars* use 5 plows and sow 7 *taghars* of wheat and 3 *taghars* of barley, which, after deducting the share of the *ranjbars*, yield 4 *taghars* for every one *taghar* sown. One mill pays 4 *taghars* of wheat and the 4 vineyards give 100 rubles a year, for a total of 2,166 rubles.

Darughegy: From the *ranjbars* of each shed, ½ *stil* of silk and from the 19 sheds 9½ *stils* of silk, for a total of 19 *stils* of silk, worth 27 rubles 71½ kopeks.

Total revenue: 2,193 rubles and 71¼ kopeks in local money, or 1,371 rubles and 6¾ kopeks in Russian currency.

28. Leki (Lak): A Tatar village.

Tax-paying families: 19. Tax-exempt families: 7.
(The families of 2 *ranjbars* belonging to the *yüzbaşi*, 4 *nokars* and 1 mullah are exempt.)

The village is the property of the mahal's *beg*, Hajji Ahmad Soltan.

Annual tribute: 30 gold rubles.

Sursat: 25 *batmans* of wheat, worth 10 rubles.

No *mal-o-jehat* or *darughegy* is collected for the treasury; it belongs to Ahmad Soltan.

Total revenue: 30 gold rubles, 10 rubles in local money, or 6 rubles and 25 kopeks in Russian currency.

29. Chirake [Chereke] (Çereke): A Tatar village.

Tax-paying families: 41. Tax-exempt families: 2.
(The families of the *yüzbaşi* and mullah are exempt).

The village is the property of the *mahal*'s *beg*, Hajji Ahmad Soltan.

Annual tribute: 50 gold rubles.

Sursat: 40 *batmans* of wheat, worth 16 rubles.

No *mal-o-jehat* or *darughegy* is collected for the treasury; it belongs to Ahmad Soltan.

Total revenue: 50 gold rubles, 16 rubles in local money, or 10 rubles in Russian currency.

30. Bevdevil [Bevdovul] (Bəydövül): A Tatar village.

Tax-paying families: 10. Tax-exempt families: 2.
(The families of the *kadkhoda* and the mullah are exempt).

The village is the property of the *mahal*'s *beg*, Hajji Ahmad Soltan.

Annual tribute: 28 gold rubles.

Sursat: 20 *batmans* of wheat, worth 8 rubles.

No *mal-o-jehat* or *darughegy* is collected for the treasury; it belongs to Hajji Ahmad Soltan.

Total revenue: 28 gold rubles, 8 rubles in local money, or 5 rubles in Russian currency.

35. Pir-Kendy [Pirkend] (Pirkənd): A Tatar village.

Tax-paying families: 12. Tax-exempt families: 2.
(The families of the *yüzbaşi* and the mullah are exempt).

The village is the property of the *mahal*'s *beg*, Hajji Ahmad Soltan.

Annual tribute: 14 gold rubles.

Sursat: 12 *batmans* of wheat, worth 4 rubles and 80 kopeks.

No *mal-o-jehat* or *darughegy* is collected for the treasury; it belongs to Hajji Ahmad Soltan.

Total revenue: 14 gold rubles, 4 rubles and 80 kopeks in local money, or 3 Russian rubles.

36. Kiuche-Gedy (Küçeçedy): A Tatar village.

Tax-paying families: 10. Tax-exempt families: 12.
(The families of the *yüzbaşi*, 4 *nokars*, the mullah and 6 *ranjbars* are exempt).

Annual tribute: 12 gold rubles and 3 rubles in local money.

Sursat: 9 *batmans* of wheat, worth 3 rubles and 60 kopeks.

The family of Qasem Beg, the brother of Hajji Ahmad Soltan, the *beg* of this *mahal*, lives in this village.

Note: The 6 *ranjbars* belong to Mostafa Khan's fugitive brother Esma`il Beg. They now have to work for the treasury. There are 6 silk farms left by the aforementioned *beg*, which yield 6 *batmans* of silk. In addition, there is a vineyard, which brings an income of 30 rubles. Furthermore 4 *taghars* of rice is planted, which yields 40 *taghars*, for a total of 777 rubles and 60 kopeks.

Mal-o-jehat: 9 *stils* of silk and 20 *batmans* of rice, worth 31 rubles and 65¾ kopeks.

Darughegy: 3 *stils* of silk, 20 *batmans* of rice and 2 rubles from a silk-weaving machine, for a total of 16 rubles and 15¼ kopeks.

Total revenue: 12 gold rubles, 828 rubles and 41 kopeks in local money, or 517 rubles and 75½ kopeks in Russian currency.

37. Kesh Khourt [Kishkhurt]: An Armenian village.

Tax-exempt families: 25.
(The 24 families and the priest immigrated from Karabagh).

The village belongs to the *mahal*'s *beg* and pays nothing to the treasury.

38. Sheker (Şeker): A Tatar village.

Tax-exempt families: 21.
(The families of 20 *ranjbars* and 1 mullah are exempt).

The village belongs to the *mahal*'s *beg* and pays nothing to the treasury.

39. Alpaut (Alpout Ucar):[8] *A Tatar village.*

Tax-exempt families: 40.
The families are immigrants from various regions.

The village belongs to the *beg* of this *mahal* and pays nothing to the treasury.

40. Arab: A Tatar village.

Tax-exempt families: 40

The village belongs to the *mahal*'s *beg* and pays nothing the treasury.

41. Shikh-Nasir [Shikh-nasyr] (Sheikh-Naser?): A Tatar village.

Tax-exempt families: 15.

The village belongs to the *mahal*'s *beg* and pays nothing to the treasury.

[8] There are a number of villages by this name in various *mahals*.

42. Bagir-Begly [Bagir-beklu] (Bağirbəylu): A nomad settlement.

Tax-exempt families: 40

The settlement belongs to the *mahal*'s *beg* and pays nothing to the treasury.

43. Miususly [Miusiusli] (Müsüslü): A nomad settlement.

Tax-exempt families: 35

The settlement belongs to the *beg* of this *mahal* and pays nothing to the treasury.

44. Dzhegirly [Dzagirly]: A nomad settlement.

Tax-exempt families: 10

The settlement belongs to the *beg* of this *mahal* and pays nothing to the treasury.

45. Shikhilly [Shikhliar]: A nomad settlement.

Tax-exempt families: 10

The settlement belongs to the *beg* of this *mahal* and pays nothing to the treasury.

46. Karabudzhak [Karabudzhag] (Qarabucaq): A [Muslim] village.

Tax-paying families: 74.

The above families had emigrated from three villages and nomadic settlements in Karabagh: Salagi, Kizilli and Haj `Ali. [All of them returned to Karabagh in 1822].[9] They originally belonged to Mostafa Khan's wife, Nakhay Begum, and now belong to the treasury. The peasants paid no taxes to the treasury, but had to plant 68 *taghars* of rice, which yielded 680 *taghars* of rice to be paid to the khan's wife.

Total revenue: 5,508 rubles in local money, or 3,442 rubles and 50 kopeks in Russian currency.

[9] See *The 1823 Russian Survey of the Karabagh Province*, trans./ed. G. Bournoutian (Costa Mesa, CA. 2012), 374, 382, 387-388.

Totals for the Sedenrud Mahal:

Tax-paying families: 813.
Tax-exempt families: 396.
Annual tribute: 567 gold rubles.
Taxes in kind: 29,834 rubles and 86 kopeks.
Taxes in cash: 370 rubles.
Mal-o-jehat: 1,347 rubles and 45¼ kopeks.
Darughegy: 1,085 rubles and 52¼ kopeks.

Total revenue: 32,670 rubles and 73½ kopeks in local currency or 20,419 rubles and 20½ kopeks in Russian currency.

Note: Since some of the villages paid their annual tribute in silver money totaling 32 rubles and 90 kopeks, the total gold rubles from this *mahal* are 573 and the total revenue is 20,398 rubles and 64½ kopeks in Russian currency.

Note: A regular *batman* of silk is 24 *stils*, while a *mizani* [or *tilani*][10] *batman* is 48 *stils*. The price for both is 70 local rubles per *batman*.[11]

Major-General Prince Madatov
Actual State Councilor, Mogilevskii

[10] The *tilani batman* was 15.43 lbs.

[11] This can be explained in two ways: either they added the weight of the *mizan* scales to the total weight, or the silk in the first instance was pure woven silk, while in the second instance it was silk cocoons.

[Register 6]

Khanchoban (Xançoban) Mahal

Revenues from the nomads of the Xançoban Mahal,[1] *populated entirely by Tatar nomads, indicating the number of tax-paying and tax-exempt families, as well as the amount paid to the Khan by each settlement—which will now go to the treasury; which settlements are under the supervision of the beg of the mahal, what part of the revenue he used to collect for the khan [which will now go to the treasury] and what part he kept for himself. Also, what other revenues are collected in the form of butter, cheese, floor mats and small rugs.*

Note: During the rule of Mostafa Khan, this mahal did not provide any *mal-o-jehat*. The *beg* and the *yüzbaşi* of this were in charge of collecting the *sursat* for the khan, as well as supervising the *nokars* and *ranjbars*, whose duty was to till and sow small allotments of land to produce the wheat needed by the nomads. In addition, each settlement provided sheep (meat) and labor when required. However, no official numbers exist for these last two dues.

Note: A *taghar* of wheat costs 20 rubles and a *batman* of wheat costs 40 kopeks. A *batman* of butter costs 4 rubles and 8 kopeks, a *batman* of cheese costs 60 kopeks, a floor mat is worth 2 rubles and 40 kopeks, and a small rug is worth 4 rubles.

Note: Malek Umud Beg supervised this *mahal*; after his flight to Iran, his relative, Kombai Beg [loyal to Russia] has assumed that position.

[1] Some of these settlements are located in the present-day Ağsu and Şamax regions of the Republic of Azerbaijan (see map 2).

1. Akhtachi (Axtaçi).

Tax-paying families: 95. Tax-exempt families: 34.
(The families of 15 *nokars*, 13 *ranjbars* belonging to the *beg*, and 6 mullahs are exempt).

Annual tribute: 76 gold rubles.

Sursat: 37 *batmans* of wheat, 7 *batmans* of butter, 4 *batmans* of cheese, 2 floor mats and 2 small rugs, worth 58 rubles and 56 kopeks.

Total revenue: 76 gold rubles and 58 rubles and 56 kopeks in local money, or 36 rubles and 60 kopeks in Russian currency.

2. Garius (Gursulu).

Tax-paying families: 150. Tax-exempt families: 33.
(The families of 15 *nokars*, 10 *ranjbars* belonging to the *yüzbaşi* and 8 mullahs are exempt).

Annual tribute: 73 gold rubles.

Sursat: 37 *batmans* of wheat, 7 *batmans* of butter, 4 *batmans* of cheese, 2 floor mats and 2 small rugs, worth 58 rubles and 56 kopeks.

Total revenue: 73 gold rubles and 58 rubles and 56 kopeks in local money, or 36 rubles and 60 kopeks in Russian currency.

3. Karakoinly [Karakoiunlu] (Qaraqoyunlu).

Tax-paying families: 50. Tax-exempt families: 12.
(The families of 5 *nokars*, 3 *ranjbars* belonging to the *yüzbaşi* and 4 mullahs are exempt).

Annual tribute: 53 gold rubles.

Sursat: 26½ *batmans* of wheat, 5½ *batmans* of butter, 3 *batmans* of cheese, 2 floor mats and 1 small rug, worth 43 rubles and 64 kopeks.

Total revenue: 53 gold rubles and 43 rubles and 64 kopeks in local money, or 27 rubles and 27 kopeks in Russian currency.

Sursat: 15 *batmans* of wheat, 3 *batmans* of butter and ½ *batmans* of cheese, 1 floor mat and 1 small rug, worth 25 rubles and 54 kopeks.

Total revenue: 36 gold rubles, 25 rubles and 54 kopeks in local money, or 15 rubles and 96¼ kopeks in Russian currency.

10. Miuskiuri [Miushkamir?] (Müsküri).

Tax-paying families: 18. Tax-exempt families: 6.
(The families of 2 *nokars*, 2 *ranjbars* and 2 mullahs are exempt).

Annual tribute: 28 gold rubles.

Sursat: 14 *batmans* of wheat, 3 *batmans* of butter, ½ *batman* of cheese, 1 floor mat and 1 small rug, worth 25 rubles and 14 kopeks.

Total revenue: 28 gold rubles, 25 rubles and 14 kopeks in local money, or 15 rubles and 17¼ kopeks in Russian currency.

11. Ovdzhili [Ovdan?] (Ovçulu).

Tax-paying families: 18. Tax-exempt families: 4.
(The families of 2 *nokars* and 2 *mullahs* are exempt).

Annual tribute: 27 gold rubles.

Sursat: 11 *batmans* of wheat, 2½ *batmans* of butter, 1 *batman* of cheese, 1 floor mat and 1 small rug, worth 20 rubles and 58 kopeks.

Total revenue: 27 gold rubles, 20 rubles and 58 kopeks in local money, or 11 rubles and 86¼ kopeks in Russian currency.

12. Molla Lar (Mollalar).

Tax-paying families: 30. Tax-exempt families: 10.
(The families of 4 *nokars*, 3 *ranjbars* and 3 mullahs are exempt).

Annual tribute: 27 gold rubles.

Sursat: 13 *batmans* of wheat, 2½ *batmans* of butter, 1¼ *batmans* of cheese, 1 floor mat and 1 small rug, worth 22 rubles and 55 kopeks.

Total revenue: 27 gold rubles, 22 rubles and 55 kopeks in local money, or 14 rubles and 9¼ kopeks in Russian currency.

13. Gik-Dalla-Gliu (Gek-dallakly].

Tax-paying families: 15. Tax-exempt families: 9.
(The families of 4 *nokars*, 3 *ranjbars* belonging to the *yüzbaşi* and 2 mullahs are exempt).

Annual tribute: 18 gold rubles.

Sursat: 7½ *batmans* of wheat, 2 *batmans* of butter, 1 *batman* of cheese, 1 floor mat and 1 small rug, worth 18 rubles and 16 kopeks.

Total revenue: 18 gold rubles, 18 rubles and 16 kopeks in local money, or 11 rubles and 35 kopeks in Russian currency.

14. Muradly (Muradlı).

Tax-paying families: 20. Tax-exempt families: 6.
(The families of 3 *nokars*, 2 *ranjbars* belonging to the *yüzbaşi* and 1 mullah are exempt).

Annual tribute: 18 gold rubles.

Sursat: 9 *batmans* of wheat, 2 *batmans* of butter, 1 *batman* of cheese, 1 floor mat and 1 small rug, worth 18 rubles and 76 kopeks.

Total revenue: 18 gold rubles, 18 rubles and 76 kopeks in local money, or 11 rubles and 72½ kopeks in Russian currency.

15. Segerlu (Səhərlu).

Tax-paying families: 15. Tax-exempt families: 8.
(The families of 5 *nokars*, 2 *ranjbars* and 1 mullah are exempt.)

Annual tribute: 18 gold rubles.

Sursat: 9 *batmans* of wheat, 2 *batmans* of butter, 1 *batman* of cheese, 1 floor mat and 1 small rug, worth 18 rubles and 76 kopeks.

Total revenue: 18 gold rubles, 18 rubles and 76 kopeks in local money, or 11 rubles and 72½ kopeks in Russian currency.

16. Kurt.

Tax-paying families: 70. Tax-exempt families: 13.
(The families of 5 *nokars*, 5 *ranjbars* and 3 mullahs are exempt.)

Annual tribute: 44 gold rubles.

Sursat: 22 *batmans* of wheat, 4½ *batmans* of butter, 2½ *batmans* of cheese, 2 floor mats and 1 small rug, worth 37 rubles and 31 kopeks.

Total revenue: 44 gold rubles, 37 rubles and 31 kopeks in local money, or 23 rubles and 31¾ kopeks in Russian currency.

17. Pir-Gasanly (Pirhəsənli).

Tax-paying families: 35. Tax-exempt families: 23.
(The families of 15 *nokars*, 5 *ranjbars*, and 3 mullahs are exempt).

Annual tribute: 36 gold rubles.

Sursat: 20 *batmans* of wheat, 4 *batmans* of butter, 2 *batmans* of cheese, 1 floor mat and 1 small rug, worth 31 rubles and 92 kopeks.

Total revenue: 36 gold rubles, 31 rubles and 92 kopeks in local money, or 19 rubles and 91 kopeks in Russian currency.

18. Ilkhichi [Ilkhichi-dag] (Ilxici).

Tax-paying families: 25. Tax-exempt families: 13.
(The families of 5 *nokars*, 5 *ranjbars*, and 3 mullahs are exempt).

Annual tribute: 21 gold rubles.

Sursat: 11 *batmans* of wheat, 2¼ *batmans* of butter, 1 *batman* of cheese, 1 floor mat and 1 small rug, worth 20 rubles and 58 kopeks.

Total revenue: 21 gold rubles, 20 rubles and 58 kopeks in local money, or 12 rubles and 86¼ kopeks in Russian currency.

19. Sarvan [Sarvan-gadzhi-kadyr].

Tax-paying families: 16. Tax-exempt families: 8.
(The families of 3 *nokars*, 3 *ranjbars*, and 2 mullahs are exempt).

Annual tribute: 16 gold rubles.

Sursat: 8 *batmans* of wheat, 1½ *batmans* of butter and 1 *batman* of cheese, worth 9 rubles and 92 kopeks

Total revenue: 16 gold rubles, 9 rubles and 92 kopeks in local money, or 6 rubles 19¾ kopeks in Russian currency.

20. Mustapaly (Mustafalı).

Tax-paying families: 30. Tax-exempt families: 7.
(The families of 3 *nokars* and 4 mullahs are exempt).

Annual tribute: 22 gold rubles.

Sursat: 11 *batmans* of wheat, 2¼ *batmans* of butter, 1 *batman* of cheese 1 floor mat and 1 small rug, worth 20 rubles and 58 kopeks

Total revenue: 22 gold rubles, 20 rubles and 58 kopeks in local money, or 12 rubles and 86¼ kopeks in Russian currency.

21. Binasli.

Tax-paying families: 25. Tax-exempt families: 8.
(The families of 3 *nokars*, 3 *ranjbars* and 2 mullahs are exempt).

Annual tribute: 18 gold rubles.

Sursat: 9 *batmans* of wheat, 2 *batmans* of butter, 1 *batman* of cheese and 1 floor mat, worth 16 rubles and 76 kopeks.

Total revenue: 18 gold rubles, 16 rubles and 76 kopeks in local money, or 10 rubles and 47½ kopeks in Russian currency.

22. Chaily (Çayili).

Tax-paying families: 20. Tax-exempt families: 6.
(The families of 2 *nokars*, 3 *ranjbars* and 1 mullah are exempt).

Annual tribute: 18 gold rubles.

Sursat: 9 *batmans* of wheat, 2 *batmans* of butter, 1 *batman* of cheese, 1 floor mat and 1 small rug, worth 18 rubles and 76 kopeks.

Total revenue: 18 gold rubles, 18 rubles and 76 kopeks in local money, or 11 rubles and 72½ kopeks in Russian currency.

23. Karama Giametli [Kara-makhmudly] (Karamamudli).

Tax-paying families: 6. Tax-exempt families: 4.
(The families of 2 *nokars* and 2 *ranjbars* are exempt).

Annual tribute: 7 gold rubles.

Sursat: 4 *batmans* of wheat, 1 *batman* of butter and ½ *batman* of cheese, worth 5 rubles and 98 kopeks.

Total revenue: 7 gold rubles, 5 rubles and 98 kopeks in local money, or 3 rubles and 73¾ kopeks in Russian currency.

24. Arabushagi [Arab-kadym] (Ərəbuşağı).

Tax-paying families: 10. Tax-exempt families: 6.
(The families of 4 *nokars* and 2 *ranjbars* are exempt).

Annual tribute: 12 gold rubles.

Sursat: 6 *batmans* of wheat, 1 *batman* of butter, ½ *batman* of cheese and 1 floor mat, worth 9 rubles and 18 kopeks.

Total revenue: 12 gold rubles, 9 rubles and 18 kopeks in local money, or 5 rubles and 73¾ kopeks in Russian currency.

25. Dalilar (Dəlilər).

Tax-paying families: 10. Tax-exempt families: 5.
(The families of 2 *nokars*, 2 *ranjbars* and 1 mullah are exempt).

Annual tribute: 12 gold rubles.

Sursat: 6 *batmans* of wheat, 1 *batman* butter, ½ *batman* cheese and 1 floor mat, worth 9 rubles and 18 kopeks.

Total revenue: 12 gold rubles, 9 rubles and 18 kopeks in local money, or 5 rubles and 73¾ kopeks in Russian currency.

26. Chovrianli.

Tax-paying families: 7. Tax-exempt families: 4.
(The families of 2 *nokars*, 1 *ranjbar* and the mullah are exempt).

Annual tribute: 7 gold rubles.

Sursat: 4 *batmans* of wheat, 1 *batman* of butter, ½ *batman* of cheese, and 1 small rug, worth 9 rubles and 98 kopeks.

Total revenue: 7 gold rubles, 9 rubles and 98 kopeks in local money, or 6 rubles and 23¾ kopeks in Russian currency.

27. Adinllu.

Tax-paying families: 8. Tax-exempt families: 2.
(The families of the 2 *nokars* are exempt).

Sursat: 1 *batman* of wheat, 1½ *batmans* of butter, ½ *batman* of cheese and 1 small rug, worth 11 rubles and 80 kopeks.

Total revenue: 12 gold rubles, 11 rubles and 80 kopeks in local money, or 7 rubles and 37½ kopeks in Russian currency.

28. Bagirlu (Bağırlı).

Tax-paying families: 6. Tax-exempt families: 6
(The families of 5 *nokars* and 1 *ranjbar* are exempt).

Annual tribute: 7 gold rubles.

Sursat: 3½ *batmans* of wheat, 1 *batman* of butter, ¼ *batman* of cheese and 1 floor mat, worth 8 rubles and 18 kopeks.

Total revenue: 7 gold rubles, 8 rubles and 18 kopeks in local money, or 5 rubles and 73¼ kopeks in Russian currency.

29. Alpaut (Alpout Pervyy).

Tax-paying families: 8. Tax-exempt families: 4.
(The families of 1 *nokar*, 2 *ranjbars*, and 1 mullah are exempt).

Annual tribute: 6 gold rubles.

Sursat: 3 *batmans* of wheat, 1 *batman* of butter, ½ *batman* of cheese and 1 small rug, worth 9 rubles and 58 kopeks.

Total revenue: 6 gold rubles, 9 rubles and 58 kopeks in local money, or 5 rubles and 23¾ kopeks in Russian currency.

30. Alidzhanly.

Tax-exempt families: 8

These families are in charge of the khan's horse herds and pay nothing. They have to be now assessed accordingly.

31. Namirly (Nəmirli).

Tax-paying families: 8. Tax-exempt families: 7.
(The families of 3 *nokars*, 2 *ranjbars* and 2 mullahs are exempt).

Annual tribute: 6 gold rubles.

Sursat: 3 *batmans* of wheat, 1 *batman* of butter, ½ *batman* of cheese, and 1 floor mat, worth 7 rubles and 98 kopeks.

Total revenue: 6 gold rubles, 7 rubles and 98 kopeks in local money, or 4 rubles and 98¾ kopeks in Russian currency.

32. Sorsor.

Tax-paying families: 6. Tax-exempt families: 5.
(The families of 2 *nokars*, 2 *ranjbars* and 1 mullah are exempt).

Annual tribute: 6 gold rubles.

Sursat: 3 *batmans* of wheat, 1 *batman* of butter, and ½ *batman* of cheese, worth 5 rubles and 58 kopeks.

Total revenue: 6 gold rubles, 5 rubles and 58 kopeks in local money, or 3 rubles 48¾ kopeks in Russian currency.

33. Eldalagli.

Tax-paying families: 6. Tax-exempt families: 5.
(The families of 4 *ranjbars* and 1 mullah are exempt).

Annual tribute: 6 gold rubles.

Sursat: 3 *batmans* of wheat, 1 *batman* of butter, ½ *batman* of cheese and 1 floor mat, worth 7 rubles and 98 kopeks.

Total revenue: 6 gold rubles, 7 rubles and 98 kopeks in local money, or 4 rubles and 98¾ kopeks in Russian currency.

34. Khanzad.

Tax-paying families: 4.

Annual tribute: 4 gold rubles.

No *sursat* in wheat is collected.

The nomads provide 1 *batman* of butter, ½ *batman* of cheese and 1 floor mat, worth 6 rubles and 78 kopeks

Total revenue: 4 gold rubles, 6 rubles and 78 kopeks in local money, or 4 rubles and 23¾ kopeks in Russian currency.

35. Shah-Sultanly (Şahsoltanlı).

Tax-paying families: 20. Tax-exempt families: 7.
(The families of 5 *nokars* and 2 *ranjbars* are exempt).

Annual tribute: 22 gold rubles.

Sursat: 11 *batmans* of wheat, 2 *batmans* of butter, 1 *batman* of cheese, 1 floor mat and 1 small rug, worth 19 rubles and 56 kopeks.

Total revenue: 22 gold rubles, 19 rubles and 56 kopeks in local money, or 12 rubles and 22½ kopeks in Russian currency.

36. Miuskurly-Molla-Gadi (Müskurlı).

Tax-paying families: 11. Tax-exempt families: 2.
(The family of the *yüzbaşi* and the mullah are exempt).

Annual tribute: 7 gold rubles

The families are all poor or immigrants and thus paid no other dues. Their status should be examined next year.

37. Shikhly (Şıxlı).

Tax-paying families: 5. Tax-exempt families: 1.
(The family of the *nokar* is exempt).

Annual tribute: 4 gold rubles.

Sursat: 2 *batmans* of wheat, ½ *batman* of butter and ½ *batman* of cheese, worth 2 rubles and 99 kopeks.

Total revenue: 4 gold rubles, 2 rubles and 99 kopeks in local money, or 1 ruble and 86¾ kopeks in Russian currency.

38. Akhundlu (Axundlu).

Tax-paying families: 8. Tax-exempt families: 1
(The family of the *yüzbaşi* is exempt).

Annual tribute: 4 gold rules.

Sursat: 2 *batmans* of wheat, 1 *batman* of butter and ½ *batman* of cheese, worth 5 rubles and 18 kopeks.

Total revenue: 4 gold rubles, 5 rubles and 18 kopeks in local money, or 3 rubles and 23¾ kopeks in Russian currency.

39. Chiragly (Çırağlı).

Tax-paying families: 30. Tax-exempt families: 10.
(The families of 4 *nokars*, 5 *ranjbars* and 1 mullah are exempt).

Annual tribute: 28 gold rubles.

Sursat: 15 *batmans* of wheat, 3 *batmans* of butter, 1½ *batmans* of cheese, 1 floor mat and 1 small rug, worth 25 rubles and 54 kopeks.

Total revenue: 28[2] gold rubles, 25 rubles and 54 kopeks in local money, or 15 rubles and 96¼ kopeks in Russian currency.

40. Akhtachi-Salian (Axtaçi-Salyan).

Tax-paying families: 20. Tax-exempt families: 4.
(The families of 2 *nokars* and 2 *ranjbars* are exempt).

Annual tribute: 10 gold rubles.

No *sursat* in wheat is collected.

Other dues are 2 *batmans* of butter and 1 *batman* of cheese, worth 8 rubles and 76 kopeks.

Total revenue: 10 gold rubles, 8 rubles and 76 kopeks in local money, or 5 rubles and 47½ kopeks in Russian currency.

41. Elli-Giuzli.

Tax-paying families: 4. Tax-exempt families: 1.
(The family of the *ranjbar* is exempt).

Annual tribute: 3 gold rubles.

[2] Text read 25 in error.

No *sursat* in wheat is collected.

Other dues are 1 *batman* of butter and ½ *batman* of cheese, worth 4 rubles and 38 kopeks.

Total revenue: 3 gold rubles, 4 rubles and 38 kopeks in local money, or 2 rubles and 73¾ kopeks in Russian currency.

42. Veisaly (Veysəlli).

Tax-paying families: 30.
The families are all immigrants from Karabagh.

The settlement is the property of Mohammad `Ali Beg

Annual tribute: 37 gold rubles.

No *sursat* is collected.

Other dues are 4 *batmans* of butter, 2 *batmans* of cheese, 1 floor mat and 1 small rug, worth 23 rubles and 92 kopeks.

Total revenue: 37 gold rubles, 23 rubles and 92 kopeks in local money, or 14 rubles and 95 kopeks in Russian currency.

43. Marzely (Mərzəli).

Tax-exempt families: 40.
The families are all immigrants from Karabagh.

They pay no dues. They have to be examined and assessed in next year's tax register.

Note: The settlement belonged to the brother of Mostafa Khan, Esma`il Beg, and now belongs to the treasury.

44. Lala-Agmetly [Akhmedly].

Tax-exempt families: 40.
The families are all immigrants from Karabagh.

They pay no dues. They have to be examined and assessed in next year's tax register.

Note: The settlement belonged to the brother of Mostafa Khan, Esma`il Beg, and now belongs to the treasury.

45. Karakhanly (Qaraxanlı).

Tax-exempt families: 20.
The families are all immigrants from Karabagh.

They pay no dues. They have to be examined and assessed in next year's tax register.

Note: The settlement belonged to Malek Umud and now belongs to the treasury.

46. Karavelly-Aga-Mamet (Qaravəlli).

Tax-exempt families: 22.
The families are all immigrants from Karabagh.

They pay no dues. They have to be examined and assessed in next year's tax register.

Note: The settlement belonged to the brother of Mostafa Khan, Esma`il Beg, and now belongs to the treasury.

Note: In addition, the *mahal* paid 100 gold rubles for the salaries of the khan's *mirzas*.

Totals for the Xançoban Mahal:

Tax-paying families: 1,085.
Tax-exempt families: 473.
Annual tribute: 1,032 gold rubles.
Dues in cash and kind: 807 rubles and 59 kopeks in local money, which equals to 504 rubles and 74¼ kopeks in Russian currency.

Major-General Madatov
Actual State Councilor Mogilevskii

[Register 7]

Elat Mahal

Revenues from the nomads of the Elat Mahal, populated entirely by Tatar nomads, indicating the number of tax-paying and tax-exempt families, as well as the amount paid by each settlement to the khan—which will now go to the treasury; which settlements are under the supervision of the beg of the mahal, what part of the revenue he collected for the khan [which will now go to the treasury] and what part he kept for himself. Also, what revenues are collected in grain, silk and other products, as well as the dues for the darugheh.

Note: Some of the settlements had to provide free labor.

Note: The *mahal* is supervised by Hajji `Ali Beg.

1. Khalach [Khaladzh] (Xələc).

Tax-paying families: 137. Tax-exempt families: 17.
(The family of the *yüzbaşi*, 4 *ranjbars* belonging to the *mahal*'s *beg*, 5 orphans and 3 mullahs are exempt).

Annual tribute: 140 gold rubles.

Sursat: 1 *taghar* and 20 *batmans* of wheat, 13 *batmans* of butter, 6 *batmans* of cheese, 2 small rugs and 2 floor mats. In addition, 1 ruble each from the 30 active plows, for total of 97 rubles and 44 kopeks in kind and 30 rubles in cash.

Mal-o-jehat: Due to the poor harvest, there was no *mal-o-jehat* collected this year. However, the average dues in the past were 4 *taghars* of wheat, 2 *taghars* of barley and a 1 ruble per *taghar* fee for the tax collector, which totals 102 rubles.

There was no *darughegy* collected for the treasury.

Note: The nomads occasionally till with more than the 30 plows; in that case a charge of 1 ruble per additional plow has to be added.

Total revenue: 140 gold rubles, 229 rubles and 44 kopeks in local money, or 143 rubles and 40 kopeks in Russian currency.

2. Kushchi (Quşçu).

Tax-paying families: 88. Tax-exempt families: 18
(The families of the 2 *kadkhodas*, 2 *ranjbars* belonging to the *yüzbaşi*, 1 *nokar*, 10 orphans and 3 mullahs are exempt).

Annual tribute: 115 gold rubles.

Sursat: 1 *taghar* and 7½ *batmans* of wheat, 10 ½ *batmans* of, 5 *batmans* of cheese, 2 small rugs and 1 floor mat. In addition, 1 ruble for each of the 75 plows, for a total of 79 rubles and 24 kopeks in kind and 75 rubles in cash.

Mal-o-jehat: Due to the poor harvest, there was no *mal-o-jehat* collected this year. However, the average dues in the past were 10 *taghars* of wheat, 5 *taghars* of barley and a 1 ruble per *taghar* fee for the tax collector, which totals 255 rubles.

There was no *darughegy* collected for the treasury.

Total revenue: 115 gold rubles, 409 rubles and 24 kopeks in local money, or 255 rubles and 77½ kopeks in Russian currency.

3. Arab-Abdul-Kerim (Ərəbabdulkerim).

Tax-paying families: 160. Tax-exempt families: 14.
(The families of 2 *yüzbaşis*, 8 *ranjbars* of the *yüzbaşis*, and 4 mullahs are exempt).

Annual tribute: 125 gold rubles.

Sursat: 1 *taghar* and 12½ *batmans* of wheat, 12½ *batmans* of butter, 5 *batmans* of cheese, 1 small rug and 2 floor mats, and 1 ruble for each of the 20 plows. In addition, out of the 160 families, 80 were *ranjbars*, who had to plant 80 *taghars* of rice in the fields of the village of Ağsu belonging to the khan, which now belongs to the treasury. The khan received more than 800 *taghars* from that harvest, at the average price of 8 rubles and 10 kopeks a *taghar* or 27 kopeks a *batman*, for a total of 6,567 rubles and 80 kopeks in kind and 20 rubles in cash.

Mal-o-jehat: Due to the poor harvest, there was no *mal-o-jehat* collected this year. However, the average dues in the past were 4 *taghars* of wheat and a 1 ruble per *taghar* fee for the tax collector, which totals 84 rubles.

There was no *darughegy* collected for the treasury; it was sent to the *mahal* supervisor, Hajji `Ali Beg.

Total revenue: 125 gold rubles, 6,671 rubles and 80 kopeks in local money, or 4,169 rubles and 87½ kopeks in Russian currency.

4. Bozavan [Bozavand] (Bozavand).

Tax-paying families: 45. Tax-exempt families: 12.
(The families of the *kadkhoda*, 10 orphans and 1 mullah are exempt).

Annual tribute: 30 gold rubles.

Sursat: 15 *batmans* of wheat, 3 *batmans* of butter, 1 small rug and 1 ruble from each of the 30 plows, for a total of 22 rubles and 24 kopeks in kind and 30 rubles in cash.

Mal-o-jehat: Due to the poor harvest, there was no *mal-o-jehat* collected this year. However, the average dues in the past were 4 *taghars* of wheat and 2 *taghars* of barley; plus a 1 ruble per *taghar* fee for the tax collector, which totals 102 rubles.

There was no *darughegy* collected for the treasury; it was sent to the *mahal* supervisor, Hajji `Ali Beg.

Total revenue: 30 gold rubles, 154 rubles and 24 kopeks in local money, or 96 rubles and 40 kopeks in Russian currency.

5. Kovlar (Qovlar).

Tax-paying families: 36. Tax-exempt families: 12.
(The families of the *kadkhoda*, 2 *ranjbars* belonging to the *yüzbaşi*, 5 orphans, and 1 mullah are exempt).

Annual tribute: 40 gold rubles.

Sursat: 20 *batmans* of wheat, 4 *batmans* of butter, 1 small rug and 1 ruble from each of the 20 plows, for a total of 28 rubles and 32 kopeks in kind and 20 rubles in cash.

Mal-o-jehat: Due to the poor harvest, there was no *mal-o-jehat* collected this year. However, the average dues in the past were 3 *taghars* of wheat and 1 *taghar* of barley; plus a 1 ruble per *taghar* fee for the tax collector, which totals 72 rubles.

There was no *darughegy* collected for the treasury; it went to the mahal supervisor, Hajji `Ali Beg.

Total revenue: 40 gold rubles, 120 rubles and 32 kopeks in local money, or 75 rubles and 20 kopeks in Russian currency.

6. Bei (Bəy).

Tax-paying families: 31. Tax-exempt families: 7.
(The families of the *yüzbaşi*, the *mo`af* and 5 orphans are exempt).

Annual tribute: 30 gold rubles.

Sursat: 15 *batmans* of wheat, 3 *batmans* of butter, 1 small rug and 1 ruble from each of the 15 plows, for a total of 22 rubles and 24 kopeks in kind and 15 rubles in cash in local money.

Mal-o-jehat: Due to the poor harvest, there was no *mal-o-jehat* collected this year. However, the average dues in the past were 2 *taghars* of wheat and 1 *taghar* of barley; plus a 1 ruble per *taghar* fee for the tax collector, which totals 51 rubles.

There was no *darughegy* collected for the treasury; it went to the *mahal* supervisor, Hajji `Ali Beg.

Total revenue: 30 gold rubles, 88 rubles and 24 kopeks in local money, or 55 rubles and 15 kopeks in Russian currency.

7. Pashaly (Ikinci Paşalı).

Tax-paying families: 22. Tax-exempt families: 2.
(The families of the *kadkhoda* and 1 orphan are exempt).

Annual tribute: 10 gold rubles.

Sursat: 5 *batmans* of wheat, 1 *batmans* of butter, for a total of 6 rubles and 8 kopeks.

Mal-o-jehat: None is collected.

There was no *darughegy* collected for the treasury; it went to the *mahal* supervisor, Hajji `Ali Beg.

Note: The inhabitants are responsible to cart the produce to the khan (now treasury) and other officials.

Total revenue: 10 gold rubles, 6 rubles and 8 kopeks in local money, or 3 rubles and 80 kopeks in Russian currency.

8. Zengena [Zangina] (Zəngənə).

Tax-paying families: 15. Tax-exempt families: 7.
(The families of 4 *mo`af* [tax-exempt] and 3 mullahs are exempt).

Annual tribute: 15 gold rubles.

Sursat: 7½ *batmans* of wheat, 1½ *batmans* of butter, 1 floor mat and 1 ruble from each of the 10 plows, for a total of 11 rubles and 72 kopeks in kind and 10 rubles in cash.

Mal-o-jehat: Due to the poor harvest, there was no *mal-o-jehat* collected this year. However, the average dues in the past were 2 *taghars* of wheat; plus a 1 ruble per *taghar* fee for the tax collector, which totals 42 rubles.

There was no *darughegy* collected for the treasury; it went to the *mahal* supervisor, Hajji `Ali Beg.

Note: The settlement has to also provide laborers, as many as required.

Total revenue: 15 gold rubles, 63 rubles and 52 kopeks in local money, or 39 rubles and 70 kopeks in Russian currency.

9. Kareimanly [Karamanlu] (Qaramanlı).

Tax-paying families: 17. Tax-exempt families: 2.
(The families of the *kadkhoda* and 1 orphan are exempt).

Annual tribute: 10 gold rubles.

Sursat: 5 *batmans* of wheat, 1 *batman* of butter, 1 floor mat and 1 ruble from each of the 15 plows, for a total of 8 rubles and 48 kopeks in kind and 15 rubles in cash.

Mal-o-jehat: Due to the poor harvest, there was no *mal-o-jehat* collected this year. However, the average dues in the past were 2 *taghars* of wheat and 1 *taghar* of barley; plus a 1 ruble per *taghar* fee for the tax collector, which totals 51 rubles.

There was no *darughegy* collected for the treasury; it went to the *mahal* supervisor, Hajji `Ali Beg.

Total revenue: 10 gold rubles, 74 rubles and 48 kopeks in local money, or 46 rubles and 55 kopeks in Russian currency.

10. Kerrar (Karrar).

Tax-paying families: 9. Tax-exempt families: 2.
(The families of the *kadkhoda* and the mullah are exempt).

Annual tribute: 5 gold rubles.

Sursat: 5 *batmans* of wheat, ½ *batman* of butter for a total of 4 rubles and 4 kopeks.

Mal-o-jehat: None collected.

There was no *darughegy* collected for the treasury; it went to the *mahal* supervisor, Hajji `Ali Beg.

Total revenue: 5 gold rubles, 4 rubles and 4 kopeks in local money, or 2 rubles and 52½ kopeks in Russian currency.

11. Boiat [Bayat] (Boyat).

Tax-paying families: 30. Tax-exempt families: 1.
(The family of the *kadkhoda* is exempt).

Annual tribute: 10 gold rubles.

Sursat: 5 *batmans* of wheat, 1 *batman* of butter and 1 small rug, for a total of 10 rubles and 8 kopeks.

Mal-o-jehat: The khan's *divan* collected nothing; the khan gave it to the local *nazer*, Hoseyn.

There was no *darughegy* collected for the treasury; the khan gave it to the local *nazer*, Hoseyn

Total revenue: 10 gold rubles, 10 rubles and 8 kopeks in local money, or 6 rubles and 30 kopeks in Russian currency.

12. Perdly (Perdilı).

Tax-paying families: 13.
(The families were all *ranjbars*; 5 families belonged to the khan and 8 to the Begum, the sister of the previous Khan of Sheki, the blind Mohammad Hasan Khan, who was married to Mostafa Khan, but who has been divorced for more than 12 years)

Annual tribute: 10 gold rubles.

Sursat: None to the treasury.
Mal-o-jehat: None to the treasury

There was no *darughegy* collected for the treasury.

The entire revenue from this village belonged to [Fatemeh][1] Begum, the khan's wife.

[1] See appendix.

13. Khinisly (Xinıslı)

Tax-paying families: 20. Tax-exempt families: 8.
(The families of the 8 *seyyeds* are exempt).

Annual tribute: 6 gold rubles.

The settlement belonged to the khan's wife Kichkin and paid no *sursat* or *darughegy*. Since the khan's flight it belongs to the treasury. However, they had to use a plow and 5 bulls belonging to the khanate and now the treasury, and till and sow 5 *taghars* of wheat and 2 *taghars* of barley, which yields 5 to 1 in the case of wheat and 6 to 1 in the case of barley, for a total of 596 rubles.

Mal-o-jehat in normal times averaged 10 *taghars* of wheat and 5 *taghars* of barley, plus the fee for the tax collector came to 255 local rubles.

Total revenue: 6 gold rubles, 851 rubles in local money, or 531 rubles and 87½ kopeks in Russian currency.

14. Mirikent [Miri-kend] (Mirikənd).

Tax-paying families: 7.

Annual tribute: 2 gold rubles and 2 rubles and 50 kopeks in local money.

No *sursat*, *mal-o-jehat* or *darughegy* was collected for the treasury.

The khan gave all the dues to the local *nazer*, Hoseyn.

Total revenue: 2 gold rubles, 2 rubles and 50 kopeks in local money, or 1 ruble and 56¼ kopeks in Russian currency.

15. Talysh (Talişli).

Tax-paying families: 65. Tax-exempt families: 6.
(The families of the *kadkhoda*, 4 orphans, and the mullah are exempt).

Annual tribute: 50 gold rubles.

Sursat: 25 *batmans* of wheat, 4½ *batmans* of butter, 1 small rug and 1 ruble from each of the 15 plows, for a total of 32 rubles and 36 kopeks in kind and 15 rubles in cash.

Mal-o-jehat: Due to the poor harvest, no assessment was made, but the average dues in the past were 2 *taghars* of wheat and 1 *taghar* of barley; plus a fee for the tax collector, for a total of 51 rubles.

There was no *darughegy* collected for the treasury; it went to the *mahal* supervisor, Hajji `Ali Beg.

Total revenue: 50 gold rubles, 98 rubles and 36 kopeks in local money, or 61 rubles and 47½ kopeks in Russian currency.

16. Shamly (Şamlı).

Tax-paying families: 20. Tax-exempt families: 1.
(The family of the *kadkhoda* is exempt).

Annual tribute: 10 gold rubles.

Sursat: 5 *batmans* of wheat, 1 *batman* of butter, 1 small rug and 1 ruble from each of the 15 plows, for a total of 10 rubles and 8 kopeks in kind and 15 rubles in cash.

Mal-o-jehat: Due to the poor harvest, there was no *mal-o-jehat* collected this year. However, the average dues in the past were 2 *taghars* of wheat and 1 *taghar* of barley; plus the fee for the tax collector, for a total of 51 rubles.

There was no *darughegy* collected for the treasury; it went to the *mahal* supervisor, Hajji `Ali Beg.

Total revenue: 10 gold rubles, 76 rubles and 8 kopeks in local money, or 47 rubles and 55 kopeks in Russian currency.

17. Dzhagirly (Cahirli).

Tax-paying families: 59. Tax-exempt families: 12.
(The families of the *kadkhoda*, 5 *ranjbars* belonging to the Hajji `Ali Beg, 4 orphans, and 2 mullahs are exempt).

Annual tribute: 60 gold rubles.

Sursat: 30 *batmans* of wheat, 5½ *batmans* of butter, 2 *batmans* of cheese, 1 small rug, 1 floor mat, and 1 ruble from each of the 30 plows, for a total of 42 rubles and 4 kopeks in kind and 30 rubles in cash.

Mal-o-jehat: Due to the poor harvest, there was no *mal-o-jehat* collected this year. However, the average dues in the past were 4 *taghars* of wheat and 2 *taghars* of barley; plus the fee for the tax collector, for a total of 102 rubles.

There was no *darughegy* collected for the treasury; it went to the *mahal* supervisor, Hajji `Ali Beg.

Total revenue: 60 gold rubles, 174 rubles and 4 kopeks in local money, or 108 rubles and 77½ kopeks in Russian currency.

18. Udzharly [Udzhary] (Ucar).[2]

Tax-paying families: 17.

Annual tribute: 12 gold rubles and 1 ruble and 60 kopeks in local money.

Sursat: 5 *batmans* of wheat and 1 *batman* of butter, for a total of 6 rubles and 8 kopeks.

No *mal-o-jehat* or *darughegy* was collected for the treasury; it belongs to Hajji Jebrail Beg, who is the owner of the settlement.

Total revenue: 12 gold rubles, 7 rubles and 68 kopeks in local money, or 4 rubles and 80 kopeks in Russian currency.

[2] These three successive villages form the present-day large town of Ucar.

19. Udzharly [Udzhary] (Ucar).

Tax-paying families: 16.
(They were all *ranjbars*, who belong to the children of Shah `Ali Beg)

Annual tribute: 10 gold rubles.

Sursat: 5 *batmans* of wheat, for a total of 2 rubles.

No *mal-o-jehat* or *darughegy* is collected for the treasury; it belongs to the children of Shah `Ali Beg.

Total revenue: 10 gold rubles, 2 rubles in local money, or 1 ruble and 25 kopeks in Russian currency.

20. Udzharly [Udzhary] (Ucar).

Tax-paying families: 17.
(They are all *ranjbars*, 4 of who belong to *`Abbas* `Ali Beg).

Annual tribute: 12 gold rubles and 1 ruble and 60 kopeks in local money.

Sursat: 5 *batmans* of wheat, 1 *batman* of butter and 1 small rug. The *ranjbars* of this settlement had to plant 13 *taghars* of rice for the owners the khan's adjutant, the fugitive Aqa Beg, and to *Abbas* `Ali Beg, which after all expenses yielded a 10-fold harvest, or 130 *taghars*, which, altogether totals 1,063 rubles and 8 kopeks.

No *mal-o-jehat* or *darughegy* was collected for the treasury; it went to the owners and the part belonging to Aqa Beg will now go to the treasury.

Total revenue: 12 gold rubles, 1,064 rubles and 68 kopeks in local money, or 665 rubles and 42½ kopeks in Russian currency.

21. Gogler (Göyler).

Tax-paying families: 56. Tax-exempt families: 10.
(The families of the khan's 2 *nokars*, 2 *mo`af*, 4 *ranjbars* belonging to Hajji Jebrail Beg, and 2 mullahs are exempt).

Annual tribute: 60 gold rubles.

Sursat: 30 *batmans* of wheat, 6 *batmans* of butter, 1 small rug and 1 floor mat, plus 1 ruble from each of the 25 plows, for a total of 42 rubles and 88 kopeks in kind and 25 rubles in cash.

Mal-o-jehat: Due to the poor harvest, there was no *mal-o-jehat* collected this year. However, the average dues in the past were 3 *taghars* of wheat and 1½ *taghars* of barley; plus the fee for the tax collector, which totals 76 rubles and 50 kopeks.

There was no *darughegy* collected for the treasury; it went Hajji Jebrail Beg.

Total revenue: 60 gold rubles, 144 rubles and 38 kopeks in local money, or 90 rubles and 23¾ kopeks in Russian currency.

22. Chapni.

Tax-paying families: 5.

Annual tribute: 2 gold rubles and 2 rubles and 50 kopeks in local money.

Due to poverty they paid no other dues.

Total revenue: 2 gold rubles, 2 rubles and 50 kopeks in local money, or 1 ruble and 56¾ kopeks in Russian currency.

Totals for the Elat Mahal:

Tax-paying families: 885.
Tax-exempt families: 131.
Annual tribute: 764 gold rubles and 8 rubles and 20 kopeks in local money, or 5 rubles and 12½ kopeks in Russian currency.
Sursat: 8,652 rubles in kind and 300 rubles in cash.
Mal-o-jehat: 1,294 rubles and 50 kopeks.
Total from the *mahal* in cash and kind: 10,254 rubles and 70 kopeks in local money, or 6,409 rubles and 18¾ kopeks in Russian currency.

Note: If we convert the 5 and 12½ kopeks in silver rubles (part of the annual tribute) into gold rubles, the annual tribute will increase to 765 gold and 1 ruble and 12½ kopeks in silver, while the total revenue in cash and kind will be reduced to 6,404 rubles and 6¼ kopeks in Russian currency.

Major-General Prince Madatov
State Councilor Mogilevskii

[Register 8]

Koshun Mahal

Revenues from the villages of the Koshun Mahal, indicating the number of tax-paying and tax-exempt families, as well as the portion [of the harvest] from each village that was assessed as the taxes paid directly to the khan, which will now go to the treasury; which villages are under the supervision of the beg of the mahal, who collected the revenue for the khan [which will now go to the treasury] and who kept a part as his salary. Also, what other revenues are collected from the grain harvest, silk production and other produce, and what are the revenues for the upkeep of the darugheh.

Note: Mahmud Beg is the supervisor.

Note: Some of the villages had to provide free labor, as many as required, by the khan.

1. Chukhany (Çuxanlı): A Tatar village.

Tax-paying families: 12. Tax-exempt families: 17.
(The families of the *kadkhoda*, 6 *nokars*, 7 *ranjbars*, belonging to the *mahal*'s *beg*,
2 orphans, and the mullah are exempt).

Annual tribute: 30 gold rubles.

Sursat: 20 *batmans* of wheat, 1 small rug and 1 floor mat and 1 ruble from each of the 25 plows, for a total of 22 rubles and 40 kopeks in kind and 25 rubles in cash.

The *mahal*'s *beg* and not the treasury collected the *mal-o-jehat* and the *darughegy*.

Total revenue: 30 gold rubles, 47 rubles and 40 kopeks in local money, or 29 rubles and 62½ kopeks in Russian currency.

2. Chagan (Inkici Çağan): A Tatar village.

Tax-paying families: 14. Tax-exempt families: 25.
(The families of the *kadkhoda*, 4 *nokars*, 3 *mo`af* families, 5 orphans, 2 mullahs and 10 immigrants from Kuba are exempt).

Annual tribute: 20 gold rubles.

Sursat: 15 *batmans* of wheat and 1 ruble from each of the 3 plows, for a total of 6 rubles in kind and 3 rubles in cash.

Mal-o-jehat: 1 *taghar* of wheat and the fee for the tax collector, for a total of 21 rubles.

Darughegy: 15 *batmans* of wheat and 2 *taghars* of barley, for 22 rubles.

Total revenue: 20 gold rubles and 52 rubles in local money, or 32 rubles and 50 kopeks in Russian currency.

3. Kala-Bogurt (Qeleybuğurd): A Tatar village.

Tax-paying families: 30. Tax-exempt families: 6.
(The families of the *kadkhoda*, 4 immigrants and the mullah are exempt).

Annual tribute: 20 gold rubles.

Sursat: 16 *batmans* of wheat and 1 ruble from each of the 7 plows, for a total of 6 rubles and 40 kopeks in kind and 7 rubles in cash.

Mal-o-jehat: 20 *batmans* of wheat, 20 *batmans* of barley and the fee for the tax collector, for a total of 13 rubles.

Darughegy: 35 *batmans* of wheat and 35 *batmans* of barley, as well as 2 *taghars* of barley as *at-arpasi* for the Mahmud Beg's horses, for 37 rubles.

Total revenue: 20 gold rubles, 63 rubles and 40 kopeks in local money, or 39 rubles and 62½ kopeks in Russian currency.

4. Dilmanlu [Dilman] (Dilman): A Tatar village.

Tax-paying families: 42. Tax-exempt families: 15.
(The families of the *kadkhoda*, 9 immigrants from Kuba, 3 orphans and 2 mullahs are exempt).

Annual tribute: 40 gold rubles.

Sursat: 32 batmans of wheat and 1 ruble from each of the 12 plows, for a total of 12 rubles and 80 kopeks in kind and 12 rubles in cash.

Mal-o-jehat: 2 *taghars* of wheat, 1 *taghar* of barley, and the fee for the tax collector, for a total of 51 rubles.

Darughegy: 2 *taghars* of barley *at-arpasi* for Mahmud Beg's horses, worth 16 rubles.

Total revenue: 40 gold rubles, 94 rubles and 80 kopeks in local money, or 57 rubles and 37½ kopeks in Russian currency.

5. Gadzhi-Manlu [Gadzhiman] (Hacıman): A Tatar village.

Tax-paying families: 23. Tax-exempt families: 5.
(The families of the *kadkhoda*, 2 immigrant families from Kuba, 1 orphan, and the mullah are exempt).

Annual tribute: 20 gold rubles.

Sursat: 16 *batmans* of wheat and 1 ruble from each of the 15 plows, for a total of 6 rubles and 40 kopeks in kind and 15 rubles in cash.

Mal-o-jehat: 1 *taghar* and 30 *batmans* of wheat and the fee for the tax collector, for a total of 33 rubles and 50 kopeks.

Darughegy: 1 *taghar* of wheat and ½ *taghar* of barley, and 15 rubles in cash for 39 rubles.

Total revenue: 20 gold rubles, 93 rubles and 90 kopeks in local money, or 58 rubles and 58½ kopeks in Russian currency.

6. Khaty-Manly (Xatman): A Tatar village.

Tax-paying families: 15. Tax-exempt families: 5.
(The families of the *kadkhoda*, 2 immigrant families from Kuba, 1 orphan and the mullah are exempt).

Annual tribute: 20 gold rubles.

Sursat: 16 *batmans* of wheat and 1 ruble from each of the 8 plows, for a total of 6 rubles and 40 kopeks in kind and 8 rubles in cash.

Mal-o-jehat: 2 *taghars* of wheat and the fee for the tax collector, for a total of 42 rubles.

Darughegy: 40 *batmans* of wheat and 20 *batmans* of barley, and 2 *taghars* of barley for *at-arpasi*, totaling 37 rubles and 60 kopeks.

Total revenue: 20 gold rubles and 94 rubles in local money, or 58 rubles and 75 kopeks in Russian currency.

7. Utugly: A Tatar village.

Tax-paying families: 33. Tax-exempt families: 7.
(The families of the *kadkhoda*, 2 *ranjbar* families belonging to the *kadkhoda*, and 4 orphans are exempt).

Annual tribute: 32 gold rubles.

Sursat: 20 *batmans* of wheat and 2 *batmans* of butter and 1 ruble from each of the 10 plows, for a total of 16 rubles and 16 kopeks in kind and 10 rubles in cash.

Mal-o-jehat: 2 *taghars* and 30 *batmans* of wheat and the fee for the tax collector, for a total of 42 rubles.

Darughegy: None for the treasury; belongs to Mahmud Beg.

Total revenue: 32 gold rubles, 68 rubles and 16 kopeks in local money, or 42 rubles and 60 kopeks in Russian currency.

8. Bekleliu [Beklia] (Bəklə): A Tatar village.

Tax-paying families: 17. Tax-exempt families: 1.
(The family of the *kadkhoda* is exempt).

Annual tribute: 14 gold rubles.

Sursat: 8 *batmans* of wheat and 2 *batmans* of butter for a total of 11 rubles and 60 kopeks in local currency.

Mal-o-jehat: None collected.

Darughegy: None collected.

Note: The villagers all live in Fitdagh and have to provide laborers for the khan, as many as required.

Total revenue: 14 gold rubles, 11 rubles and 60 kopeks in local money, or 7 rubles and 10 kopeks in Russian currency.

9. Charagan (Çarağan): A Tatar village.

Tax-paying families: 8. Tax-exempt families: 10.
(The family of the *kadkhoda*, 4 immigrant families from Kuba and 5 *ranjbars* belonging to the treasury are exempt).

Annual tribute: 15 gold rubles.

Sursat: 12 *batmans* of wheat, 2 *batmans* of butter and 1 small rug, as well as 1 ruble from each of the 12 plows, for a total of 16 rubles and 96 kopeks in kind and 12 rubles in cash.

Mal-o-jehat: 1 *taghar* of wheat and the fee for the tax collector, for 21 rubles.

Darughegy: 1 *taghar* and 10 *batmans* of wheat and 1 *taghar* and 8 *batmans* of barley, for a total of 33 rubles.

Total revenue: 15 gold rubles, 83 rubles and 56 kopeks in local money, or 52 rubles and 22½ kopeks in Russian currency.

10. Niuidi [Nuidy] (Nüydı): A Tatar village.

Tax-paying families: 13. Tax-exempt families: 5.
(The family of the *kadkhoda* and 5 *ranjbars* belonging to the *darugheh* are exempt).

Annual tribute: 14 gold rubles.

Sursat: 12 *batmans* of wheat, 2 *batmans* of butter and 1 small rug, as well as 1 ruble from each of the 8 plows, for a total of 16 rubles and 96 kopeks in kind and 8 rubles in cash.

Mal-o-jehat: 2 *taghar* of wheat and the fee for the tax collector, for 42 rubles.

Darughegy: None collected for the treasury.

Total revenue: 14 gold rubles, 66 rubles and 96 kopeks in local money, or 41 rubles and 85 kopeks in Russian currency.

11. Mengalekhany: A Tatar village.

Tax-paying families: 6.

Annual tribute: 4 gold rubles.

Sursat: None is collected, only 1 ruble from each of the 4 plows, for a total of 4 rubles in cash.

Mal-o-jehat: 26 *batmans* of wheat and the fee for the tax collector, for 9 rubles.

Darughegy: None collected for the treasury.

Total revenue: 4 gold rubles and 13 rubles in local money, or 8 rubles and 12½ kopeks in Russian currency.

12.Tuluch [Tuludzh]: A Tatar village.

Tax-paying families: 3. Tax-exempt families: 2.
(The families of the *kadkhoda* and the mullah are exempt).

Annual tribute: 3 gold rubles.

Sursat: Only 1 ruble from each of the 3 plows, for a total of 3 rubles in cash.

Mal-o-jehat: 20 *batmans* of wheat and the fee for the tax collector, for a total of 9 rubles.

Darughegy: None is collected.

Total revenue: 3 gold rubles and 12 rubles in local money, or 7 rubles and 50 kopeks in Russian currency.

13. Shagradyl [Shagdagi?]: A Tatar village.

Tax-paying families: 1.

Annual tribute: 2 gold rubles.

Note: Due to its poverty the village paid nothing, except the annual tribute to the treasury.

14. Talysh (Malyy Talyş): A Tatar village.

Tax-paying families: 2.

Annual tribute: 2 rubles and 50 kopeks in local money, or 1 ruble and 56¼ kopeks in Russian currency.

Note: Due to its poverty the village paid only the annual tribute.

15. Archiman (Ərçiman): A Tatar village.

Tax-paying families: 11. Tax-exempt families: 1.
(The family of the *kadkhoda* is exempt).

Annual tribute: 9 gold rubles.

Sursat: 6 *batmans* of wheat, as well as 1 ruble from each of the 6 plows, for a total of 2 rubles and 40 kopeks in kind and 6 rubles in cash.

Mal-o-jehat: 1 *taghar* of wheat and the fee for the tax collector, for 21 rubles.

Darughegy: None for the treasury.

Total revenue: 9 gold rubles, 29 rubles and 40 kopeks in local money, or 18 rubles and 37½ kopeks in Russian currency.

16. Engekharan (Əngəxaran): A Tatar village.

Tax-paying families: 24. Tax-exempt families: 4.
(The family of the *kadkhoda* and the 3 *nokars* belonging to the *beg* are exempt).

Annual tribute: 20 gold rubles.

Sursat: 16 *batmans* of wheat, 2½ *batmans* of butter, 1½ *batmans* of cheese and 3 small rugs, and 1 floor mat as well as 1 ruble from each of the 15 plows, for a total of 31 rubles and 90 kopeks in kind and 15 rubles in cash.

Mal-o-jehat: 2 *taghar* of wheat and 1 *taghar* of barley and the fee for the tax collector, for 51 rubles.

Darughegy: None for the treasury.

Total revenue: 20 gold rubles, 97 rubles and 90 kopeks in local money, or 61 rubles and 18½ kopeks in Russian currency.

17. Zarat: A Tatar village.

Tax-paying families: 26. Tax-exempt families: 5.
(The families of the *kadkhoda* and 4 mullahs are exempt).

Annual tribute: 20 gold rubles.

Sursat: 16 *batmans* of wheat, 2 *batmans* of butter, 1 *batman* of cheese, and 1 small rug and 1 floor mat, as well as 1 ruble from each of the 12 ploughed fields for a total of 21 rubles and 56 kopeks in kind and 12 rubles in cash.

Mal-o-jehat: 1 *taghar* of wheat and the fee for the tax collector, for a total of 21 rubles.

Darughegy: None for the treasury

Total revenue: 20 gold rubles, 56 rubles and 20 kopeks in local money, or 35 rubles and 10 kopeks in Russian currency.

18. Chilov: A Tatar village.

Tax-paying families: 22. Tax-exempt families: 6.
(The families of the *kadkhoda*, 2 immigrants and 3 orphans are exempt).

Annual tribute: 30 gold rubles.

Sursat: 20 *batmans* of wheat, 6 *batmans* of butter, 3 *batmans* of cheese, 3 small rugs, 1 floor mat, as well as 1 ruble from each of the 21 plows, for a total of 51 rubles and 8 kopeks in kind and 21 rubles in cash.

Mal-o-jehat: 3 *taghars* of wheat, 2 *taghars* of barley, and the fee for the tax collector, for a total of 81 rubles.

Darughegy: None for the treasury.

Total revenue: 30 gold rubles, 153 rubles and 8 kopeks in local money, or 95 rubles and 67½ kopeks in Russian currency.

19. Dzhabani (Cabanı): A Tatar village.

Tax-paying families: 7. Tax-exempt families: 1.
(The family of the *kadkhoda* is exempt).

Annual tribute: 14 gold rubles.

Sursat: 10 *batmans* of wheat, 1½ *batmans* of butter, 1 *batman* of cheese as well as 1 ruble from each of the 10 plows, for a total of 10 rubles and 72 kopeks in kind and 10 rubles in cash.

Mal-o-jehat: 2 *taghars* of wheat and 1 *taghar* of barley and the fee for the tax collector, for 51 rubles.

Darughegy: None for the treasury.

Total revenue: 14 gold rubles, 71 rubles and 72 kopeks in local money, or 44 rubles and 82½ kopeks in Russian currency.

20. Siundi [Sundi] (Syundi): A Tatar village.

Tax-paying families: 61. Tax-exempt families: 14.
(The families of the *kadkhoda* and his 4 *ranjbars*, 2 immigrant families from Kuba, 5 *mo`afs* and 2 mullahs are exempt).

Annual tribute: 48 gold rubles.

Sursat: 40 *batmans* of wheat, 4 *batmans* of butter, 2 *batmans* of cheese, 1 small rug and 1 floor mat, as well as 1 ruble from each of the 60 plows, for a total of 39 rubles and 92 kopeks in kind and 60 rubles in cash.

Mal-o-jehat: 5 *taghar* of wheat and 3 *taghars* of barley and the fee for the tax collector, for 132 rubles.

Darughegy: 2 *taghars* of wheat and 2 *taghars* of barley, for a total of 56 rubles.

Total revenue: 48 gold rubles, 287 rubles and 92 kopeks in local money, or 179 rubles and 95 kopeks in Russian currency.

21. Merzendyge [Marzandige]: A Tatar village.

Tax-paying families: 23. Tax-exempt families: 5.
(The families of the *kadkhoda*, 3 *mo`afs* and 1 mullah are exempt).

Annual tribute: 30 gold rubles.

Sursat: 20 *batmans* of wheat, 3 *batmans* of butter, 1½ *batmans* of cheese, 2 small rugs, and 1 floor mat, as well as 1 ruble from each of the 25 plows, for a total of 31 rubles and 54 kopeks in kind and 25 rubles.

Mal-o-jehat: 2 *taghars* of wheat, 1 *taghar* of barley, plus the fee for the tax collector, for a total of 51 rubles.

Darughegy: None for the treasury.

Total revenue: 30 gold rubles, 107 rubles and 54 kopeks in local money, or 57 rubles and 21½ kopeks in Russian currency.

22. Nabur: A Tatar village.

Tax-paying families: 35. Tax-exempt families: 7.
(The families of the *kadkhoda*, his *ranjbar*, 4 orphans and the mullah are exempt).

Annual tribute: 30 gold rubles.

Sursat: 24 *batmans* of wheat, as well as 1 ruble from each of the 30 plows, for a total of 9 rubles and 60 kopeks in kind and 30 rubles in cash.

Mal-o-jehat: 2 *taghars* of wheat and 1 *taghar* of barley and the fee for the tax collector, for a total of 51 rubles.

Darughegy: 2 *taghar* of wheat and 2 *taghars* of barley, for a total of 56 rubles.

Total revenue: 30 gold rubles, 146 rubles and 80 kopeks in local money, or 91 rubles and 62½ kopeks in Russian currency

23. Matrasy: An Armenian village.

Tax-paying families: 28. Tax-exempt families: 25.
(The family of 3 priests, the *kevkha*, 2 *ranjbars* belonging to the treasury who work on the khan's field in Ağsu, 9 *ranjbars* belonging to the *beg*, and 10 *mo`afs* are exempt).

Annual tribute: 80 gold rubles.

Sursat: 1 *taghar* of wheat worth 20 rubles,

Since the village is the property of Ebrahim Aqa no *mal-o-jehat* or *darughegy* is collected.

Total revenue: 80 gold rubles and 20 rubles in local money, or 12 rubles and 50 kopeks in Russian currency.

24. Kerkench [Kerkendzh] (Kərkənc): An Armenian village.

Tax-paying families: 58. Tax-exempt families: 15.
(The families of the *kevkha*, 4 *ranjbars* belonging to the treasury, who are currently working on the khan's field in Ağsu, 4 *ranjbars* belonging to the *darugheh* and the *kevkha*, 4 orphans, 1 priest, and 1 foreman are exempt).

Annual tribute: 70 gold rubles.

Sursat: 40 *batmans* of wheat, 200 rubles in *kharaj*, as well as 1 ruble from each of the 50 plows, for a total of 16 rubles in kind and 250 rubles in cash.

Mal-o-jehat: 12 *taghars* of wheat and 6 *taghars* of barley, and the fee for the tax collector, for a total of 288 rubles.

Darughegy: Belongs to Hajji Aqa Beg.

Note: The village has to provide laborers for 3 days a year to the khan, now the treasury.

Total revenue: 70 gold rubles and 554 rubles in local money, or 346 rubles and 25 kopeks in Russian currency.

25. Kelakhani [Kalakhany]: An Armenian village.

Tax-paying families: 29. Tax-exempt families: 13.
(The families of the *kevkha* 4 ranjbars belonging to Aqa Reza Beg, the priest, 4 orphans, and 3 immigrants from Karabagh are exempt).

The village is the property of Aqa Reza Beg.

Annual tribute: 30 gold rubles.

Sursat: 30 *batmans* of wheat, worth 12 rubles.

Mal-o-jehat: Belongs to Aqa Reza Beg

Darughegy: Belongs to Aqa Reza Beg.

Total revenue: 30 gold rubles, 30 rubles and 12 kopeks in local money, or 7 rubles and 50 kopeks in Russian currency.

26. Meisary (Meysəri): An Armenian village.

Tax-paying families: 7. Tax-exempt families: 11.
(The families of the kevkha, and the 10 immigrants from Karabagh are exempt).

Annual tribute: 12 gold rubles.
Sursat: 8 *batmans* of wheat, 15 rubles in *kharaj* as well as 1 ruble from each of the 8 plows, for a total of 3 rubles and 23 kopeks in kind and 23 rubles in cash.

Mal-o-jehat: 1 *taghar* of wheat and 23 *batmans* of barley, and the fee for the tax collector, for 26 rubles and 30 kopeks

Darughegy: 1 *taghar* of wheat and 28 *batmans* of barley, for a total of 25 rubles and 60 kopeks.

Total revenue: 12 gold rubles, 78 rubles and 30 kopeks in local money, or 48 rubles and 93½ kopeks in Russian currency.

27. Lengevis [Lengebiz] (Ləngəbiz): A Tatar village.

Tax-paying families: 27. Tax-exempt families: 3.
(The families of the *kadkhoda*, an orphan and a mullah are exempt).

Annual tribute: 33 gold rubles.

Sursat: 26 *batmans* of wheat, worth 10 rubles and 40 kopeks.

Mal-o-jehat: None

Darughegy: None
The village belongs to Shah `Ali Beg

Total revenue: 33 gold rubles, 10 rubles and 40 kopeks in local money, or 6 rubles and 50 kopeks in Russian currency.

28. Kashat [Kashad]: A Tatar village.

Tax-paying families: 10. Tax-exempt families: 1.
(The family of the *kadkhoda* is exempt).

Annual tribute: 22 gold rubles.

Sursat: 18 *batmans* of wheat, worth 7 rubles and 20 kopeks.

Mal-o-jehat: None

Darughegy: None

The village belongs to Shah `Ali Beg

Total revenue: 22 gold rubles, 7 rubles and 20 kopeks in local money, or 4 rubles and 50 kopeks in Russian currency.

29. Geshtymez: A Tatar village.

Tax-paying families: 17. Tax-exempt families: 3.
(The families of the *kadkhoda* and 2 orphans are exempt).

Annual tribute: 22 gold rubles.

Sursat: 18 *batmans* of wheat, worth 7 rubles and 20 kopeks.

Mal-o-jehat: None

Darughegy: None

The village belongs to Shah `Ali Beg

Total revenue: 22 gold rubles, 7 rubles and 20 kopeks in local money, or 4 rubles and 50 kopeks in Russian currency.

30. Bidzhov (Bico): A Tatar village.

Tax-paying families: 33. Tax-exempt families: 2.
(The families of the *kadkhoda* and the mullah are exempt).

Annual tribute: 33 gold rubles.

Sursat: 26 *batmans* of wheat, worth 10 rubles and 40 kopeks.

Mal-o-jehat: None.

Darughegy: None.

The village belongs to Shah `Ali Beg

Total revenue: 33 gold rubles, 10 rubles and 40 kopeks in local money, or 6 rubles and 50 kopeks in Russian currency.

31. Sagiany [Sagian] (Saqiyan): An Armenian village.

Tax-paying families: 30. Tax-exempt families: 2.
(The families of the *kevkha* and the priest are exempt).

Annual tribute: 35 gold rubles.

Sursat: 30 *batmans* of wheat, the *kharaj* of 20 rubles, the *bagh-bashi* of 20 rubles, as well as 1 ruble from each of the 20 plows, for a total of 12 rubles and in kind and 120 rubles in cash.

Mal-o-jehat: 4 *taghars* of wheat and 2 *taghars* of barley, and the fee for the tax collector, for a total of 102 rubles.

Darughegy: belongs to Vahid Beg, who is in charge of this village.

Total revenue in Russian currency: 146 rubles and 25 kopeks.

32. Kunakent [Konakh-kend]: A Tatar village.

Tax-exempt families: 52.
(They are all immigrant families from Kuba; they include 2 *yüzbaşis*,
2 *ranjbars*, and 2 mullahs).

Note: Mostafa exempted the village from taxes, but with the exception of the 6, the rest have to be assessed now. They pay nothing to the treasury and are under the supervision of Mahmud Beg.

Totals for the Koshun Mahal:

Tax-paying families: 730
Tax-exempt families: 268
Annual tribute: 772 gold rubles and 2 rubles and 60 kopeks.
Sursat: 419 rubles and 96 kopeks in kind and 679 rubles in cash.
Mal-o-jehat: 1,159 rubles in local money.
Darughegy: 322 rubles and 80 kopeks in local money

Total collected in local money: 2,582 rubles and 26 kopeks, which equals to 1,613 rubles and 91½ kopeks in Russian currency.

Note: The 2.50 rubles in Shirvani money toward the annual tribute, increases the total to 772½ gold rubles, while it decreases the total silver to 1,612 rubles and 35 kopeks.

Major-General Prince Madatov
State Councilor Mogilevskii

[Register 9]

Karasubasar [Qarasubasar] Mahal

Revenues from the villages of the Qarasubasar Mahal, indicating the number of tax-paying and tax-exempt families, as well as the portion [of the harvest] from each village that was assessed as the taxes paid directly to the khan, which will now go to the treasury; which villages are under the supervision of the beg of the mahal, who collected the revenue for the khan [which will now go to the treasury] and who kept a part as his salary. Also, what other revenues are collected from the grain harvest, silk production and other produce.

1–2. Shilian (Şilyan) and Karabiurkliu [Karabiuk] (Qarabürk): Tatar villages.

Note: Ibrahim Beg was in charge of these 2 villages.

Note: No *darughegy* was collected from this *mahal*, for each two villages are under the supervision of a different *beg*, who collects the *darughegy* dues.

Note: Most of the villages had to provide free laborers to the khan.

Tax-paying families: 80. Tax-exempt families: 41.
(20 newcomers, 5 *nokars* belonging to the *begs*, 10 widows with small children, and 6 mullahs are exempt).

Annual tribute: 154 gold rubles.

Sursat: 1½ *taghars* of wheat and 1 ruble for each of the 80 plows, for 30 rubles in kind and 80 rubles in cash.

Mal-o-jehat: 10 *taghars* of wheat and 1 ruble per *taghar* for the tax collector, for a total of 210 rubles.

Total revenue: 154 gold rubles and 320 rubles in local money, or 200 rubles in Russian currency.

3–4. Leki (Ləki 1 and Ləki 2): Tatar villages.

Amir Allah Qoli Beg and Aslan Beg were in charge of these 2 villages.

Tax-paying families: 90. Tax-exempt families: 29.
(6 *ranjbars* belonging to Amir Allah Qoli Beg, 3 *nokars*, 4 mullahs, 5 orphans, 5 widows with small children, 3 *nokars* of the *begs* and 3 *nokars* of the khan are exempt).

Annual tribute: 154 gold rubles.

Sursat: 30 *batmans* of wheat and 1 ruble for each of the 30 plows and in Leki 1; 45 *batmans* of wheat from Leki 2 and 1 ruble from each of its 50 plows. In addition, in Leki 1 there are 4 plows and 4 pairs of oxen and 4 families of *ranjbars* belonging to the khan; in Leki 2 there are 6 plows, 6 pair of oxen and 6 families of *ranjbars* belonging to the khan. The two villages have to provide 10 *ranjbars* to till the 10 fields for the khan (and now the treasury). They have to sow 10 *taghars* of wheat and 5 *taghars* of barley, with a yield of 15 to 1. The same *ranjbars* have to plant 10 *batmans* of cotton for every pair of oxen, that is, 100 *batmans*, which produces 84 *batmans* of cleaned cotton. The total in kind comes to 1,053 rubles and 36 kopeks in kind and 80 rubles in cash.

Mal-o-jehat: 30 *taghars* of wheat, 20 *taghars* of barley and 1 ruble per *taghar* for the tax collector, for a total of 810 rubles.

The villages also have to supply as many workers as needed to the khan.

Total revenue: 154 gold rubles, 4,943 rubles and 36 kopeks in local money, or 3,089 rubles and 60 kopeks in Russian currency.

5–6. Alvent (Əlvənd): A Tatar village.

Nowruz `Ali Beg was in charge of these 2 villages.

Tax-paying families: 80. Tax-exempt families: 58.
(30 newcomers belonging to the *beg*, 6 *ranjbars*, 5 *nokars* belonging to the *beg*, 12 widows with small children, 2 *seyyeds* and 3 mullahs are exempt).

Annual tribute: 154 gold rubles.

Sursat: 1½ *taghars* of wheat and 1 ruble for each of the 40 plows. In addition, a part of a silk farm, which belonged to the fugitive `Abdollah Beg and now the treasury, and produces 2 *batmans* of silk, and 1 ruble from each of the 90 silk sheds. Moreover, 1 ruble and 60 kopeks from each of the 40 large orchards and 80 kopeks from each of the 50 small ones, for a total of 170 rubles in kind and 234 rubles in cash.

Mal-o-jehat: 12 *batmans* of silk, 5 *taghars* of wheat and 1 ruble per *taghar* for the tax collector, for a total of 1,000 rubles.

Total revenue: 154 gold rubles and 1,404 rubles in local money, or 877 rubles and 50 kopeks in Russian currency.

Note: When the Kur River overflows its banks, the above 2 villages have to more sow wheat and pay additional *mal-o-jehat* in wheat, which increases the total of the *mal-o-jehat* considerably.

6–7. Tilan and Kiugiun: Tatar villages.

Umay Beg was in charge of these villages.

Tax-paying families: 80. Tax-exempt families: 68.
(15 widows with small children, 15 *nokars* and *mo`afs*, 10 *seyyeds*, 8 mullahs and 20 newcomers are exempt).

Annual tribute: 154 gold rubles.

Sursat: 1½ *taghars* of wheat and 1 ruble for each of the 50 silk farms and 1 ruble and 60 kopeks from each of the large orchards and 80 kopeks from the small ones. In addition, Ja`far Beg of Talin owned 3 silk farms with sheds, which now belong to the treasury, and which produce 3 *batmans* of silk. In addition, after the flight of Kemal, a *nokar*, the treasury took over his silk farm and shed, which produces 1 *batman* of silk. The total is 310 rubles in kind and 110 in cash.

Mal-o-jehat: 10 *batmans* of silk, worth 700 rubles.

Total revenue: 154 gold rubles and 1,120 rubles in local money, or 700 rubles in Russian currency.

8. Muratkhan [Muradkhan] (Muradxan): A Tatar village.

The belonged to Esma`il Beg, the brother of Mostafa Khan, and now belongs to the treasury.

Tax-paying families: 35. Tax-exempt families: 28.
(The families of 10 newcomers, the *yüzbaşi* and the *darugheh*, both of who have 4 *ranjbar* families, 3 *seyyeds*, 2 mullahs and 7 widows with small children are exempt).

Sursat: 5 *taghars* of wheat, 4 *taghars* of barley, which, after deduct-ing the share of the laborers, yields 10 *taghars* per *taghar* planted. In addition, 200 *batmans* of cotton had to be sown, which produced 150 *batmans* of pure cotton. There are 6 plows in this village, which belonged to Esma`il Beg and now the treasury. In addition the village had to pay 225 rubles from the production and sale of madder. Moreover, instead of the annual tribute, the village gave 150 rubles in *toujih* dues. The total comes to 2,076 rubles in kind and 375 in cash.

Mal-o-jehat: 15 *taghars* of wheat and 5 *taghars* of barley and 50 *batmans* of cotton, 1 ruble per *taghar* for the tax collector, for a total of 592 rubles. The above *mal-o-jehat* is collected in good years when there is adequate rainfall. In the last two years the drought has resulted in no *mal-o-jehat*.

Total revenue: 3,043 rubles in local money, or 1,901 rubles and 87½ kopeks in Russian currency.

Note: The above harvest from this village is when the Musa River overflows its banks due to plenty of rain. In the last two years there has been little rain and the harvest was negligible.

9. Khalach [Khaladzh] (Xalaç): A Tatar village.

Yüzbaşis `Ali-Panah and Mohammad are in charge of this village.

Tax-paying families: 22. Tax-exempt families: 12.
(The families of the *yüzbaşis* and their 4 *ranjbars*, 4 widows with small children, and 2 mullahs are exempt).

Note: The inhabitants of this village fled to the Khanate of Sheki some 20 years ago. Half of them returned 8 years ago and the other half last year. The khan exempted all of them from taxes, but now we have to assess the 22 families depending on their condition.

10. Zardob (Zərdab): A Tatar village.

Rahim Beg is in charge of this village.

Tax-paying families: 70. Tax-exempt families: 104.
(The families of 13 orphans, 13 newcomers, 8 *nokars*, 5 *ranjbars* belonging to the *beg*, 2 *mo`afs*, 2 village elders, and 6 mullahs are exempt).

Note: In addition, 40 families belonging to the cousin of the *beg*, Khalil and 15 families belonging to his other cousin, Rostam Beg, are exempt. They are all silk producers and pay their dues in silk to the *begs*.

Annual tribute: 154 gold rubles.

Sursat: 1½ *taghars* of wheat and 1 ruble for each of the 70 silk farms. In addition, 1 ruble and 60 kopeks from each of the 30 large orchards, and 80 kopeks from each of the 40 small ones, for a total of 30 rubles in kind and 150 rubles in cash

Mal-o-jehat: 18 *batmans* of silk, which the khan gave as the annual salary to Rahim Beg, worth 1,260 rubles.

Total revenue: 154 gold rubles and 1,440 rubles in local money, or 900 rubles in Russian currency.

11. Chally (Çallı): A Tatar village.

Rahim Beg is in charge of this village.

Tax-exempt families: 20.
They all came from the Ağdaş *Mahal* in Sheki and pay no dues. They now have to be assessed depending on local conditions.

Totals for the Qarasubasar Mahal:

Tax-paying families: 457.
Tax-exempt families: 360
Annual tribute: 770.
Dues in kind: 6,669 rubles and 36 kopeks.
Dues in cash: 1,029 rubles
Mal-o-jehat: 4,572 rubles

Total in cash and kind: 12,270 rubles in local money, which equals to 7,668 rubles and 97½ kopeks in Russian currency.

Major-General Prince Madatov
State Councilor Mogilevskii

[Register 10]

Kasan (Kessan) Mahal

Revenues from the villages of the Kessan Mahal, indicating the number of tax-paying and tax-exempt families, as well as the portion [of the harvest] from each village that was assessed as the taxes paid directly to the khan, which will now go to the treasury; which villages are under the supervision of the beg of the mahal, who collected the revenue for the khan [which will now go to the treasury] and who kept a part as his salary. Also, what other revenues are collected from the grain harvest, silk production and other produce

Note: Since all the villages of this *mahal*, except for Kirk and Genza—which now belong to the treasury—are the patrimony of the superintendent of the *mahal*, Mostafa Beg, all the revenues, except for the annual tribute and the *sursat* belong to him.

1. Kiupakent[d]: An Armenian village.

Tax-paying families: 40. Tax-exempt families: 5.
(The family of the *yüzbaşi* and his 4 *ranjbars* are exempt).

Annual tribute: 24 gold rubles.

Sursat: 18 *batmans* of wheat, worth 7 rubles and 20 kopeks in local money, or 4 rubles and 50 kopeks in Russian currency.

2. Tubi [Tuba] (Tubikənd): An Armenian village.

Tax-paying families: 19.

Annual tribute: 16 gold rubles.

Sursat: 12 *batmans* of wheat, worth 4 rubles and 80 kopeks in local money, or 3 rubles in Russian currency.

3. Fetagly: An Armenian village.

Tax-paying families: 6.
The village paid no dues whatsoever.

4. Engikent [Engikend] (Yenikənd): An Armenian village.

Tax-paying families: 25. Tax-exempt families: 6.
(The 6 Tatar families are exempt).
They all work on a farm called Shiukurchi.

Annual tribute: 23 gold rubles.

Sursat: 20 *batmans* of wheat, worth 8 rubles in local money, or 5 rubles in Russian currency.

5. Upper Ismailly (Ismayıllı) A Tatar village.

Tax-paying families: 54. Tax-exempt families: 20.
(The families of 13 *mo`afs* and the *beg*'s *nokars*, and 7 immigrant families from Kuba are exempt).

Annual tribute: 80 gold rubles.

Sursat: 1 *taghar* of wheat and ½ *taghar* of barley worth 24 rubles in local money, or 15 rubles in Russian currency.

6. Talystan (Talıstan): A Tatar village.

Tax-paying families: 23. Tax-exempt families: 7.
(The families of 1 *mo`af* and 4 of the *beg*'s *nokars* and 2 immigrants from Sheki are exempt).

Annual tribute: 26 gold rubles.
Sursat: 25 *batmans* of wheat, worth 6 rubles in local money, or 3 rubles and 75 kopeks in Russian currency.

7. Kush-Iangidzha: A Tatar village.

Tax-paying families: 25. Tax-exempt families: 7.
(3 *mo`af* families, the *yüzbaşi* and his 2 brothers and a *ranjbar* are exempt).

Annual tribute: 38 gold rubles.

Sursat: 35 *batmans* of wheat, worth 14 rubles in local money, or 8 rubles and 75 kopeks in Russian currency.

8. Dially (Diyallı): A Tatar village.

Tax-paying families: 20. Tax-exempt families: 4.
(The families of the 4 *nokars* of the *beg* are exempt).

Annual tribute: 6 gold rubles.

Sursat: 7 *batmans* of wheat, worth 10 rubles in local money, or 6 rubles and 25 kopeks in Russian currency.

9. Dzhulian (Cülyan): A Tatar village.

Tax-paying families: 8.

Annual tribute: 24 gold rubles.

Sursat: 18 *batmans* of wheat, worth 2 rubles and 80 kopeks in local money, or 1 ruble and 75 kopeks in Russian currency.

10–11. Dakhar (Daxar) and Niugedi [Niugdy] (Nügdı): Tatar villages.

Tax-paying families: 6. Tax-exempt families: 3.
(The families of 3 *nokars* are exempt).

Annual tribute: 13 gold rubles.

Sursat: 12½ *batmans* of wheat, worth 5 rubles in local money, or 3 rubles and 12½ kopeks in Russian currency.

12. Magakhi: A Tatar village.

Tax-exempt families: 25.
(The 20 native families and 5 immigrants from Karabagh are exempt).

The village belongs to the *beg* and his brothers and pays no dues.

13. Degma-Dagly [Dagmadagly]: An Armenian village.

Tax-exempt families: 10.
(They are all immigrants).

The village belongs to the *beg* and his brothers and pays no dues.

14. Miushkurly (Müşkürlı): A nomad settlement.

Tax-exempt families: 16

The settlement belongs to the *beg* and his brothers and pays no dues.

15. Bedally: A Tatar village.

Tax-exempt families: 3

The village belongs to the *beg* and his brothers and pays no dues.

16. Karadygin [Kara-digin]: A Tatar village.

Tax-exempt families: 4
(All immigrants from Sheki).

The village belongs to the *beg* and his brothers and pays no dues.

17. Velibina: A Tatar village.

Tax-exempt families: 4

The village belongs to the *beg* and his brothers and pays no dues.

18. Gazili: A Tatar village.

Tax-exempt families: 4

The village belongs to the relatives of the *beg*'s mother and pays no dues.

19. Kirk: An Armenian village.

Tax-paying families: 10. Tax-exempt families: 25.
(25 immigrant families from Karabagh are exempt).

The village belonged to Mostafa Khan's wife and now to the treasury.

Annual tribute: 7 gold rubles.

Sursat: 10 *batmans* of wheat. In addition the village has a plow with 6 pairs of oxen, which belonged to Mostafa Khan's wife, Kichkin and now to the treasury. Four *ranjbars* families from this village have to till the land and sow 5 *taghars* of wheat and 2 *taghars* of barley seeds belonging to the treasury. The yield, after the share of the *ranjbars*, is 5 to 1 for wheat and 6 to 1 for barley. The village also pays a *kharaj* of 200 rubles. The *sursat* from this village is 598 rubles and 40 kopeks in kind and 200 rubles in cash.

Mal-o-jehat: 25 *taghars* of wheat and 15 *taghars* of barely, worth 620 rubles.

Total revenue: 7 gold rubles, 1,418 rubles and 40 kopeks in local money, or 886 rubles and 50 kopeks in Russian currency.

20. Genza (Kənzə): An Armenian village.

Tax-paying families: 35.

The village belonged to Naft `Ali Beg, who fled with Mostafa Khan and now belongs to the treasury. It is currently administered by `Omar Soltan, the son of Naft `Ali Beg.

Annual tribute: 13 gold rubles

Kharaj: 70 rubles.

Mal-o-jehat: 13 *taghars* of wheat and 4 *taghars* of barely, worth 332 rubles.

Darughegy: The treasury received 3 *taghars* of wheat and 3 *taghars* of barley, worth 84 rubles, the rest belongs to `Omar Soltan.

Total revenue: 13 gold rubles, 486 rubles in local money, or 303 rubles and 75 kopeks in Russian currency.

Totals for the Kessan Mahal:

Tax-paying families: 271.
Tax-exempt families: 143.
Annual tribute: 272 gold rubles.
Dues in kind: 764 rubles and 20 kopeks.
Dues in cash: 270 rubles.
Mal-o-jehat: 952 rubles.

Total revenues in cash and kind: 1,986 rubles and 20 kopeks in local money, which equals to 1,241 rubles and 37½ kopeks in Russian currency.

Major-General Prince Madatov
State Councilor Mogilevskii

[Register 11]

Akerat [Ekeret] Mahal

Revenues from the villages of the Akerat Mahal, indicating the number of tax-paying and tax-exempt families, as well as the portion [of the harvest] from each village that was assessed as the taxes paid directly to the khan, which will now go to the treasury; which villages are under the supervision of the beg of the mahal, who collected the revenue for the khan [which will now go to the treasury] and who kept a part as his salary. Also, what other revenues are collected from the grain harvest, silk production and other produce, and what are the revenues for the upkeep of the darugheh.

Note: Karim Beg is the *mahal* supervisor.

Note: Some of the villages had to provide laborers for the khan.

1. Incha (Inçe): A Tatar village.

Tax-paying families: 20. Tax-exempt families: 17.
(The families of 10 *nokars* and *mo`afs*, 2 *ranjbars* belonging to the *beg*, 2 mullahs and 3 orphans are exempt)

Annual tribute: 38 gold rubles.

Sursat: 15 *batmans* of wheat, 1 ruble from each of the 15 silk farms, and 1 ruble from each of the 10 plows, for a total of 6 rubles in kind and 25 rubles in cash.

Mal-o-jehat: 1 *batman* of silk, 1½ *taghars* of wheat, plus 1 ruble per *taghar* for the fee of the tax collector, for a total of 101 rubles and 50 kopeks.

Darughegy: None for the treasury, collected by the *beg* of the *mahal*.

Total revenue: 38 gold rubles, 132 rubles and 50 kopeks in local money, or 82 rubles and 81¼ kopeks in Russian currency.

2. Kiurt-Mashi (Kürdmaşı): A Tatar village.

Tax-paying families: 20. Tax-exempt families: 10.
(The families of the 4 *mo`af*, 2 *ranjbars* belonging to the *yüzbaşi*,
the mullah and 3 orphans are exempt).

Annual tribute: 38 gold rubles.

Sursat: 15 *batmans* of wheat, 1 ruble from each of the 12 silk farms and 1 ruble from each of the 11 plows, for a total of 6 rubles in kind and 23 rubles in cash.

Mal-o-jehat: 1½ *taghars* of wheat, ½ *taghar* of barley, and 1 *batman* of silk, for a total of 106 rubles.

Darughegy: 12 *stils* of silk, 5 *batmans* of wheat and 4 *batmans* of barley, for a total of 65 rubles and 81 kopeks.

Total revenue: 38 gold rubles, 200 rubles and 81 kopeks in local money, or 125 rubles and 50½ kopeks in Russian currency.

3. Eke Khana (Yekəxana):[1] *A Tatar village.*

Tax-paying families: 15. Tax-exempt families: 6.
(The families of the *kadkhoda*, 4 orphans and the mullah are exempt).

Annual tribute: 24 gold rubles.

Sursat: 10 *batmans* of wheat, 1 ruble each from the 6 silk work-shops and 1 ruble each from the 8 plows, which totals 4 rubles in kind and 14 rubles in cash.

Mal-o-jehat: 15 *stils* of silk, 1 *taghar* and 10 *batmans* of wheat, which with the fee for the tax collector, totals 68 rubles and 96½ kopeks.

Darughegy: 8 *stils* of silk and 5 *batmans* of wheat and 4 *batmans* of barley, worth 45 rubles and 74 kopeks.

Total revenue: 24 gold rubles, 132 rubles and 70½ kopeks in local money, or 82 rubles and 93½ kopeks in Russian currency.

---

[1] There are a number of villages called Yekekhana, see Qobustan Mahal.

4. Karamarianly [Karamarian] (Qaraməryəm): A Tatar village.

Tax-paying families: 18. Tax-exempt families: 8.
(4 *mo`af* and 4 orphans are exempt).

Annual tribute: 38 gold rubles.

Sursat: 15 *batmans* of wheat, 1 ruble each from the 13 silk workshops and 1 ruble each from the 12 plows, for a total of 6 rubles in kind and 25 rubles in cash.

Mal-o-jehat: 1½ *batmans* of silk, 1½ *taghars* of wheat, and ½ *taghar* of barley which with the fee for the tax collector, totals 125 rubles and 50 kopeks.

Darughegy: 15 *stils* of silk and 5 *batmans* of wheat and 4 *batmans* of barley, worth 77 rubles and 36½ kopeks.

Total revenue: 38 gold rubles, 231 rubles and 86½ kopeks in local money, or 144 rubles and 91½ kopeks in Russian currency.

Note: 30 families from this village live in the village of Alkhas in the Sedenrud *Mahal* and work in silk farms belonging to the khan's wife, Kichkin, and now to the treasury. According to the records they were to pay 30 gold rubles in tribute but the khan paid it on their behalf. The treasury now has to take on this expense.

5. Karabakkal [Karabakhkal] (Qarabaqqal): A Tatar village.

Tax-paying families: 20. Tax-exempt families: 6.
(The families of the *kadkhoda*, 3 orphans and 2 mullahs are exempt).

Annual tribute: 38 gold rubles.

Sursat: 15 *batmans* of wheat, 1 ruble each from the 15 silk work-shops, which totals 6 rubles in kind and 15 rubles in cash.

Mal-o-jehat: 1½ *batmans* of silk, 30 *batmans* of wheat, and 1 *taghar* of rice which with the fee for the tax-collector, totals 126 rubles and 70 kopeks.

Darughegy: 16 *stils* of silk and 2½ *taghars* of rice, worth 66 rubles and 93 kopeks.

Total revenue: 38 gold rubles, 214 rubles and 63 kopeks in local money, or 134 rubles and 14½ kopeks in Russian currency.

6. Karaman (Qaraman): A Tatar village.

Tax-paying families: 12. Tax-exempt families: 3.
(The families of the *kadkhoda*, 1 orphan and the mullah are exempt).

Annual tribute: 14 gold rubles.

Sursat: 5 *batmans* of wheat, 1 ruble each from the 6 silk workshops, which totals 2 rubles in kind and 6 rubles in cash.

Mal-o-jehat: 15 *stils* of silk, 24 *batmans* of rice, which with the fee for the tax collector, totals 50 rubles and 94½ kopeks.

Darughegy: 8 *stils* of silk and 24 *batmans* of rice, worth 29 rubles and 82 kopeks.

Total revenue: 14 gold rubles, 88 rubles and 76½ kopeks in local money, or 55 rubles and 47½ kopeks in Russian currency.

7. Saatly-Seitler (Saatlı-Seidlyar): A Tatar village.

Tax-exempt families: 8.

Since the inhabitants of this village are all *seyyeds*, they pay no dues.

Totals for the Ekeret mahal:

Tax-paying families: 105.
Tax-exempt families: 58.
Total in Annual tribute: 190 gold rubles.
Total revenue in kind: 30 rubles.
Total revenue in cash: 108 rubles.
Total *mal-o-jehat*: 577 rubles and 60½ kopeks.
Total *darughegy* dues: 285 rubles and 66½ kopeks.

Total revenues in local money: 1,001 rubles and 26½ kopeks, which equals to 625 rubles and 79½ kopeks in Russian currency.

Major-General Prince Madatov
State Councilor Mogilevskii

[Register 12]

Kabristan [Qobustan] Mahal

Revenues from the nomad settlements of the Qobustan Mahal, indicating the number of tax-paying and tax-exempt families, as well as the amount paid by each village to the khan—which will now go to the treasury; which villages are under the supervision of the beg of the mahal, what part of the revenue he used to collect for the khan [which will now go to the treasury] and what part he kept for himself. Also, what other revenues are collected from the grain harvest, silk production and other produce, and what are the revenues for the upkeep of the darugheh.

Note: Malek Baqesh Beg, who has fled with Mostafa Khan to Iran, was the original supervisor of the *mahal*. Jebrail Beg is the current supervisor. The nomads have to supply laborers, horses for carts, and sheep as many as required.

1. Araba-Kadym [Arab-kadym] (Ərəbqədim).

Tax-paying families: 58. Tax-exempt families: 12.
(The families of 7 sheikhs and mullahs, and 5 families of *ranjbars* belonging to Jebrail Beg are exempt).

Annual tribute: 63 gold rubles.

Sursat: 35 *batmans* of wheat, 7 *batmans* of butter, 3½ *batmans* of cheese, 1 small rug and 1 floor mat and 1 ruble from each of the 40 plows, for a total of 51 rubles and 6 kopeks in kind and 40 rubles in cash.

Mal-o-jehat: This year the locust destroyed the harvest and thus only 5 *taghars* of wheat, which with the fee for the tax collector came to 105 rubles.

No *darughegy* is collected for the treasury.

Total revenue: 63 gold rubles, 196 rubles and 6 kopeks in local money, or 122 rubles and 53½ kopeks in Russian currency.

2. Arab-Bala-Oglan [Balaoglan].

Tax-paying families: 52. Tax-exempt families: 28.
(The family of *Yüzbaşi* Bala-Oghlan, 19 families of his relatives and their *nokars*, as well as his 5 *ranjbars*, and the 3 mullahs are exempt).

Annual tribute: 63 gold rubles.

Sursat: 35 *batmans* of wheat, 7 *batmans* of butter, 3½ *batmans* of cheese, 1 small rug and 1 floor mat and 1 ruble from each of the 40 plows, for a total of 51 rubles and 6 kopeks in kind and 40 rubles in cash.

Mal-o-jehat: This year the locust destroyed the harvest and thus only 5 *taghars* of wheat, which with the fee for the tax collector came to 105 rubles.

No *darughegy* is collected. The settlement belongs to *Yüzbaşi* Bala-Oghlan.

Total revenue: 63 gold rubles, 196 rubles and 6 kopeks in local money, or 122 rubles and 53½ kopeks in Russian currency.

3. Shikh Zagirlu-Chul [Shikh-zagerli].

Tax-paying families: 10. Tax-exempt families: 4.
(The families of 4 *nokars* are exempt).

Annual tribute: 16 gold rubles.

Sursat: 10 *batmans* of wheat, 2 *batmans* of butter, 1 *batman* of cheese, 1 small rug, 1 floor mat and 1 ruble from each of the 12 plows, for a total of 17 rubles and 96 kopeks in kind and 12 rubles in cash.

Mal-o-jehat: This year the locust destroyed the harvest and thus only 2 *taghars* of wheat and 20 *batmans* of barley, which with the fee for the tax collector, totals 46 rubles and 50 kopeks.

No *darughegy* is collected.

Total revenue: 16 gold rubles, 76 rubles and 46 kopeks in local money, or 47 rubles and 78 kopeks in Russian currency.

4. Shikh Zagirlu Sheger.

Tax-paying families: 20. Tax-exempt families: 5.
(The families of 4 *nokars* and the mullah are exempt).

Annual tribute: 21 gold rubles.

Sursat: Having no grain, they pay only 3 *batmans* of butter, for a total of 12 rubles and 24 kopeks in kind and 12 rubles in cash.

Mal-o-jehat: None collected for the treasury

No *darughegy* is collected.

Total revenue: 21 gold rubles, 12 rubles and 24 kopeks in local money, or 7 rubles and 65 kopeks in Russian currency.

5. Kelagaily [Kalagainy].

Tax-paying families: 15. Tax-exempt families: 4.
(The families of the *nokar*, 2 *ranjbars* and the mullah are exempt).

Annual tribute: 18 gold rubles.

Sursat: 15 *batmans* of wheat, 2 *batmans* of butter, 1 *batman* of cheese, 1 small rug, 1 floor mat and 1 ruble from each of the 18 plows, for a total of 21 rubles and 16 kopeks in kind and 18 rubles in cash.

Mal-o-jehat: This year the locust destroyed the harvest and thus only 3 *taghars* of wheat and 30 *batmans* of barley, which with the fee for the tax collector totals 69 rubles and 75 kopeks.

No *darughegy* is collected.

Total revenue: 18 gold rubles, 108 rubles and 91 kopeks in local money, or 68 rubles and 6¾ kopeks in Russian currency.

6. Khile (Xıllı).

Tax-paying families: 54. Tax-exempt families: 7.
(The families of the *nokar*, 4 *ranjbars* belonging to the *yüzbaşi*, and 2 mullahs are exempt).

Annual tribute: 70 gold rubles.

Sursat: 1½ *taghars* of wheat, 8 *batmans* of butter, 4 *batmans* of cheese, 3 small rugs, 3 floor mats and 1 ruble from each of the 20 plows, for a total of 84 rubles and 24 kopeks in kind and 20 rubles in cash.

Mal-o-jehat: 15 *taghars* of wheat and 5 *taghars* of barley, which with the fee for the tax collector totals 360 rubles.

No *darughegy* is collected.

Total revenue: 70 gold rubles, 464 rubles and 24 kopeks in local money, or 290 rubles and 15 kopeks in Russian currency.

7. Takle-Safi [Teklia] (Təklə).

Tax-paying families: 5. Tax-exempt families: 2.
(The families of 2 *ranjbars* belonging to the *yüzbaşi* are exempt).

Annual tribute: 9 gold rubles.

Sursat: 10 *batmans* of wheat, 1 *batman* of butter, ½ *batman* of cheese, 1 floor mat and 1 ruble from each of the 4 plows, for a total of 10 rubles and 78 kopeks in kind and 4 rubles in cash.

Mal-o-jehat: 1 *taghar* of wheat, which with the fee for the tax collector totals 21 rubles.

No *darughegy* is collected.

Total revenue: 9 gold rubles, 35 rubles and 78 kopeks in local money, or: 22 rubles and 3¼ kopeks in Russian currency.

8. Eka-Khany-Talyb (Yekaxana Taleb).

Tax-paying families: 43. Tax-exempt families: 9.
(The families of 4 *nokars* and 5 *ranjbars* are exempt).

Annual tribute: 46 gold rubles.

Sursat: 30 *batmans* of wheat, 6 *batmans* of butter, 3 *batmans* of cheese, 2 small rugs, 3 floor mats and 1 ruble from each of the 30 plows, for a total of 53 rubles and 48 kopeks in kind and 30 rubles in cash.

Mal-o-jehat: 5 *taghars* of wheat and 1 *taghar* of barley, which with the fee for the tax collector totals 114 rubles in local.

No *darughegy* is collected.

Total revenue: 46 gold rubles, 197 rubles and 48 kopeks in local money, or 123 rubles and 55½ kopeks in Russian currency.

9. Karadzhauzly.

Tax-paying families: 80. Tax-exempt families: 10.
(The families of 9 *nokars* and the mullah are exempt).

Annual tribute: 104 gold rubles.

Sursat: 1½ *taghars* of wheat, 12 *batmans* of butter, 6 *batmans* of cheese, 5 small rugs, 5 floor mats and 1 ruble from each of the 90 plows, for a total of 114 rubles and 56 kopeks in kind and 90 rubles in cash.

Mal-o-jehat: 15 *taghars* of wheat and 5 *taghars* of barley, which with the fee for the tax collector, totals 360 rubles.

No *darughegy* is collected.

Total revenue: 104 gold rubles, 564 rubles and 56 kopeks in local money, or: 352 rubles and 85 kopeks in Russian currency.

10. Arab-Dzhabralu.

Tax-paying families: 70. Tax-exempt families: 13.
(The families of 5 *ranjbars*, 3 families who are relatives of the *yüzbaşi*,
2 *nokars*, the mullah and 2 immigrants from Kuba are exempt).

Annual tribute: 63 gold rubles.

Sursat: 30 *batmans* of wheat, 7 *batmans* of butter, 4 *batmans* of cheese, 3 small rugs, 3 floor mats and 1 ruble from each of the 30 plows, for a total of 62 rubles and 16 kopeks in kind and 30 rubles in cash.

Mal-o-jehat: 4 *taghars* of wheat and 2 *taghars* of barley, which with the fee for the tax collector totals 102 rubles.

No *darughegy* is collected.

Total revenue: 63 gold rubles, 194 rubles and 16 kopeks in local money, or 121 rubles and 35 kopeks in Russian currency.

11. Takly Adzhi-Mamad-Ussein (Təklə Hajji Mohammad Hoseyn).

Tax-paying families: 81. Tax-exempt families: 14.
(The families of 6 *nokars*, 5 *ranjbars* belonging to the *yüzbaşi* and
3 mullahs and sheikhs are exempt).

Annual tribute: 79 gold rubles.

Sursat: 1 *taghar* of wheat, 9 *batmans* of butter, 4½ *batmans* of cheese, 3 small rugs, 4 floor mats and 1 ruble from each of the 75 plows, for a total of 80 rubles and 75 kopeks in kind and 75 rubles in cash.

Mal-o-jehat: 10 *taghars* of wheat and 5 *taghars* of barley, which with the fee for the tax collector, totals 255 rubles.

No *darughegy* is collected.

Total revenue: 79 gold rubles, 411 rubles and 2 kopeks in local money, or 256 rubles and 88¾ kopeks in Russian currency.

12. Dzhash-Dzhamli.

Tax-paying families: 14. Tax-exempt families: 2.
(The families of 2 *nokars* are exempt).

Annual tribute: 12 gold rubles.

Sursat: 15 *batmans* of wheat, 2 *batmans* of butter, 1 *batman* of cheese, 1 small rug, 1 floor mat and 1 ruble from each of the 10 plows, for a total of 21 rubles and 16 kopeks in kind and 10 rubles in cash.

Mal-o-jehat: 1½ *taghars* of wheat, ½ *taghar* of barley, which with the fee of the tax collector totals 36 rubles.

No *darughegy* is collected.

Total revenue: 12 gold rubles, 67 rubles and 16 kopeks in local money, or 41 rubles and 97½ kopeks in Russian currency.

13. Kiurdamich (Kürdamiç).

Tax-paying families: 20. Tax-exempt families: 5.
(The families of 2 *nokars*, 2 *ranjbars* and the mullah are exempt).

Annual tribute: 29 gold rubles.

Sursat: 20 *batmans* of wheat, 4 *batmans* of butter, 2 *batmans* of cheese, 1 small rug, 2 floor mats and 1 ruble from each of the 35 plows, for a total of 34 rubles and 32 kopeks in kind and 35 rubles in cash.

Mal-o-jehat: 5 *taghars* of wheat, and 2 *taghars* of barley, which with the fee for the tax collector, totals 123 rubles.

No *darughegy* is collected.

Total revenue: 29 gold rubles, 192 rubles and 32 kopeks in local money, or 120 rubles and 20 kopeks in Russian currency.

14. Arabi-Shakh-Verdi [Arab-shakhverdi] (Ərəbşahverdi).

Tax-paying families: 77. Tax-exempt families: 8.
(The families of 2 *nokars*, 5 *ranjbars* and the mullah are exempt).

Annual tribute: 63 gold rubles.

Sursat: 40 *batmans* of wheat, 7 *batmans* of butter, 4 *batmans* of cheese, 3 small rugs, 3 floor mats and 1 ruble from each of the 60 plows, for a total of 66 rubles and 16 kopeks in kind and 60 rubles in cash.

Mal-o-jehat: 8 *taghars* of wheat and 4 *taghars* of barley, which with the fee of the tax collector, totals 204 rubles.

No *darughegy* is collected.

Total revenue: 63 gold rubles, 330 rubles and 16 kopeks in local money, or 206 rubles and 35 kopeks in Russian currency.

15. Takle-Mirza Baba (Təklə Mirzababa).

Tax-paying families: 63. Tax-exempt families: 15.
(The families of 8 *nokars*, 3 *ranjbars* and 4 mullahs are exempt).

Annual tribute: 44 gold rubles.

Sursat: 25 *batmans* of wheat, 6 *batmans* of butter, 4 *batmans* of cheese, 3 small rugs, 3 floor mats and 1 ruble from each of the 30 plows, for a total of 56 rubles and 8 kopeks in kind and 30 rubles in cash.

Mal-o-jehat: 4 *taghars* of wheat and 2 *taghars* of barley, which with the fee for the tax collector totals 102 rubles.

No *darughegy* is collected.

Total revenue: 44 gold rubles, 188 rubles and 8 kopeks in local money, or 117 rubles and 55 kopeks in Russian currency.

16. Marazali.

Tax-paying families: 75. Tax-exempt families: 15.
(The families of 4 *nokars*, 5 *ranjbars*, and 4 *seyyeds* and mullahs are exempt).

Annual tribute: 104 gold rubles.

Sursat: 1½ *taghars* of wheat, 12 *batmans* of butter, 6 *batmans* of cheese, 5 small rugs, 5 floor mats and 1 ruble from each of the 90 plows, for a total of 114 rubles and 56 kopeks in kind and 90 rubles in cash.

Mal-o-jehat: 14 *taghars* of wheat and 4 *taghars* of barley, which with the fee for the tax collector totals 330 rubles.

No *darughegy* is collected.

Total revenue: 104 gold rubles, 534 rubles and 56 kopeks in local money, or 334 rubles and 10 kopeks in Russian currency.

17. Kiurt Kendy [Kiurd-kend] (Kürdkənd).

Tax-paying families: 26. Tax-exempt families: 17.
(The families of 5 *nokars*, 10 *ranjbars* belonging to the khan, now treasury, 2 *ranjbars* belonging to the *darugheh* are exempt).

Annual tribute: 32 gold rubles.

Sursat: 30 *batmans* of wheat, 3 *batmans* of butter, 1½ *batmans* of cheese, 1 small rug, 1 floor mat and 1 ruble from each of the 16 plows, for a total of 54 rubles and 16 kopeks in kind and 16 rubles in cash.

Mal-o-jehat: 4 *taghars* of wheat and 1 *taghar* of barley, which with the fee for the tax collector totals 93 rubles.

No *darughegy* is collected.

Total revenue: 32 gold rubles, 140 rubles and 54 kopeks in local money, or 87 rubles and 83¾ kopeks in Russian currency.

18. Kurbanchi (Qurbançı).

Tax-paying families: 30. Tax-exempt families: 6.
(The 5 *mo`af* families and the mullah are exempt).

Annual tribute: 32 gold rubles.

Sursat: 30 *batmans* of wheat, 4 *batmans* of butter, 2 *batmans* of cheese, 2 small rugs, 2 floor mats and 1 ruble from each of the 25 plows, for a total of 42 rubles and 32 kopeks in kind and 25 rubles in cash.

Mal-o-jehat: 4 *taghars* of wheat and 1 *taghar* of barley, which with the fee for the tax collector totals 93 rubles.

No *darughegy* is collected.

Total revenue: 32 gold rubles, 160 rubles and 32 kopeks in local money, or 100 rubles and 20 kopeks in Russian currency.

19. Tesii (Təsi).

Tax-paying families: 37.
(They are all *ranjbars*).

Annual tribute: 32 gold rubles.

As *ranjbars* they do not have to pay any dues, but they have to use 2 plows, and 10 oxen belonging to the treasury, and till and sow 20 *taghars* of wheat and 10 *taghars* of barley seeds, which after deducting the share of the *ranjbars*, yields 4 to 1 for wheat and 5 to 1 for barley. In addition, the *ranjbars*, near the village of Dülbarcan have to sow 15 *taghars* of wheat belonging to the treasury and harvest it, which from every *taghar* yields not less than 40[1] *taghars* for a total of 11,000 rubles in kind.

Mal-o-jehat: 10 *taghars* of wheat and 5 *taghars* of barley, which with the fee for the tax collector, totals 255 rubles.

---

[1] The total revenue, however, assumes a yield of 30 *taghars*.

Total revenue: 32 gold rubles and 11,255 rubles in local money, or 7,034 rubles and 37½ kopeks in Russian currency.

Note: The settlement belonged to Mostafa Khan's wife, Kichkin, who fled with him to Iran and now belongs to the treasury.

Note: The yield in grain from the village of Dülbarcan is sometimes 100 fold, for when the Kur River overflows, the fields can produce a harvest, which will be enough to provide seeds for 3 years and, at times, grows grain without sowing.

20. Eke-Khany-Ibragim (Yekəxana Ibrahim)

Tax-paying families: 14. Tax-exempt families: 1.
(1 *mo`af* family is exempt).

Annual tribute: 7 gold rubles.

Sursat: 10 *batmans* of wheat, 1 *batman* of butter, 1 *batman* of cheese, 1 small rug, 1 floor mats and 1 ruble from each of the 10 plows, for a total of 15 rubles and 8 kopeks in kind and 10 rubles in cash.

Mal-o-jehat: 1 *taghar* of wheat and 1 *taghar* of barley, which with the fee for the tax collector, totals 30 rubles.

No *darughegy* is collected.

Total revenue: 7 gold rubles, 55 rubles and 8 kopeks in local money, or 34 rubles and 42½ kopeks in Russian currency.

21. Gamiia [Gamially].

Tax-paying families: 30. Tax-exempt families: 1.
(The family of the mullah is exempt).

Annual tribute: 35 gold rubles.

Sursat: 25 *batmans* of wheat, 4 *batmans* of butter, 2 *batmans* of cheese, 2 small rugs, 1 floor mat and 1 ruble from each of the 20 plows, for a total of 37 rubles and 92 kopeks in kind and 20 rubles in cash.

Mal-o-jehat: 3 *taghars* of wheat and 1 *taghar* of barley, which with the fee for the tax collector, totals 72 rubles.

No *darughegy* is collected.

Total revenue: 35 gold rubles, 129 rubles and 92 kopeks in local money, or 81 rubles and 20 kopeks in Russian currency.

22. Khydyrly [Khidyrlu] (Xidırılı).

Tax-paying families: 20. Tax-exempt families: 3.
(The families of a *nokar* and 2 mullahs are exempt).

Annual tribute: 13 gold rubles.

Sursat: 15 *batmans* of wheat, 2 *batmans* of butter, 1 *batman* of cheese, 1 small rug, 1 floor mat and 1 ruble from each of the 15 plows, for a total of 21 rubles and 16 kopeks in kind and 15 rubles in cash.

Mal-o-jehat: 2 *taghars* of wheat and 1 *taghar* of barley, which with the fee for the tax collector, totals 51 rubles.

No *darughegy* is collected from this settlement.

Total revenue: 13 gold rubles, 87 rubles and 16 kopeks in local money, or 54 rubles and 47½ kopeks in Russian currency.

23. Sharbachi.

Tax-paying families: 20. Tax-exempt families: 1.
(The family of the *yüzbaşi* is exempt).

Annual tribute: 20 gold rubles.

Sursat: 15 *batmans* of wheat, 3 *batmans* of butter, 1½ *batmans* of cheese, 1 small rug, 1 floor mat and 1 ruble from each of the 15 plows, for a total of 25 rubles and 51 kopeks in kind and 15 rubles in cash.

Mal-o-jehat: 2 *taghars* of wheat and 1 *taghar* of barley, which with the fee for the tax collector, totals 51 rubles.

No *darughegy* is collected.

Total revenue: 20 gold rubles, 91 rubles and 51 kopeks in local money, or 57 rubles and 21½ kopeks in Russian currency.

24. Siazanlu (Siyəzən?).

Tax-paying families: 20.
(They are all *ranjbars*).

Note: As *ranjbars* they pay no dues, but they have to plant 20 *taghars* of rice for Baghesh Beg (now for the treasury), which after their share nets a 4-fold yield. Since a *taghar* of rice is 8 rubles and 10 kopeks, the harvest is worth 648 rubles in local money, or 405 rubles in Russian currency

25. Pulatty [Polatly] (Poladlı).

Tax-paying families: 12.
(They are all *ranjbars*).

Note: As *ranjbars* they pay no dues, but they have to work on a silk farm, belonging to the treasury, which yields a *batman* of silk, worth 70 rubles in local money, or 43 rubles and 75 kopeks in Russian currency.

Except for the silk yield, these nomads have to work for the supervisor of the *mahal*, Jebrail Beg.

26. Chaily (Çaylı).

Tax-exempt families: 5.
(They are all *nokars* of the treasury).

As *nokars* they pay no dues.

27. Uduly (Üdullı).

Tax-exempt families: 40+3 mullahs.

Mostafa Khan gave this settlement to Bala-Oghlan Beg, through a *ta`liqeh,* which is saved at the City (Shari`a) Court.

Totals for the Qobustan Mahal:

Tax-paying families: 946.
Tax-exempt families: 230.
Annual tribute: 975 gold rubles +100 (1,075), see below
Dues in kind: 12,743 rubles and 56 kopeks.
Dues in cash: 685 rubles.
Mal-o-jehat: 2,978 rubles and 25 kopeks.
Darughegy: 0

Total revenue: 16,406 rubles and 81 kopeks in local money, or 10,254 rubles and 25½ kopeks in Russian currency.

Note: In addition to the above gold rubles, another 100 gold rubles were paid by the *mahal* for the upkeep of the *mirzas*.

Note: The Tesi settlement had to pay 32 gold rubles, but since the khan always took that upon himself, it is necessary to divide it among all inhabitants of the *mahal*, since the settlement provides much grain to the treasury.

Major-General Prince Madatov
State Councilor Mogilevskii

[Register 13]

Lagich [Lahıc] Mahal

Revenues from the villages of the Lahıc Mahal, indicating the number of tax-paying and tax-exempt families, as well as the amount paid by each village to the khan—which will now go to the treasury; which villages are under the supervision of the beg of the mahal, what part of the revenue he used to collect for the khan [which will now go to the treasury] and what part he kept for himself. Also, what other revenues are collected from the grain harvest, silk production and other produce, and what are the revenues for the upkeep of the darugheh.

Note: The *mahal* supervisor is Malek Taher Beg.

Note: The villages had to provide free laborers to the khan (now the treasury).

1. Lagich (Lahıc): A town.

Tax-paying families: 180. Tax-exempt families: 60.
(The exempt families belong to the *seyyeds*, *akhunds*, immigrants and so forth).

Annual tribute: 240 gold rubles.

Sursat: 3 *taghars* of wheat and 1 ruble from each of the 36 plows for the *mirzas*. The above lands produce 80 loads of straw, which belonged the khan's son, Ja`far Qoli Aqa, and now the treasury, worth 80 kopeks per load, for a total of 124 rubles in kind and 36 rubles in cash

Mal-o-jehat: 4 *taghars* of wheat, worth 80 rubles.

Darughegy: 2 rubles were collected for the *darugheh* (Malek Taher Beg) from each of the 36 plows. In addition, he receives 30 rubles worth of firewood and charcoal, as well as 80 loads of straw, all worth 166 rubles.

Total revenue: 240 gold rubles and 406 rubles in local money, or 253 rubles and 75 kopeks in Russian currency.

Note: This *mahal* used to belong to Ja`far Qoli Aqa, the son of Mostafa Khan. After his flight it now belongs to the treasury and is supervised by Malek Taher. The town of Lahıc pays little in *sursat* and *mal-o-jehat* dues, because it has almost no farmers. Its inhabitants are mostly master craftsmen, gunsmiths and coppersmiths. The main dues consisted of up to 100 guns and pistols and copper utensils, which the khan and his sons took, sometimes with pay, others times, free. It is impossible to figure the accurate taxes, but we have in the future determine the exact amount to be collected, if not in cash, in arms and copper utensils.

2. Gautasiub (Haftasov?): A Tatar village.

Tax-paying families: 60.

Annual tribute: 80 gold rubles.

Sursat: 1 *taghar* of wheat, 40 loads of straw, and 1 ruble from each of the 40 plows, for a total of 52 rubles in kind and 40 rubles in cash.

Mal-o-jehat: 4 *taghars* of wheat and 2 *taghars* of barley, worth 96 rubles.

Darughegy: 40 loads of straw, 2 rubles from each of the 40 plows for the *mirzas*, 10 rubles worth of charcoal and 2 *batmans* of butter, for a total of 130 rubles and 16 kopeks.

Total revenue: 80 gold rubles, 318 rubles and 6 kopeks in local money, or 198 rubles and 85 kopeks in Russian currency.

3. Aganly: A Tatar village.

Tax-paying families: 30. Tax-exempt families: 2.
(The families of the *kadkhoda* and the mullah are exempt).

Annual tribute: 40 gold rubles.

Sursat: ½ *taghar* of wheat and 1 ruble from each of the 25 plows for the *mirzas*, and 25 loads of straw, all worth 30 rubles in kind and 25 rubles in cash.

Mal-o-jehat: 3 *taghars* of wheat and 3 *taghars* of barley, which total 76 rubles.

Darughegy: 2 rubles from each of the 25 plows, 5 rubles in firewood and charcoal, 25 loads of straw, and 1 *batman* of butter, all worth 79 rubles and 3 kopeks.

Total revenue: 40 gold rubles, 210 rubles and 8 kopeks in local money, or 131 rubles and 30 kopeks in Russian currency.

4. Khimran (Ximran): A Tatar village.

Tax-paying families: 16. Tax-exempt families: 2.
(The families of the *kadkhoda* and the mullah are exempt).

Annual tribute: 20 gold rubles.

Sursat: 10 *batmans* of wheat and 1 ruble from each of the 15 plows, for the *mirzas*, and 15 loads of straw, all worth 16 rubles in kind and 15 rubles in cash.

Mal-o-jehat: 1 *taghar* of wheat and 10 *batmans* of barley, which totals 22 rubles.

Darughegy: 2 rubles from each of the above 15 plows, 2 rubles in firewood and charcoal, 15 loads of straw, and ½ *batman* of butter, all worth 46 rubles and 4 kopeks.

Total revenue: 20 gold rubles, 99 rubles and 4 kopeks in local money, or 61 rubles and 90 kopeks in Russian currency.

5. Miudry (Müdri): A Tatar village.

Tax-paying families: 10. Tax-exempt families: 2.
(The families of the *kadkhoda* and the mullah are exempt).

Annual tribute: 10 gold rubles.

Sursat: 5 *batmans* of wheat and 1 ruble from each of the 8 plows for the *mirzas*, and 8 loads of straw, all worth 8 rubles and 40 kopeks in kind and 8 rubles in cash.

Mal-o-jehat: 1½ *taghars* of wheat and 15 *batmans* of barley, for a total of 22 rubles.

Darughegy: 2 rubles from each of the above 8 plows, 1 ruble in firewood and charcoal, 8 loads of straw, and ½ *batman* of butter, all worth 33 rubles.

Total revenue: 10 gold rubles, 73 rubles and 82 kopeks in local money, or 46 rubles and 13¾ kopeks in Russian currency.

6. Dakhar (Daxar): A Tatar village.

Tax-paying families: 10. Tax-exempt families: 2.
(The families of the *kadkhoda* and the mullah are exempt).

Annual tribute: 10 gold rubles.

Sursat: 5 *batmans* of wheat and 1 ruble from each of the 8 plows for the *mirzas*, and 8 loads of straw, all worth 8 rubles and 40 kopeks in kind and 8 rubles in cash.

Mal-o-jehat: 1½ *taghars* of wheat and 15 *batmans* of barley, worth 33 rubles.

Darughegy: 2 rubles from each of the above 8 plows, 1 rubles in firewood and charcoal, 8 loads of straw, and ½ *batman* of butter, all worth 24 rubles and 42 kopeks.

Total revenue: 10 gold rubles, 73 rubles and 80 kopeks in local money, or 46 rubles and 13¾ kopeks in Russian currency.

Totals for the Lahıc Mahal:

Tax-paying families: 306.
Tax-exempt families: 68.
Annual tribute: 400.
Dues in kind: 238 rubles and 80 kopeks.
Dues in cash: 132 rubles.
Mal-o-jehat: 340 rubles.
Darughegy: 470 rubles and 12 kopeks.

Total revenues in local currency: 1,180 rubles and 92 kopeks, or 738 rubles and 7½ kopeks in Russian currency.

Major-General Prince Madatov
State Councilor Mogilevskii

[Register 14]

Rudbar Mahal

The villages of the Rudbar Mahal, indicating the number of tax-paying and tax-exempt families, as well as the gold rubles they paid toward the tribute, which are the only dues they pay to the treasury.

Note: All other revenues belong to of the *mahal* supervisor (*darugheh*), Mamad (Mohammad) Khan.

1. Dzhavat [Dzhevat] (Javad): A Tatar village.

Tax-paying families: 62. Tax-exempt families: 30.
(The families of 3 *kadkhoda*, the *darugheh*, 5 immigrants from Karabagh, 11 *ranjbars* and 10 *nokars* belonging to *darugheh*, the khan's son, and the *kadkhodas* are exempt).

Annual tribute: 70 gold rubles.

2. Belvan: A Tatar village.

Tax-paying families: 9. Tax-exempt families: 1.
(The family of the *kadkhoda* is exempt).

Annual tribute: 7 gold rubles.

3. Dabakhlar: A Tatar village.

Tax-paying families: 4.

Annual tribute: 4 gold rubles and 1 ruble.

4. Karally [Karaly] (Qaralı): A nomad settlement.

Tax-paying families: 14. Tax-exempt families: 1.
(The family of the *kadkhoda* is exempt).

Annual tribute: 14 gold rubles.

5. Engikent (Yenikənd): A Tatar village.

Tax-paying families: 35. Tax-exempt families: 4.
(The families of the *darugheh*, 2 *ranjbars* and 1 immigrant are exempt).

Annual tribute: 35 gold rubles.

6. Kazylu (Qazilu): A Tatar village.

Tax-paying families: 40. Tax-exempt families: 18.
(The families of the *darugheh*, the *kadkhoda*, 4 *ranjbars*, 10 *nokars* belonging to the *mahal*'s chief and 2 mullahs are exempt).

Annual tribute: 35 gold rubles.

7. Agmed-Beglu (Ahmədbəy): A Tatar village.

Tax-paying families: 4.

Annual tribute: 5 gold rubles.

8. Kuruzmanly [Kuruzma] (Kuruzma): A Tatar village.

Tax-paying families: 19. Tax-exempt families: 3.
(The families of the *kadkhoda*, the *darugheh*, and the *mullah* are exempt).

Annual tribute: 28 gold rubles.

9. Abdulian (Abdullu): A Tatar village.

Tax-paying families: 35. Tax-exempt families: 14.
(The families of the *kadkhoda*, the *darugheh*, 4 *ranjbars*, 2 mullahs and 6 *mo`afs* are exempt).

Annual tribute: 42 gold rubles.

10. Engidzhe [Engidzha]: A Tatar village.

Tax-paying families: 5.

Annual tribute: 7 gold rubles.

11. Mustafalu (Mustafalı): A Tatar village.

Tax-paying families: 22. Tax-exempt families: 4.
(The families of 3 mullahs and 1 *ranjbar* are exempt).

Annual tribute: 14 gold rubles.

12. Akhtachi (Axtaçi): A Tatar village.

Tax-paying families: 5.

Annual tribute: 7 gold rubles.

13. Meineman [Meiniman]: A Tatar village.

Tax-paying families: 6. Tax-exempt families: 3.
(The families of the *kadkhoda*, a *nokar* and a *mo`af* are exempt).

Annual tribute: 7 gold rubles.

14. Kosrat: A Tatar village.

Tax-paying families: 45. Tax-exempt families: 6.
(The families of 2 *ranjbars*, the *darugheh*, the *kadkhoda* and 2 mullahs are exempt).

Annual tribute: 49 gold rubles.

15. Siurra-Agamoglan: A Tatar village.

Tax-paying families: 4. Tax-exempt families: 3.
(The families of the *kadkhoda* and 2 *ranjbars* are exempt).

Annual tribute: 3 gold rubles.

16. Siurra-Agabedal: A Tatar village

Tax-paying families: 5. Tax-exempt families: 3.
(The families of the *kadkhoda* and 2 *ranjbars* are exempt).

Annual tribute: 3 gold rubles.

17. Siurra-Mammet (Mohammad): A Tatar village.

Tax-paying families: 3. Tax-exempt families: 2.
(The families of 2 *ranjbars* are exempt).

Annual tribute: 3 gold rubles.

18. Siurri-Abdulla-(`Abdollah) Beg: A Tatar village.

Tax-paying families: 17. Tax-exempt families: 6.
(The families of the 4 *ranjbars*, the *kadkhoda* and the mullah are exempt).

Annual tribute: 12 gold rubles.

Totals for the Rudbar Mahal:

Tax-paying families: 324.
Tax-exempt families: 98.
Annual tribute: gold rubles 345 and 1 ruble.

Major-General Prince Madatov
State Councilor Mogilevskii

[Register 15]

Mughan Mahal

The Mughan domain, which lies on the right bank of the Kur River and which belonged to the fugitive Hasan Khan, and now belongs to his cousin Mostafa Beg, indicating the number of families and the gold rubles paid in tribute.

The names of the forts and the *begs* who rule over the nomads:

Kalakain (Qalağayin), which is a fort, and the residence by the *beg* of the *mahal*. There are no native people who reside there; however from every nomad settlement in the Mughan a number of families reside there, which with the nokars total up to 100 families.

There are 44 nomad settlements, totaling some 400 families, in the Mughan, which are indicated by the names of the *begs* who supervise them.

1. Mohammad-Reza Beg
2. Melik
3. Mohammad `Ali
4. `Abdul
5. Yolchi
6. Safa-Mirza
7. Ahmad
8. Mullah-`Abdol
9. Jamshid
10. Mohammad Hoseyn Beg
11. Aqa Beg
12. Assadollah
13. Mohammad Khalifeh
14. Shah Morad
15. Kalb-`Ali
16. `Abdol-Hoseyn Beg
17. Malek Mohammad Beg
18. `Ali Khan
19. Ahmad `Ali
20. `Ali

21. Taleb
22. Sharif
23. Mohammad Nevi
24. Hoseyn
25. Ja`far
26. Mashhadi-Nejer `Ali
27. Ahmad
28. Mohammad
29. Kegiyek
30. Siz Beg
31. `Ali Mohammad
32. Neti Beg
33. `Ali Mirza
34. Akhund Qasem
35. Aqa Rahim
36. Seyyed Qasem
37. Allah-Verdi
38. Ebrahim

There is a dye workshop in Kalakayin (Qalağayin), which is leased out for 150 rubles in local currency. Mostafa Khan used to get that money, but when the Russian government began to demand *chapar-khaneh* (relay station for couriers) from Shirvan, the khan then gave this money for the inhabitants of Mughan to pay for the *chapar-khaneh.*

Every caravan from Iran or other places passing through here has to pay 6 *`abbasis* for every load for the *beg* of the *mahal.*

There are 6 salt lakes, 4 *aghach* from Qalağayin. No one supervises them and the inhabitants of Mughan use the salt free of charge, while the other people of Shirvan have to pay 1 *`abbasi* per load. The inhabitants of Talesh, sometimes secretly take it.

After the flight of Mostafa Khan, 50 families fled to Talesh and 60 to Karabagh, fearing that the khan may carry them along. Those from Talesh have already returned, but Mahdi Qoli Khan of Karabagh does not let the others leave his domain.

Since the population of Mughan resides on the other side of the Kur River, they pay only the tribute in gold rubles and nothing else, except for guards (*qaravuls*) to watch the Iranian border and be on constant guard. The khan always returned 100 gold rubles from the 450 they had to pay annually, which they will now have to pay.

Major-General Prince Madatov
State Councilor Mogilevskii

[Register 16]

Navagi [Navahi] Mahal

The revenues from the Navahi Mahal which belonged to the fugitive Mostafa Khan of Shirvan. The mahal is composed of only one village, Navahi, which is divided into 3 quarters. The register indicates the tax-paying and tax-exempt families and their dues.

1. Mughanly (Muğanlı) Quarter.

Tax-paying families: 30. Tax-exempt families: 16.
(The families of the *yüzbaşi*, the foreman, 4 mullahs and 10 *ranjbars* of the khan, now of the treasury, are exempt).

2. Kushchi (Quşçi) Quarter.

Tax-paying families: 30. Tax-exempt families: 13.
(The families of the *yüzbaşi*, the foreman, the mullah and 10 *ranjbars* belonging to the khan and now the treasury, are exempt).

3. Navagly [Navagi] (Navahi) Quarter.

Tax-paying families: 30. Tax-exempt families: 9.
(The families of the *yüzbaşi*, foreman, 2 mullahs and 5 *ranjbars* belonging to the khan, and now to the treasury, are exempt).

The *mahal* is supervised by the *darugheh*, Aqa Beg of Xançoban.

Annual tribute: 90 gold rubles.

Dues in kind: Each of the 3 quarters provided 1 *taghar* of wheat and 1 ruble from each of the 80 plows. In addition, there are 25 *ranjbars* in these quarters; they have to work use 25 plows with 25 pairs of oxen belonging to the treasury, till and sow 1 *taghar* of wheat and ½ *taghar* of barley seeds per a pair of oxen. The minimum harvest from wheat is 30-fold and barley is 40-fold, after deducting the share of the *ranjbars*. In addition, the *ranjbars* have to plant 200 *batmans* of cotton, which yield a minimum of 200 *batmans* of pure cotton, after deducting the share of the *ranjbars*. Finally, in the marsh of Dülbarcan, the *ranjbars* have to sow 30 *taghars* of wheat and sometimes more, which yield a harvest of 30 fold. Since a *taghar* of wheat is sold for 20 local rubles and a *batman* for 40 kopeks and a *taghar* of barley is sold for 8 rubles and 20 kopeks a *batman*, and a *batman* of cotton is worth 5 rubles and 4 kopeks, the total dues in kind is 38,248 rubles.

Mal-o-jehat: The *mal-o-jehat* depends on the harvest, but it is no less than 60 *taghars* of wheat and 40 *taghars* of barley, which with the addition of 1 ruble per *taghar* for the tax collector, totals 1,620 rubles.

The *darughegy* belongs to Aqa Beg.

Totals for the Navahi Mahal:

Annual tribute: 90 Gold rubles.
Tax-paying families: 90.
Tax-exempt families: 38

Dues in cash and kind: 39,868 rubles in local currency, or 24,917 rubles and 50 kopeks in Russian currency.

Note: In the Navahi *Mahal* and the marsh of Dülbarcan, the harvest is out of the ordinary and according to local inhabitants it can reach 100 to 1. The seeds provided can be used on the land for three years. In fact the land does not have to be ploughed. When the river overflows, they just cast the seeds on the land and they produce a harvest.

Major-General Prince Madatov
State Councilor Mogilevskii

[Register 17]

Karabaghlar (Qarabağlar) Mahal

Revenues from the villages of the Qarabağlar Mahal, indicating the number of tax-paying and tax-exempt families, as well as the amount paid by each village to the khan—which will now go to the treasury; which villages are under the supervision of the beg of the mahal, what part of the revenue he used to collect for the khan [which will now go to the treasury] and what part he kept for himself. Also, what other revenues are collected from the grain harvest, silk production and other produce.

Note: The village was administered by the fugitive Soltan Beg and now by the treasury.

Note: In addition to the dues listed in this register, each village had to provide workers, as many as required to the khan.

1. Engi-Arkh (Yeniarx): A Tatar village.

Tax-paying families: 8. Tax-exempt families: 1.
(The family of the *yüzbaşi* is exempt).

Annual tribute: 9 gold rubles and 2 rubles and 50 kopeks in local money.

Sursat: 23½ *batmans* of wheat, worth 9 rubles and 40 kopeks.

Mal-o-jehat: 8 *stils* of silk and 2 *taghars* of rice, for a total of 39 rubles and 51 kopeks.

Darughegy: 4 *stils* of silk and 1 *taghar* and 12 *batmans* of rice, worth 23 rubles and 1 kopek.
Total revenue: 9 gold rubles, 74 rubles and 45 kopeks in local money, or 46 rubles and 53 kopeks in Russian currency.

Note: The nomads from the Ucar settlement in the Elat *Mahal* produced 13 *taghars* of rice in this village for the khan's adjutant, Aqa Beg, who has fled with him, thus, it now belongs to the treasury. The income is listed in the Elat *Mahal*.

2. Charadzha [Charadzhi] (Cərəcə): A Tatar village.

Tax-paying families: 5. Tax-exempt families: 1.
(The family of the *yüzbaşi* is exempt).

Annual tribute: 6 gold rubles and 1 ruble and 50 kopeks in local money.

Sursat: 16½ *batmans* of wheat, worth 6 rubles and 60 kopeks.

Mal-o-jehat: 6 *stils* of silk and 1 *taghars* of rice, for a total of 25 rubles and 60½ kopeks.

Darughegy: 2½ *stils* of silk and 24 *batmans* of rice, worth 13 rubles and 77 kopeks.

Total revenue: 6 gold rubles, 47 rubles and 17 ½ kopeks in local money, or 29 rubles and 48½ kopeks in Russian currency.

3. Karabaglar (Qarabağlar): A Tatar village.

Tax-paying families: 13. Tax-exempt families: 2.
(The families of the *yüzbaşi* and *effendi* are exempt).

Annual tribute: 13 gold rubles and 2 rubles and 50 kopeks in local money.

Sursat: 33 *batmans* of wheat and 1 ruble from each of the 3 plows, for a total of 13 rubles and 20 kopeks in kind and 3 rubles in cash.

Mal-o-jehat: 11 *stils* of silk and 1 *taghar* and 18 *batmans* of rice, for a total of 45 rubles and 5½ kopeks.

Darughegy: 7 *stils* of silk and 1 *taghar* and 18 *batmans* of rice, worth 33 rubles and 38½ kopeks.

Total revenue: 13 gold rubles, 27 rubles and 13½ kopeks in local money, or 60 rubles and 70½ kopeks in Russian currency.

4. Kiurt (Kürd): A Tatar village.

Tax-paying families: 9. Tax-exempt families: 4.
(The families of the *yüzbaşi*, 2 orphans and one *mo`af* are exempt).

Annual tribute: 11 gold rubles and 2 rubles and 50 kopeks in local money.

Sursat: 27 *batmans* of wheat, worth 10 rubles and 80 kopeks.

Mal-o-jehat: 10 *stils* of silk and 1 *taghar* of rice, for a total of 42 rubles and 13½ kopeks.

Darughegy: 6 *stils* of silk and 12 *batmans* of rice, worth 28 rubles and 84½ kopeks.

Total revenue: 11 gold rubles, 18 rubles and 78 kopeks in local money, or 51 rubles and 11½ kopeks in Russian currency.

5. Poti (Potu): A Tatar village.

Tax-exempt families: 18.

The village belongs to Aghasi Beg and pays no dues to the treasury.

There are 8 *ranjbar* families belonging to the *beg* and the rest are his relatives.

6. Rastadzhi [Rastadzha] (Rastacı): A Tatar village.

Tax-paying families: 13. Tax-exempt families: 7.
(The families of 5 *nokars*, the *kadkhoda* and the mullah are exempt)
The rest are all *ranjbars*, who belonged to Soltan Beg and now the treasury).

Dues: 4 *batmans* of silk from the 4 silk farms and sheds, worth 280 rubles in local money, or 175 rubles in Russian currency.

No other dues are collected for the treasury.

Note: From the 13 *ranjbar* families, only 4 belonged to the fugitive Soltan Beg, the rest belong to Amatull Khanum and the orphans of Qahraman.

7. Shadat (Səhadət): A Tatar village.

Tax-paying families: 12. Tax-exempt families: 4.
(The families of the 3 *nokars* and the *darugheh*, Soltan Aqa, are exempt).

The rest are all *ranjbars*, who belonged to the fugitive Soltan Beg and now to the treasury. They all work on the 12 new silk farms, which have not produced anything yet. It is estimated that 12 *batmans* of silk should be produced, worth 840 rubles in local money, or 525 rubles in Russian currency.

8. Khosh Abat (Xoşabad): An Armenian village.

Tax-paying families: 4. Tax-exempt families: 1.
(The family of the *kevkha* is exempt).

The inhabitants had to us 4 plows and sow 1½ *taghars* of wheat and ½ *taghar* of barely for the tax collector. The yield for each is 5-fold. Only half of the harvest belongs to the tax collector, the other half is the share of the villagers. The total worth is 340 rubles in local money, or 212 rubles and 50 kopeks in Russian currency.

Note: The village is inhabited solely by immigrants. Soltan Beg brought them here and they pay their dues only to him and nothing to the treasury.

Totals for the Qarabağlar Mahal:

Tax-paying families: 64.
Tax-exempt families: 38.
Annual tribute: 39 gold rubles and 6.20 rubles.
Dues in kind: 1,500 rubles.
Dues in cash: 3 rubles.
Mal-o-jehat: 152 rubles and 33½ kopeks.
Darughegy: 99 rubles and ¼ kopek.

Total revenue: 1,760 rubles and 54 kopeks in local money, or 1,100 rubles and 33½ kopeks in Russian currency.

Note: When the 6.20 local rubles for the annual tribute is converted to 1 gold ruble and 1.20 local rubles, the total tribute is 40 gold rubles and 1.20 local rubles, while the total for the regular dues is 1,754.34 in local money, or 1,096 rubles and 4½ kopeks Russian currency.

Major-General Prince Madatov
State Councilor Mogilevskii

[Register 18]

Biulket [Boluket] Mahal

Revenues from the villages of the Boluket Mahal, indicating the number of tax-paying and tax-exempt families, as well as the amount paid by each village to the khan—which will now go to the treasury; which villages are under the supervision of the beg of the mahal, what part of the revenue he used to collect for the khan [which will now go to the treasury] and what part he kept for himself. Also, what other revenues are collected from the grain harvest, silk production and other produce.

Ja`far Beg is the *mahal* supervisor (*darugheh*).

1. Akhsu (Ağsu): A Tatar village:

Tax-paying families: 30.
(In addition there were *ranjbars* from various villages who had to till the fields of the khan's family. They included 5 *ranjbars* from the nomad settlement of Nardeli, 10 from Navahi, 5 from Borbor, where they also took the miller for the mill, 10 *ranjbars* for Ja`far Qoli Aqa, the khan's son, from Salyan and 5 *ranjbars* for the khan's wife, Kichkin, from the village of Khnis).

Annual tribute: 30 gold rubles.

Dues: The village has 4 plows and 40 oxen, which belonged to the khan and now to the treasury. The inhabitants sow 20 *taghars* of wheat and 8 *taghars* of barley; the yield from the first, after deducting the share of the *ranjbars* is 5 fold, the second 6 fold. They also sow 4 *taghars* of millet, yielding 15 fold, after the share of the *ranjbars*. In addition, the two mills, each with 2 pairs of grinding stones, give 20 *taghars* of wheat a year.

The son of Mostafa Khan, Ja`far Qoli Aqa, had 2 plows in this village with 10 pairs of oxen, all of which now belong to the treasury. They sowed 10 *taghars* of wheat and 5 *taghars* of barley, with the same yields as above. In addition, an orchard, with various fruit and a vineyard, brings an income of 200 rubles.

The khan's wife, Kichkin, had one plow and 5 pairs of oxen, which now belong to the treasury. They sowed 5 *taghars* of wheat and 2 *taghars* of barley, with the same yield as above. In addition, she owned half of a large orchard, bringing an income of 150 rubles.

Since a *taghar* of wheat is worth 20 rubles and a *taghar* of barley and millet is worth 8 rubles a *taghar*, the total revenue in kind comes to 5,100 rubles and 350 rubles in cash.

Mal-o-jehat: A minimum of 8 *taghars* of wheat, 2 *taghars* of barley, 3 *taghars* of millet, 1 *batman* of silk, for a total of 270 local rubles.

No *darughegy* is collected for the treasury. It belongs to the *beg* of the *mahal*.

Total revenue: 30 gold rubles and 5,720 rubles in local money, or 3,575 rubles in Russian currency.

2. Kiurdamir (Kürdəmir): A Tatar village.

Tax-paying families: 100. Tax-exempt families: 8.
(The families of the 2 *yüzbaşis* and 6 mullahs are exempt).

Annual tribute: 130 gold rubles.

Sursat: 2½ *taghars* of wheat, worth 50 rubles.

No *mal-o-jehat* or other dues are collected for the treasury.

The village is the private property of Fatemeh Begum, the former wife of Mostafa Khan, who was divorced 12 years ago and has no children.

3. Karasakally [Kara-sakhkal] (Qarasaqqal): A Tatar village.

Tax-paying families: 35. Tax-exempt families: 2.
(The families of the *yüzbaşi* and the mullah are exempt).

Annual tribute: 42 gold rubles.

Sursat: 30 *batmans* of wheat, 4 silk workshops, each producing 1 *batman* of silk, a vineyard, which after all expenses has an income of 50 rubles, 80 kopeks from each of the 15 plows, *bagh-bashi* from the orchards 20 rubles, all worth 292 rubles.

Mal-o-jehat: 2½ *taghars* of wheat, a *taghar* of barley, ½ *batman* of silk, and 1 ruble per *taghar* for the tax collector, for a total of 166 rubles and 50 kopeks.

The village is supervised by Ja`far Beg, the *beg* of the *mahal*. It originally belonged to the nephew of Mostafa Khan, who has fled with him to Iran and now belongs to the treasury.

4. Neudzhi: A Tatar village.

Tax-paying families: 5.

Annual tribute: 3 gold rubles.

The village pays no other dues, for the khan gave the irrigation canal of the village to the sons of Sheikh `Ali Beg.

5. Dzhagly: A Tatar village.

Tax-paying families: 15. Tax-exempt families: 25.
(25 immigrant families from various places are exempt).

Annual tribute: 11 gold rubles.

Sursat: 10 *batmans* of wheat, worth 4 local rubles or 2.50 Russian rubles.

The village paid nothing else; all income went to the *beg* of the *mahal* and his brothers.

6. Kiululy [Kiuliuli] (Külüllü): A Tatar village.

Tax-paying families: 25. Tax-exempt families: 3.
(The families of the *yüzbaşi* and 2 mullahs are exempt).

Annual tribute: 11 gold rubles.

Sursat: 30 *batmans* of wheat, worth 12 local rubles or 7.50 Russian rubles.

The village belongs to Hajji Mostafa Beg and was given to him by the father of Mostafa Khan as his private property.

7. Samuilly (Isamuilli): A Tatar village.

Tax-paying families: 20.
(All Kangarlu tribesmen from Karabagh)

Annual tribute: 32 gold rubles.

Sursat: 20 *batmans* of wheat. In addition, there are 2 plows with 10 pairs of oxen, which belonged to the khan's wife Kichkin, and now the treasury. They sow 10 *taghars* of wheat, 4 *taghars* of barley and 1 *taghar* of millet seeds. Furthermore, 20 *taghars* of rice is planted. The yield, after deducting the share of the *ranjbars*, is 5-fold for wheat and 6-fold for barley, 35-fold for millet, 35-fold, and 25-fold for rice. Moreover, there are 17 silk farms and sheds, which produce 17 *batmans* of silk. There are also 3 large vineyards, which can yield 250 rubles annually. Finally, from the hollow of Esrafil, half of which belonged to the khan's wife, 10 *taghars* of rice is produced. The entire dues in kind are 8,785 rubles and 250 rubles in cash.

Mal-o-jehat: 20 *taghars* of wheat and 15 *taghars* of barley, produced by the *ranjbars*, worth 520 rubles.

Total revenue: 32 gold rubles and 9,555 rubles in local money, or 5,971 rubles and 87½ kopeks in Russian currency.

8. Mullah[1]-`Ali-Ogli: A Tatar village.

Tax-exempt families: 10
(All are vagrants or *ranjbars* from various parts of Shirvan).

The village is the property of *Yüzbaşi* Yusef and pays no dues whatsoever to the treasury.

9. Agri: A nomad settlement.

Tax-paying families: 14. Tax-exempt families: 7.
(5 *mo`af* families and 2 mullahs are exempt).

[1] The 1913 gazetteer has the Persian *molla* for mullah.

The village belonged to the fugitive Qader Beg and now to the treasury.

The inhabitants, all *ranjbars*, are responsible for producing grain and rice for the former owner. But no grain grew for three years and there was not enough water for growing rice. Therefore, there was no income for 3 years. The village has now to be assessed for future dues.

10. Shakhmezit (Sheikmizid): A Tatar village.

Tax-paying families: 4.

The village belonged to the various members of the khan's family and now to the treasury. It is administered by Ja`far Beg.

Dues: The village has 3 mills, which belonged to Mostafa Khan's brother, Esma`il Beg, who fled with him to Iran. Two of the mills have a pair of millstones, the other one. They bring an income of 12 *taghars* of wheat a year. In addition, there are also 3 large fruit orchards and vineyards, with an income of 200 rubles a year. Below this village, near Ağsu, there is a mill with 2 millstones, which is leased out for 10 *taghars* of wheat a year. The khan's sister Zeyveh Khanum has a water mill with 2 millstones, with an income of 10 *taghars* of wheat. But it only works during rainy season. There are also 4 orchards, one young and the others old; two of which are leased for 200 rubles a year, while the other two can produce 100 rubles. All the dues in kind total 840 rubles and in cash, 500 rubles, for a total 1,340 rubles in local money, or 837 rubles and 50 kopeks in Russian currency.

Note: The mill near Ağsu belonged to Esma`il Khan, who gave it to his wife for her own income long time ago. Thus, no figures exist as to its income.

Totals for the Boluket Mahal:

Tax-paying families: 248.
Tax-exempt families: 55.
Annual tribute: 290 gold rubles.
Dues in kind: 15,083 rubles.
Dues in cash: 1,182 rubles.

Total dues: 17,221 rubles and 50 kopeks in local money, or 10,763 rubles and 43 kopeks in Russian currency

Major General Prince Madatov
State Councilor Mogilevskii

[Register 19]

Khozourt [Khazarud] Mahal

Revenues from the villages and nomad settlements of the Khazarud Mahal, indicating the number of tax-paying and tax-exempt families, as well as the amount paid by each village to the khan—which will now go to the treasury; which villages are under the supervision of the beg of the mahal, what part of the revenue he used to collect for the khan [which will now go to the treasury] and what part he kept for himself. Also, what other revenues are collected from the grain harvest, silk production and other produce.

Note: The *mahal* supervisor is Azay Soltan.

1. Gaputty [Gaputly]: A nomad settlement.

Tax-paying families: 150. Tax-exempt families: 100.
(The families of 20 *nokars* and 80 immigrant *ranjbars* are exempt).

Annual tribute: 232 gold rubles.

Sursat: 3 *taghars* of wheat, 20 *batmans* of butter, 10 *batmans* of cheese, 10 small rugs, 2 coverings for mules, 10 woolen cords (worth 80 kopeks each), 1 ruble from each of the 150 plows, for a total of 195 rubles and 60 kopeks in kind and 150 rubles in cash.

Mal-o-jehat: 15 *taghars* of wheat, 5 *taghars* of barley, plus 1 ruble per *taghar* for the salary of the *mirzas*, for a total of 360 rubles.

Total revenue: 232 gold rubles, 705 rubles and 60 kopeks in local money, or 441 rubles in Russian currency.

2. Shikhly (Şıxlı): A nomad settlement.

Tax-paying families: 150. Tax-exempt families: 4.
(The families of the 3 *yüzbaşis* and the mullah are exempt).

Annual tribute: 194 gold rubles.

Sursat: 3 *taghars* of wheat, 10 *batmans* of butter, 5 *batmans* of cheese, 5 small rugs, 5 woolen cords, 1 ruble from each of the 150 plows, for a total of 127 rubles and 80 kopeks in kind and 150 rubles in cash.

Mal-o-jehat: 7 *taghars* of wheat, 3 *taghars* of barley, plus 1 ruble per *taghar* for the salary of the *mirzas*, for a total of 174 rubles.

Total revenue: 194 gold rubles, 451 rubles and 80 kopeks in local money, or 282 rubles and 37½ kopeks in Russian currency.

3. Midzhan (Mican): A Tatar village.

Tax-paying families: 8. Tax-exempt families: 4.

Annual tribute: 12 gold rubles.

Sursat: 15 *batmans* of wheat and 1 *batman* of butter, worth 10 rubles and 8 kopeks.

Mal-o-jehat: It is collected by the local *beg*, none for the treasury.

Total revenue: 12 gold rubles, 10 rubles and 8 kopeks in local money, or 6 rubles and 30 kopeks in Russian currency.

4. Kalynchakh [Kalynchag] (Qalıncaq): A Tatar village.

Tax-paying families: 12. Tax-exempt families: 2.

Annual tribute: 12 gold rubles.

Sursat: 15 *batmans* of wheat and 1 *batman* of butter, worth 10 rubles and 8 kopeks.

Mal-o-jehat: To the local *beg*, none to the treasury.

Total revenue: 12 gold rubles, 10 rubles and 8 kopeks in local money, or 6 rubles and 30 kopeks in Russian currency.

5. Khanagely (Xanağalı): A Tatar village.

Tax-exempt families: 8.
(They are all immigrant sheikhs from Kuba).

As sheikhs they were exempt from all dues.

6. Gialage (Qalagah): An Armenian village.

Tax-paying families: 55. Tax-exempt families: 2.
(The families of the *kevkha* and the priest are exempt).

Annual tribute: 87 gold rubles.

Sursat: 2 *taghars* of wheat, *kharaj* of 200 rubles, 1 ruble from each of the 50 plows. In addition there is a plow and 3 pairs of oxen belonging to the treasury, with which the villagers are obliged to till and sow 3 *taghars* of wheat, which yields a minimum 5-fold harvest, after deducting the share of the peasants for a total of 340 rubles in kind and 250 in cash.

Mal-o-jehat: 25 *taghars* of wheat, 10 *taghars* of barley, plus the *darugheh* received 5 *taghars* of wheat and 5 *taghars* of barley, all of which, with the fees, totals 755 rubles.

Total revenue: 87 gold rubles and 1,345 rubles in local money, or 840 rubles and 62½ kopeks in Russian currency.

In addition, the villagers had to perform 3 free days of labor for the *darugheh*. He could also demand firewood, charcoal and straw, as needed without payment.

The village belonged to the khan's sister, Balash Khanum, and now to the treasury.[1]

7. Ushtal (Uştal): An Armenian village.

Tax-paying families: 25. Tax-exempt families: 1.
(The family of the *kevkha* is exempt).

[1] This and the next village had paid *qullughi* dues in the past.

Annual tribute: 43 gold rubles.

Sursat: 1 *taghars* of wheat, 100 rubles in *kharaj*, 1 ruble from each of the 25 plows. In addition there are 2 plows with 2 pairs of oxen belonging to the treasury, with which the villagers are obliged to till and sow 3 *taghars* of wheat seeds, for a total of 320 rubles in kind and 125 rubles in cash.

Mal-o-jehat: 12½ *taghars* of wheat, 5 *taghars* of barley, plus 2½ *taghars* of wheat and 2½ *taghars* of barley for the *darugheh*, which with the tax collector's fees totals 377 rubles and 50 kopeks.

Total revenue: 43 gold rubles and 825 rubles in local money, or 515 rubles and 62½ kopeks in Russian currency.

In addition, the villagers had to perform 3 free days of labor for the *darugheh*. He could also demand firewood, charcoal and straw, as needed without payment.

The village belonged to the khan's sister, Balash Khanum and now to the treasury.

8. Engikent (Yenikənd): An Armenian village.

Tax-exempt families: 30.
(All are immigrants from Karabagh).

The village is the private property of Azai Soltan and pays no dues to the treasury.

9. Urushan: An Armenian village.

Tax-exempt families: 8.
(All are immigrants from Karabagh).

The village is the private property of Azai Soltan and pays no dues to the treasury.

Totals for the Khazarud Mahal

Tax-paying families: 300.
Tax-exempt families: 104.
Annual dues: 580 gold rubles.
Dues in kind: 1,003 rubles and 56 kopeks
Dues in cash: 675 rubles.
Mal-o-jehat: 1,666 rubles and 50 kopeks.

Total revenue 3,347 rubles and 56 kopeks in local money, or 2,092 rubles and 22½ kopeks in Russian currency

Major-General Prince Madatov
State Councilor Mogilevskii

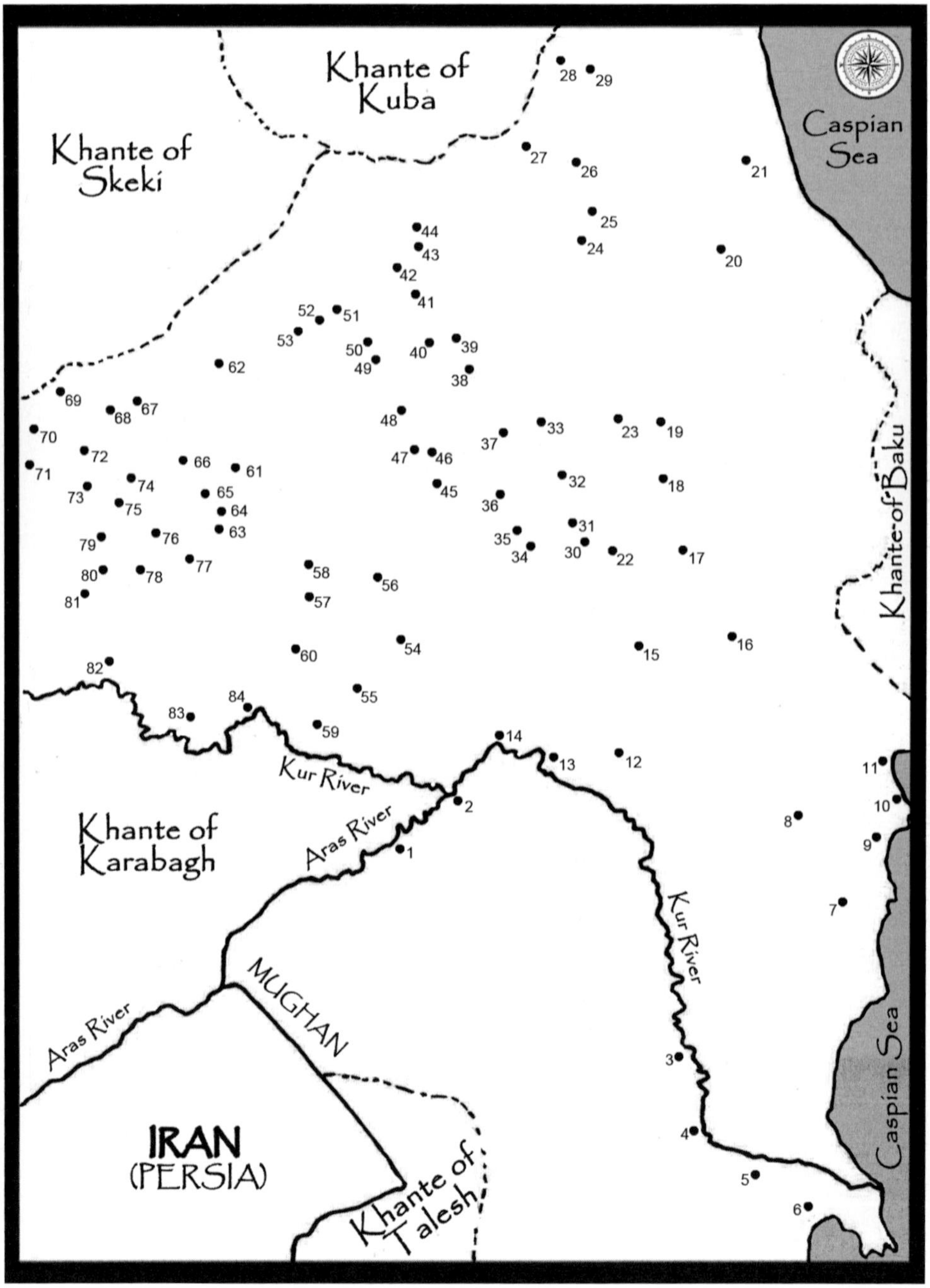
Khante of
Kuba
Khante of
Skeki
Caspian
Sea
Khante of Baku
Kur River
Aras River
Khante of
Karabagh
MUGHAN
Aras River
Kur River
Caspian Sea
IRAN
(PERSIA)
Khante of
Talesh
1
2
3
4
5
6
7
8
9
10
11
12
13
14
15
16
17
18
19
20
21
22
23
24
25
26
27
28
29
30
31
32
33
34
35
36
37
38
39
40
41
42
43
44
45
46
47
48
49
50
51
52
53
54
55
56
57
58
59
60
61
62
63
64
65
66
67
68
69
70
71
72
73
74
75
76
77
78
79
80
81
82
83
84

Map 2: Some of the Place Names Mentioned in the Text

1. Saatli
2. Javad
3. Salyan
4. Surra
5. Xıllı
6. Neftçala
7. Xıdırlı
8. Navahi
9. Ələt
10. Şıxlar
11. Qobustan
12. Mugan
13. Abdulyan
14. Qovlar
15. Birinci Udulu
16. Hacivali
17. Ərəbqədim
18. Mərəzə
19. Nabur
20. Xələc
21. Siyəzən
22. Qoşçu
23. Sündü
24. Muçu
25. Zarat
26. Dəhnə
27. Qonaqkənd
28. Zargava
29. Zəyvə
30. Poladi
31. Çaylı
32. Məlıkçobanli
33. Şamaxi
34. Göylər
35. Ovçulu
36. Buco
37. Mədrəsə
38. Kalva
39. Sulut
40. Basqal
41. Lahic
42. Müdri
43. Varna
44. Burovdal
45. Ərəbuşağı
46. Ağsu
47. Pirhəsənli
48. Gürcüvan
49. Tircan
50. Tazəkənd
51. Talistan
52. Ismaılı
53. Mican
54. Karrar
55. Pirili
56. Qarasaqqal
57. Kürdəmir
58. Yenikənd
59. Mollakənd
60. Incə
61. Sorsor
62. Qalagah
63. Müsuslü
64. Alpout
65. Baydəvil
66. Mırtı
67. Göyçay
68. Qarabağlar
69. Ərəb
70. Qülbəndə
71. Ləki
72. Yeniarx
73. Ucar
74. Gərələ
75. Alpi
76. Ciyni
77. Bargüşad
78. Boyat
79. Qazyan
80. Lak
81. Ikinci
82. Zərdab
83. Əlvənd
84. Süsün

ВѢДОМОСТЬ

доходамъ съ деревень и кочевьевъ Садарынскаго магала, съ показаніемъ числа семействъ—платящихъ подать и неплатящихъ; также сколько съ какой деревни или кочевья по раскладкѣ собиралось собственно въ пользу Хана окладныхъ податей, долженствующихъ нынѣ поступать въ казну, и съ объясненіемъ—какія изъ сихъ деревень состоятъ подъ управленіемъ магальнаго бека, плати всѣ доходы Хану, и изъ какихъ часть оныхъ предоставлена въ его пользу; равнымъ образомъ какимъ еще обложены сборомъ съ урожая хлѣба, шелку и другихъ произведеній и какіе имѣютъ таругскіе доходы.

№	ЗВАНІЕ КОЧЕВЬЕВЪ и ДЕРЕВЕНЬ. Татарскихъ и Армянскихъ.	Число семействъ, платящихъ подать.	Число семействъ, не платящихъ подать.	ОКЛАДНЫЯ ПОДАТИ. Хлѣбныя и другихъ произведеній, съ показаніемъ цѣнъ. Руб. Коп.	Денежная подать. Руб. Коп.	Червонцы въ раиь слѣдующіе. Чер. Руб. К.	Малджекатъ или десятая часть съ урожая хлѣба, и пятая съ урожая шелку и хлопчатой бумаги. Руб. К.	Торугскіе доходы. Руб. К.	ИТОГО ВСЕГО. На червонцы и ханское серебро. Чер. Руб. К.	На россійское серебро, полагая 1 р. россійскій въ 1 р. 60к. ханскими. Чер. Руб. К.	Кѣмъ управляется или кому принадлежитъ.	ПРИМѢЧАНІЕ.
24.	Кочевье КЮРТЪ. Въ немъ пришельцевъ изъ Шекинской провинціи 20 семей	20	—	Съ жителей сего кочевья, по ихъ бѣдности, не было взимаемо никакихъ податей, такъ какъ они были неоплачиваемые поступахами. — —	— —	— — —	Малджекатъ не берется.	Таругскихъ доходовъ не имѣется.	— — —	— — —	Принадлежало бывшему Касымъ-беку, а нынѣ казнѣ.	Если ихъ въ Ширванѣ оставить, то должно, по усмотрѣнію, обложить податью, или перевесть въ Шекинскую провинцію, гдѣ они считаются въ окладѣ.
25.	Кочевье ХАЛИЛЛЫ. Въ немъ пришельцевъ изъ Кубы 45 семей	45	—	Все кочевье сіе состоитъ изъ бекскихъ поступовъ, и потому никакихъ другихъ податей не платили. — —	— —	— — —	Малджекатъ не берется.	Таругскихъ доходовъ не имѣется.	— — —	— — —	Принадлежало бывшему Касымъ-беку, а нынѣ казнѣ.	Такъ какъ жители сего кочевья 25 лѣтъ вышли изъ Кубы, то оставя ихъ на жительствѣ въ Ширванѣ, слѣдуетъ обложить податью въ казну, по состоянію.
26.	Кочевье МАРТЫ. Въ немъ 30 семействъ . .	30	—	Всѣ жители сего кочевья были почтовщики табунщики, а потому никакихъ податей не платили. — —	— —	— — —	Малджекатъ не берется.	Таругскихъ доходовъ не имѣется.	— — —	— — —	Принадлежало бывшему Касымъ-беку, а нынѣ казнѣ.	Такъ какъ кочевье сіе состоитъ изъ природныхъ ширванцевъ, то и слѣдуетъ обложить ихъ наравнѣ съ другими податью въ казну.

Explanatory Remarks

Shirvan's geographical location, between the so-called "Iron Gates" of Derbent and the Mughan-Karabagh Steppe, gave it a strategic importance. It thus served as a corridor between the Caucasus Mountains, the Caspian littoral and Iran. It is not surprising therefore, that the Sassanid kings, Arab governors, and the Sharvanshahs, had all been concerned about the control of this corridor.[1] In the eighteenth century, Iranian military commanders were well aware of the strategic importance of this corridor, which separated Iran's northern marches from the unruly Sunni tribes living in the north Caucasus. It is also not surprising that Nader, distrustful of the Shirvanis, destroyed Shemakha, the capital of the province, and established a new town, New Shemakha or Ağsu. In the nineteenth century Russian generals saw Shirvan and the other khanates in the eastern part of the South Caucasus, together with the Georgian Military Highway, as a route to subdue the Chechens and other rebellious tribes in the high Caucasus.[2]

As noted, Tsitsianov's military threats convinced the khans of Karabagh and Sheki to accept Russian protection. Both received Russian military ranks, medals and salaries for themselves and their elder sons. More importantly, Ebrahim Khan of Karabagh not only hoped to assert his claim to the town of Javad, but also claimed the Qapanat, in southern Zangezur, as well as the part of the Mughan Steppe south of the Aras (Arax) River. In addition, he demanded the return of a number of his subjects who had settled in Shirvan.[3]

By delaying his submission to Russia, Mostafa Khan of Shirvan, in addition to receiving a military rank, medal and salary, also convinced Tsitsianov to permit him to keep the lucrative district of Salyan, which Mostafa had taken from its *soltan*.[4] The town of Javad and its environs, which had been a small khanate in the eighteenth century, as well as all the Mughan south of the Aras River also remained part of the khanate of Shirvan. Several villages on or within the borders of Kuba and Sheki were also incorporated into the tax-rolls of the chancery (*divan*) of Shirvan. The large territory was divided into seventeen *mahals* (districts).

[1] For details, see A. E. Krymskii, "Stranitsy iz istorii severnogo ili Kavkazskogo Azerbeidzhana (klassicheskoi Albanii)," *Sbornik statei k piatidesiatiletiiu nauchno-obshchestvennoi deiatel'nosti Sergeio Fedorovichu Ol'denburgu* (Leningrad, 1934), 280-30; V. Minorsky, *A History of Sharvan and Darband in the 10th-11th centuries* (Cambridge, 1958).

[2] General Yermolov spent five years trying to subdue the Chechens and other tribes in Daghestan, see J. Baddeley, *The Russian Conquest of the Caucasus* (London, 1908), chapter IX.

[3] See Article VI of the treaty in the Appendix.

[4] *Ibid.*, Article V.

Yermolov, as noted, was determined upon his return from his diplomatic mission in Iran in 1817, to end the autonomy of the three surviving khanates located south of the Caucasus. The first opportunity came following the death of the khan of Sheki, who had died in 1819 without an heir. The khanate was immediately annexed outright and Yermolov dispatched Major-General Fedor Akhverdov and State Councilor Paul Mogilevskii to conduct a detailed survey on the revenues collected in the fiscal year 1819, which would now be under the direct supervision of the treasury in Tiflis, Yermolov's military and administrative headquarters.[5]

Circumstances and Purpose of the 1820 Russian Survey

The next opportunity arrived a year later, when on September 1, 1820 Mostafa Khan of Shirvan fled his khanate and sought refuge with Crown Prince `Abbas Mirza Qajar in Iran.[6] On September 7, Yermolov sent the following order to Major-General Prince Valerian Madatov:

> *As a just punishment for the terrible betrayal committed by Mostafa Khan by his flight to Iran, the Shirvan Province is now under direct Russian rule. I appoint Your Excellency to lead this transition. For more than three years the province has been included in your administrative region[7] and you, more than anyone, are familiar with it. We have asked the first secretary of the chancery, State Councilor Mogilevskii,[8] to assist you in this task. I ask you to report on the following:*
>
> *To set the new administration on the same basis as was done in the Kuba Province; to ascertain the actual revenues of the khanate and to continue to collect them. The increase or decrease of these revenues in the future will depend on your findings. As far as farmed out revenues of the khanate are concerned, it is imperative to have a detailed account, especially proof concerning the sum paid to the khan for the fishing rights in Salyan leased to the court councilor, Ivanov.*
>
> *To determine, as soon as possible, the validity of the khan's decrees concerning villages, lands or other private properties. Such decrees can easily be fake, or may have expired. The swindlers are often those begs whom the khan, because he needed them to carry out some evil deed, raised from a low status and are not from among the original citizens or state functionaries of Shirvan.*

---

[5] An annotated English translation is forthcoming.

[6] Mostafa Khan, together with Mahdi Qoli Khan of Karabagh, joined `Abbas Mirza and at the start of the Second Russo-Iranian War crossed the Aras River with the Iranian army, hoping to regain their domains. Following the Iranian defeat they remained in Iran until the death of `Abbas Mirza in 1833. They then both received permission to return to their domains as Russian pensioners.

[7] In 1817 Madatov was appointed the commander of the forces in the khanates of Karabagh, Shirvan, Sheki and Kuba.

[8] Paul Mogilevskii, as noted, was one of the compilers of the Russian survey of Sheki in 1819.

Are there any close attendants and functionaries of the khan who have remained? If so, keep the trustworthy ones, but not as parasites, and send the dangerous ones to Persia (Iran).

Ascertain the reasons that the khan has exempted anyone from paying taxes. Make sure it is for a good reason but accept them with caution.

The revenues from the silk farms and rice fields belonging to the khan are to remain as is, until we can assess the conditions of the peasants and perhaps be able to lighten their load. Try to find ways to increase silk production by encouragement and not through oppression. We have to look to the future. It is better to lower our profits for now in order to increase them later.

As to the salt from the lakes near Salyan, you must set up a special arrangement without runing the income of the contractor or increasing the sum paid for his lease. Please let me know as soon as possible your opinion on this matter.

Major-General Vlasov the Third is to take care of the khan's stud farms, for I plan to turn them into Imperial stud farms. I have ordered that the khan's sheep and cattle be sold, for keeping them is not profitable for the treasury. It would be good, however, if we were able to choose the best bulls to be used as transport animals for the treasury. I await your information.

The property of those who have taken part in the khan's treachery must be seized immediately by the treasury. The grain should be given to the troops and the rest sold. The property of the poorest begs should be given to their nearest relatives. There has to be an exact account of all of this.

Make a list of the khan's relatives who did not follow him [to Iran] and send it to me. Beware, and make certain that they have not been left behind by the khan in order for him to maintain contact with the province...[9]

I am delaying the apppointment of a commandant and hope you can find a capable person from among the officers serving in the [local] treasury.[10] *As to the revenues of this province, until the establishment of a new order, you should follow my special authority and keep them in a safe place.*

You should also set up a customs house, find an appropriate place for it, and inform me of your ideas...[11]

On the same day, Yermolov also sent a directive to Councilor Paul Mogilevskii, which read:

Wishing to speed up the Russian administration of the Shirvan Province and to end the confusion caused by the khan's flight, I am sending Major-General Prince

[9] Madatov and Mogilevskii prepared two lists: The first included those who had left with the khan, the second (mostly women and children) who were left behind but were sent to Iran at a later date, see numbers 4 and 6 in the Appendix.

[10] Captain Prince Makaev was chosen as the commandant.

[11] *Akty*, VI/1, doc. no. 1217, order number 184.

Madatov to Shirvan. To bring about an orderly transition, I am appointing you, who have already proven your worth in organizing the Sheki Province, to assist him in this endeavor. In my instructions to Major-General Prince Madatov, I have listed the most important objectives which he has to undertake without delay. I am sending you a copy of those instructions.[12]

After arriving in Shirvan and assessing the situation, Madatov and Mogilevskii sent the following report to Yermolov on September 20 from Fitdagh, the administrative center of the khanate:

Upon arrival at the borders of the Shirvan province, we were informed that the traitor Mostafa Khan, in his hurry to flee, had left a major part of his belongings in his residences in Fitdagh and Sulut. In order to keep the property secure we rushed to Fitdagh, where we arrived on the 4th [16th] of this month. Here we found the said property, which, on the orders of Major-General Vlasov, was itemized by Captain Prince Makaev, a copy of which we have the honor to send to Your Exalted Excellency.

As to the dresses of women and the beddings listed in the copy, which belonged to the wives of Mostafa Khan who have fled with him, we ask your permission to give them to his remaining wives or to the poorest of his relatives who have remained here, since selling them in a public sale offends Asiatic customs. Moreover, in our opinion, such an act is unseemly for the Russian State. The rest of the khan's property, as well as his livestock, is known and will be sold in public auction. We have already announced the date throughout Shirvan and the neighboring states...

The majority of the begs of the mahals have, at our demand, already arrived in Fitdagh. The rest are expected today. The moment they all arrive we will immediately start to elect the members of the city court and the said court will open its doors. We have already made all the necessary preparations...

...We have already prepared the necessary lists of the districts and await only the arrival of the battalion with officers who will immediately go with the begs to each mahal, to require the population to swear allegiance to His Imperial Majesty.

As to the farmed out revenues, we have already made a list of some and will soon complete the rest. The khan had leased some of them to individuals who have fled with him. Among them is the tax farmer who purchased the revenues from the sale of madder. We have decided to lease the orchards belonging to the khan, his family, and the begs who fled with him. We have already found willing lessees.

[12] *Ibid.*, doc. no. 1218.

As to the numerous decrees handed out by the khan regarding the possession of land or other property owned by individuals as private property [molk], we have announced throughout the mahals that such individuals have a fifteen day time period to present valid documents.

In addition to demanding from the khan's mirzas the tax rolls for the revenues from silk production, grain and rice which belonged to the khan, we also are asking for the list of the revenues for the darughehs (police superintendents of the bazaar, or supervisors of a mahal). We do not plan to alter any of the taxes and, in fact, hope to improve their collection. We have received information that some of the population who had to work on the above lands, especially the Armenians, had stopped working after the khan's flight. We have sent strict orders, with threats of heavy punishment, stating that everyone has to perform his labor as was required in the past.[13]

Since the main income of the khan was from Salyan we need to ascertain the exact amount, as well as establish the most convenient framework for extraction of salt from the salt lakes of the region. Thus, we have summoned the nayeb (deputy) of Salyan with all the available instructions from the khan. Although according to the local begs, Lt.-Colonel Bulgakov has already made a list of the revenues from Salyan, we do not know what directives he received from Your Excellency.

Upon our arrival in Fitdagh we learned from Captain Prince Makaev that Major-General Vlasov had dispatched Cossack officers to enumerate the remaining cattle and sheep belonging to the khan and those begs who had fled with him... We have no information on the khan's stud farms. According to the local inhabitants it would be difficult to keep the horses here. They will not survive the coming of winter and the lack of fodder, caused by the destruction of grain and grass by locusts. It would be better if Your Excellency would order the Cossacks to transport the horses to Georgia to remain there until they can be sent to the Imperial stud farms. In this manner the treasury [of Shirvan] will not have to spend the money to maintain the khan's horse herders.

We should have no difficulty in feeding the [Russian] troops here, for, according to the records handed by Captain Prince Makaev, there are 2,970 chetverts[14] *of wheat and 579 chetverts of barley left behind by the khan and the begs who fled with him. In addition, according to the inhabitants, there is plenty of grain belonging to the khan and the various begs who have fled, in Salyan which has yet to be collected,*[15] *as well as the mal-o-jehat, or a tenth part of the harvest, which will be more than enough.*

[13] The registers list free labor performed by the peasants for the khan, which now belong to the treasury.

[14] Text refers to a Russian measure equal to 126.41 lbs.

[15] Since the khan fled in September during the harvest season, some of the revenues from the land were yet to be collected.

> *The major difficulty concerns the khan's income, for there are few written documents... The khan was illiterate and relied on his advisors. There are few ta`liqehs [certificates of tax-exemption] or barats [receipts of quittance], even for farmed out revenues. Most contracts were made orally. Thus, even the tax farmers, whom we are now questioning in order to prepare a register, do not present any papers. They know only the period of the contract and the sum they paid, which had been agreed orally. The khan's nazer (steward), Hoseyn, has some barats, but their accuracy cannot be determined. Some of the leases have not been renewed and have continued at the same sum as in previous years. The khan's mirzas and the attendants of the begs have no documents for some of this year's leases. In spite of this, we are thoroughly examining everything on which we can lay our hands.*
>
> *The khan's residence in Fitdagh was left open after his flight. Many of the citizens went inside and stole various items. We have now issued an announcement that they must return these items, as well as any sums owed to the khan, within ten days, or face severe punishment... Similar announcements have been sent to all the mahals.*
>
> *In conclusion, it is our duty to inform you that the traitor Mostafa Khan did not manage to take most of his belongings. Kombai Beg, the same man who, during our expedition against the Qazi-qumuq, served us well as the commander of the Shirvani cavalry, and who upon his return was tortured and hunted by Mostafa Khan, learned of his flight, gathered the Shirvani cavalry and caught up with the khan at the crossing [at the Kur River], while the entire baggage train was still on this side... Anyway the booty was retrieved by Lt.-Colonel Saginov*[16] *and his Cossacks, who after his arrival took away some of the items which were looted by the Shirvanis.*[17]

Yermolov's instructions to Madatov and Mogilevskii were very clear. They were to make a detailed list of all the revenues collected for the khan from the inhabitants of the Shirvan khanate. The survey continously states the fact that these revenues would now belong to the treasury. What is unclear is what part of the revenues would remain in the treasury of the newly-annexed Russian province of Shirvan for its administrative expenses; what part would be sent to Tiflis to cover the expenses of military and civilian apparatus of the Russian administration in the Caucasus; and what, if any, part would be sent to the imperial treasury in St. Petersburg.[18]

[16] He was a major in the Apsheron Infantry Corps and, later, the commandant of Kuba.

[17] Report number 11 of September 8 [20], 1820, in *Akty*, VI/1, doc. no. 1221.

[18] Although there is information on the revenues collected following the complete Russian takeover in 1828 (see below and appendix), further research in the archives of Tbilisi, Moscow and St. Petersburg to ascertain the amount of revenues received from all the former khanates located south of the Caucasus Mountains is in order. It would be interesting to find out what percentage was used to improve local socioeconomic conditions and how much was sent to Tiflis or St. Petersburg.

For the next three months, Madatov and Mogilevskii, with the help of Mirza Hasan and Mirza Hoseyn, the chief secretaries (*mirzas*) of the *divan* (chancery) examined the tax rolls (*daftar*), (*barats*), (*ta`liqehs*) and conducted interviews with the landowners, local officials and the *darughehs* (prefects) of the districts, some of whom had replaced the former officials who had fled with the khan. On December 9, 1820, they presented their findings, arranged in nineteen registers, to General Yermolov and to Prince Makaev, the Russian commandant in the town of Fitdagh, the administrative center of Shirvan.

The survey, entitled *The Description of the Shirvan Province*, compiled in 1820, was eventually published in 1867 by the press of the Viceroy of the Caucasus in Tiflis.[19] The number of copies printed must have been very few, for it, like the similar Russian surveys conducted in the Sheki (1819) and, later, in Karabagh (1823) provinces, soon became extremely rare.

Population of Shirvan in 1820

It is obvious that the survey's main purpose was to determine the number of people and the revenues of a province, which would now be administered by Russian officials. Therefore, the survey does not demonstrate any bias in favor of one group or another. It follows the same procedure as the earlier Russian survey of Sheki and the later one conducted in Karabagh; that is, it lists the Tatar,[20] nomad and Armenian families in each village or nomad settlements located in the various *mahals* of Shirvan. It also indicates the number of tax-paying and tax-exempt families in each locality. In the absence of any other reliable earlier data on the number of villages and nomad settlements and the people who inhabited the Shirvan Province, the Russian survey of 1820 is our best primary source.

In their report Madatov and Mogilevskii stated that they had not included the five registers of the farmed out or leased properties.[21] Instead, they had provided a summary of the total revenues from such properties in two registers.[22] They added that they had not included two other registers. The first register dealt with the khan's residences [in the town of Fitdagh and the hamlet of Sulut], his movable properties and flocks, which they had sold.[23] Unfortunately, there is no information on the amount of cash received from these sales. The second absent register was the total number of families in, and the total revenue received from the seventeen *mahals* of Shirvan.[24] The two officials

[19] *Opisanie Shirvanskoi Provintsii sostavlennoe v' 1820 godu.*

[20] The survey of Shirvan refers to the various Turkic groups as Tatars, while other Muslims are identified as Kurds or by their tribal names. The term Tatar is primarily used to identify those who spoke the local Turkish dialect (*Torki*). All Russian sources refer to them as Tatars, while the sources in Persian refer to them by their tribal or regional names.

[21] See page 13 in the text.

[22] Indicated as Registers 1 and 3 by the translator-editor of this volume.

[23] See pages 190–191.

[24] See page 13 in the text.

justified their action by stating that the first register had nothing to do with the total annual revenues from the province, which after all was the purpose of their survey, and that the second could be ascertained by adding the total revenues from each *mahal*.[25]

The following table recreates the latter missing register:

Location	Tax-paying families	Tax-exempt families
Fitdagh*	60	2,000 (estimate)
Salyan	1,400 (estimate)	-
Houz	480	161
Sedenrud	813	396
Khanchoban	1,085	473
Elat	885	131
Koshun	730	268
Karasubasar	457	360
Kessan	271	143
Ekeret	105	58
Qobustan	946	230
Lahic	306	68
Rudbar	324	98
Mughan	500 (estimate)	-
Navahin	90	38
Karabaghlar	64	38
Boluket	248	55
Khazarud	300	104
Totals	**9,064**	**4,621**

* See register 2.

[25] *Ibid.* Three years later Yermolov ordered Mogilevskii, together with Colonel Peter Yermolov, Yermolov's own cousin, to conduct a survey of the last surviving autonomous khanate, that of Karabagh, whose khan had also fled to Iran at the end of 1822. The shortcomings of the first two surveys were not repeated. The 1823 survey of the Karabagh khanate is not only twice the size of the earlier efforts, but, in addition to the population numbers and the revenues collected, also contains information on the various professions, a detailed list of the property of the khan and his family, the complete revenues from concessions; see G. Bournoutian, ed./trans., *The 1823 Russian Survey of the Karabagh Province: A Primary Source on the Demography and Economy of Karabagh in the Early 19th Century* (Costa Mesa, CA., 2012).

The above totals enumerate the number of tax-paying and tax-exempt families who lived in the various *mahals* of Shirvan in 1820. The survey also mentions the 60 Jewish families who resided on the outskirts of Fitdagh. Although the survey has concrete population figures for 16 of the *mahals*, it lacks exact figures for the Salyan *Mahal* and the city of Fitdagh. The total population of the 16 *mahals* was 10,285 families. The survey estimates that there were 1,000 original families in Fitdagh, while the remaining 1,000 families belonged to artisans or craftsmen who had come there from various *mahals*. They were also an estimated 1,400 families (more according to the local official) in Salyan.

Thus, if we add the above figures for Salyan and Fitdagh, the total population of Shirvan in 1820 consisted of 13,685 families. If we accept that the average family size in the region during that period was six, the total population numbered 82,110. However, the numbers listed in the survey are debatable. For if we accept the testimony of local officials, who claimed that the population was undercounted in some places,[26] the estimated population probably reached some 15,000 families,[27] or some 90,000 inhabitants.

The survey, as noted, lists the number of Tatar, nomad and Armenian families who resided in their respective villages or pastures in the 16 *mahals*. Although there are no figures on how many Tatars, nomads or Armenians lived in Fitdagh or Salyan, the great majority (based on the information in the survey) must have been Muslims, followed by some Armenians and a handful of Russians, Jews and Iranians.

The total Muslim population (Tatars and nomads) was probably around 81,000. The settled Tatars counted for more than 42,000, while there were some 39,000 Tatar and Kurdish nomads in the khanate. The Armenian population was not over 5,500 inhabitants, and the Jews numbered some 500. The Muslims thus formed 93.10% of the population (48.27% settled and 44.83% nomads), the Armenians 6.32% and the Jews 0.58%.[28]

There were a total of 370 villages and pastures: 187 Tatar villages, or 50.54%; 154 Kurdish and Tatar nomadic settlements, or 41.62%; 28 Armenian villages, or 7.57%; and one Jewish village or 0.27%.

According to the survey, almost half (48.39%) of Shirvan's population living in the sixteen *mahals* was composed of Kurds and various Tatar tribes. The largest tribe was that of Khan-Chopan (Xançoban). Four of the *mahals*: Xançoban, Elat, Qobustan and Mughan were populated entirely by nomads. The Sedenrud *Mahal* had five nomad

---

26 This was especially true among the roaming nomadic population.

27 In 1828 the population was 18,444 households; see appendix.

28 In 1842 the head of the Caspian Province published the population figures for the cities of Shemakha, Kuba, Derbent, Lenkoran, Baku and Nukha. The city of Shemakha had 15,602 Muslims (84.7% of the population); there were 2,759 Christians (Armenians, Catholics and Russian Orthodox), or 15% of the total; the rest, (0.3%), were the 73 Raskolniks (dissenters from the Russian Orthodox Church) and an insignificant number of Jews, see D. I. Ismail-zade, *Naselenie gorodov zakavkazskogo kaira v xix-nachale xx v.* (Moscow, 1991), 79, 120. In 1856 the city of Shemakha had 20,433 (a 10% increase) inhabitants, *ibid.*, 60.

settlements, while the *mahals* of Kessan, Howz and Khazarud had only four nomad settlements altogether. The nomads were, therefore, concentrated in specific locations that could sustain their pastoral existence. An average nomad settlement had 31 families.

The *mahals* of Salyan, Koshun, Qarasubasar, Ekeret, Lahıc, Navahin and Qarabağlar, were totally devoid of nomads. No Armenians resided in the Salyan, Qarasubasar, Ekeret, Lahic, Navahin, Boluket, or Rudbar *mahals*. Apart from one Jewish village, the settled population was divided between Tatars and Armenians. They resided in 215 villages, each populated entirely by their own religious and ethnic group. As noted, there were 187 Tatar villages and 28 Armenian villages. An average Armenian village had 27 families, while and average Tatar village had 24 families.

Unfortunately, unlike the Russian surveys of the khanates of Yerevan and Karabagh, there is no information on the various skilled professions. This may be explained by the fact that few Armenians resided in Shirvan and almost none in the town of Fitdagh, for, in the cities of Yerevan and Shushi, the Armenians formed the majority of the skilled artisans.[29] In fact, except for Talesh, Armenians resided in every khanate of South Caucasus. They, and, to a lesser extent, the Jews, played a central role in the economic and commercial life of the region.[30]

Land Tenure in Early Nineteenth-Century Shirvan

The Russian survey of Shirvan is a valuable primary source on the various forms of land ownership in the South Caucasus in the final years of Iranian suzerainty. Unlike some other khanates, Shirvan had numerous rivers to irrigate its agricultural base. The Salyan region, watered by the Kur River and its various tributaries was ideal for growing rice. There is, therefore, no evidence of undeground water channels, known as *qanat*, which was so prevalent in other parts of Iran. The abundance of mullberry trees encouraged silk farms and, starting in the mid-sixteenth century, Shirvan's silk was exported to the Ottoman Empire, Europe, and Russia.[31]

Social life in Shirvan was based in and around the village and on nomad settlements close to the village. The peasants had common holdings and were assessed based on the amount of land which could be cultivated by a wooden plow attached to a pair of oxen, called *juft* in Persian. The villagers had the right to use the pastures and to collect scrub for fuel.

Overall, the land tenure system was similar to the other khanates in the region and was divided into:

---

[29] See G. Bournoutian, *The Khanate of Erevan Under Qajar Rule, 1795–1828* (New York, 1992), 181, 238–242; G. Bournoutian, *The 1823 Russian Survey of the Karabagh Province* (Costa Mesa, CA., 2012), 34–87.

[30] M. Atkin, Russia and Iran, 1780–1828 (Minneapolis, 1980), 12.

[31] See G. Bournoutian, *The Journal of Zak`aria of Agulis* (Costa Mesa, CA, 2003).

a. Movable and immovable property belonging to Mostafa Khan and his family: The Russo-Shirvani treaty recognized Mostafa Khan as the hereditary ruler of the khanate. He thus held proprietory rights over the territory of his domain. He distributed it among his family members, assigned it to administrators or military officers in lieu of service (*toyul*, see below), or gifted it as personal estates.[32] These propreties consisted of cultivated fields, irrigation canals, mills, orchards, silk farms, stud farms and herds, which were administered directly by the *divan* or treasury of the khan.[33]

Since Mostafa Khan and some members of his family fled the khanate, all of these properties were confiscated, sold or leased and the income was transferred to the new Russian administration. Only a handful of Mostafa Khan's family members managed to keep their hereditary properties.[34] In fact, following the death of `Abbas Mirza, Mostafa Khan petitioned Russia to allow him to return to Shirvan. The permission was granted and the khan received a pension from the Russian government.[35]

b. Private property (*molk*): Such properties could have been purchased or inherited by their owners or could have been granted, through a *ta`liqeh* by the khan, or a former ruler, as a gift to reward a service. The Russian survey identifies the holders of private property in Shirvan by the term *prinadlezhit'* ("belongs to"). Private property could include cultivated lands, irrigation canals, mills, orchards, silk farms and other similar belongings.[36] It is important to note that some private properties in reality had been usurped by their owners. In fact, that is the main reason that new khans, as well as the Russians, demanded proof of ownership. Once again, the survey indicates that some of these *molks* were confiscated following the flight of the *molkdars* to Iran.

c. Income from land: Mostafa Khan allocated the income from certain lands to various military officers and civil officials in lieu of salary/service (*toyul*). In some cases it was a grant of the revenue attached to certain offices, such as that of the *darugheh*. The Russian survey identifies such office holders by the term *upravlaiutsia* ("administered by") and indicates them as being tax-exempt (*mo`af*). Some of these administrative or military land grants could,

---

[32] The notion that the ruler was the sole owner of the soil went back to the Seljuq era (11th century). Such allocations were known as *iqta`*.

[33] Such lands are referred to as *divani* in sources in Persian.

[34] It is interesting to note that unlike the situation in Shirvan, the family members of the last khan of Sheki, who had remained loyal to Russia and had died in office (1819) continued to receive income from their properties based on *vaqfs* and testaments, see forthcoming survey on Sheki. In order to retain their large properties, wealthy notables in nineteenth-century Iran devised various tactics in order not to divide it among various family members, see N. Abe's excellent article, "Preserving a Qajar Estate: Analysis of Fath `Ali Khan Donboli's 'Property Retention Tactics'," *Studia Iranica*, 43, 2014), 129–150.

[35] Other Shirvani notables, such as Esma`il Beg also returned (1833) and petitioned Russia to return their property, see, II, 38.

[36] Such properties are also referred to as *arbabi* in Persian sources.

in time, turn into *de facto* private possessions. The Russian survey repeatedly states the need to ascertain the right of ownership from a number of such landholdings. Once more, according to the survey, some of these *toyuls* were abolished following the flight of the *toyuldars* to Iran, while others (those of *toyuldars* who continued to serve under the Russian administration) remained intact for decades.[37]

d. Summer (*yeylaq*) or winter pasturelands (*qeshlaq/kishlak*): Turcoman and Kurdish nomads paid dues to the khan and his family, major officials, or local administrators for the use of such pastures.

e. Properties in the form of charitable trusts to support religious institutions:[38] Such properties were tax-exempt. Since the Russian survey is primarily interested in the revenues collected by khan's *divan*, there is little mention of such holdings in Shirvan.

f. The peasants (*ra`iyats*) and nomads, who lived and labored on the above categories of lands, paid dues in cash, agricultural produce, animals or services in form of *corvée*, either to Mostafa Khan, his family, the landowner, the fief-holder, the local administrator, or the religious institution. The above landholders, unless they were totally exempt, also paid a part of the revenues collected from their subjects to the khan's *divan*. The Russians noted that serfdom did not exist in the South Caucasus.[39]

The *ranjbars*[40] were landless peasants who worked as sharecroppers or seasonal workers. The landowners provided the seeds, animals and implements and the *ranjbars* took from one-third to one half of the harvest in return for their labor.

On December 31, 1828 (January 12, 1829) General Paskevich ordered an assessment of the property damages suffered by the Karabagh, Sheki and Shirvan provinces in 1826, during the Iranian incursions in the Second Russo-Iranian War. The process took more than a year and on May 6 (18), 1830, at a cost of 1,500 rubles, a report was prepared of the claims of Muslims, Armenians, Russian officials, [Armenian] clergy, inhabitants of some Georgian districts, people who had come to the region for various reasons from Russian provinces, and Iranian merchants who had come for trade.

[37] In 1858 two *mirzas* (Nasrollah Beg and Qorban Beg) asked for the use of a field measuring 50 *desiatins* as a lifetime *toyul* in exchange for their services; see Petrushevskii, Bogdanova and Pritykin, eds. *Kolonial'naia politika rosiiskogo tsarizma v Azerbaidzhane v 20-60-kh gg. XIX v.* Part II (Moscow, 1937), 183.

[38] These are known as *vaqf* (Arabic *waqf*).

[39] The khans, however, did not allow their peasants, the main base of their revenues, to migrate to other khanates and demanded their return; see Article VI of the Russo-Shirvani treaty in Appendix.

[40] *Ranjbar* translates as "he who toils." Some Russian historians erroneously viewed the *ranjbars* as serfs.

The report concluded that although the number of claims could not be determined accurately, they totaled 1,168,284 silver rubles. According to the various Russian local commandants, however, the total was 292,681 silver rubles and 804,637 in *assignat*[41] rubles.

It was decided that the treasury should reimburse all the losses of the local administrations, landlords, villagers, tax farmers and merchants from the indemnity paid by the Iranian government.[42]

Taxes Collected in Shirvan in 1820

The Russian survey of Shirvan is also an important source for the various taxes collected in cash, produce and services from the inhabitants in the last year of Mostafa Khan's governorship. Although some of these taxes are similar to those collected in Iran or other khanates south of the Caucasus Mountains, others are unique to Shirvan. The survey mainly indicates the assessed revenues collected by the khan's *divan*. Unfortunately, only in some instances does it mention the share collected by the landholder or local official, which, if known, would give a more accurate picture of the burden imposed on the tax-paying population.

[41] A form of paper money used from 1769–ca. 1849.

[42] Article VI of the Turkmanchay Treaty fixed the indemnity at 20,000,000 silver rubles.

The following chart is recreated from the totals of each *mahal* register:

	Taxed	Exempt	Gold rubles	Russian silver rubles
Fitdagh*	60	2,000	144	-
Contracts†	-	-	11,223	0.62½
Salyan	1,400	-	37,036	1.04
Howz	480	131	898	1,397.42¾
Sedenrud	813	396	573	20,398.64½
Xançoban	1,085	473	1,032	504.74¼
Elat	885	131	765	6,404.06¼
Koshun	730	268	772½	1,612.35
Qarasubasar	457	360	770	7,668.97½
Kessan	271	143	272	1,241.37½
Ekeret	105	58	190	625.79¼
Qobustan	946	230	1,075	10,254.25½
Lahıc	306	68	400	738.07½
Rudbar	324	98	345	1
Mughan	500	-	450	-
Navahin	90	38	90	24,917.50
Qarabağlar	64	38	39	1,100.33¾
Boluket	248	55	290	10,763.43¾
Khazarud	300	104	580	2,092.22½
Totals	**9,064**	**4,621**	**56,944½**	**80,021.86½**

* See register 2.

† See register 1. The above concessions do not include the farmed out revenues from the Salyan *Mahal*.

According to these figures 51% of the families were tax-exempt (*mo`af*). The numbers, however, can be deceiving. For, if one leaves out the town of Fitdagh and the Salyan *Mahal*, which as will be noted, had special status, and concentrates solely on the remaining sixteen *mahals* the tax-exempt percentage drops to 34.2%. Nevertheless, a little over one-third of the population of Shirvan did not have to pay any taxes to the khan. As will be noted below, the presence of a large bureaucracy, as well as some questionable certificates, indicated by Madatov and Mogilevskii in their reports, was the main reason for such an unusual large tax-exempt percentage.

There were 4,831 nomad families in the 16 *mahals*: 3,755 families (77.73%) paid taxes, while 1,076 families (22.27%) were tax exempt.

There were 4,534 Tatar families in the 16 *mahals*: 3,103 families (68.44%) paid taxes; 1431 families (31.56%) were tax-exempt.

There were 761 Armenian families in the 16 *mahals*: 557 families (73.30%) paid taxes, while 205 families (26.70%) were tax-exempt.

There were 60 Jewish families outside Fitdagh; they paid their taxes in a lump sum.

Taxes were paid either in cash, kind, or various services. Taxes were levied on households or families (apparently regardless of size). We have no concrete numbers of the tax-paying and tax-exempt families in Salyan or Fitdagh. The total number of families in the 16 mahals who paid taxes was 7,664, while 2,621 families were tax-exempt.

The survey indicates that 53 widows, and 104 orphans were exempt from paying taxes to the khan. The same was true for the 7 Armenian priests, 217 Muslim mullahs, 15 sheikhs, 3 *akhunds* (theologian, preacher), and 40 *seyyeds* (those who claimed to be descendants of the Prophet Mohammad through his daughter Fatima). In addition, the khan sometimes extended a special tax-exempt status to various individuals through a *ta`liqeh*, which was an official document given to the individual or attached to the tax register. There were 75 such families in Shirvan.

The families and the retainers of the *begs*, the 35 *darughehs*, *nazers* (stewards), *nayebs* (deputies), *mirzas*, the khan's 404 servitors (*nokars*), the 74 *yüzbaşis* (local officers), 4 foremen, the 67 Muslim *kadkhodas* and 12 Armenian *kevkhas* (village elders) did not pay any taxes to the khan or to the landholder, but were required to perform their administrative duties.

The largest group of tax-exempt families (905) was the *ranjbars*. The second prominent tax-exempt group was the immigrants (705). The khan and other major officials would encourage regular peasants to flee neighboring khanates, especially Kuba and Karabagh, and settle in Shirvan in exchange for tax-exemption. Unlike the Russian survey of Karabagh, which indicates the number of years such immigrants were exempt from taxes, the survey of Shirvan is silent in this regard. The two Russian surveyors stress that some of these "immigrants" have lived in Shirvan for decades and had to be reassessed.

The following is a list of the various taxes and services collected by the khan's *divan* in Shirvan in 1820:

1. Annual Tribute: Dues totaling 8,000 gold rubles, which equaled 24,000 Russian silver rubles or 38,400 silver coins in Shirvani currency. The sum was paid in two installments by the Shirvan Province to the Russian administration in Tiflis. As noted, the 1805 treaty stipulated the payment of this annual tribute to Russia in exchange for permitting Mostafa Khan to maintain his governorship of the province under Russian supervision and to collect the revenues from it.[43]

[43] See number 1 in Appendix.

According to the survey, the khan, in 1820, collected 8,685 gold rubles from the villages and nomad pastures. The town of Fitdagh and the Salyan *Mahal* formed a separate category. In order to encourage people to settle in his new capital of Fitdagh, the khan exempted its citizens from all dues. The khan viewed the Salyan *Mahal* as his private property (see below). Thus after deducting the 8,000 gold rubles annual for the tribute the khan was left with only 685 gold rubles.

It is interesting to note that the Jews paid the largest percentage per capita (7.2 Russian silver rubles); the Armenians were next with 2.83 silver rubles; the Tatar villagers paid 2.73 silver rubles, while the nomads paid the least 2.34 silver rubles.[44]

2. Contracts and farmed out revenues: The khan's main source of income came from various contracts, leases and rentals, most of which were located in the Salyan *Mahal*. The survey indicates that he received 48,259 gold rubles, or eight times the amount of his annual tribute to Russia.[45] Yermolov, even prior to the Russian annexation of Shirvan, had his eye on this lucrative income.[46]

3. *Sursat*: Mostafa Khan had to maintain between 600 and 1,000 troops at his own expense and provide for the 500-man Russian garrison. In nineteenth-century Shirvan, the *sursat* was collected as purveyance for the khan's family, household, administration and the upkeep of the troops. Although the *sursat* was collected mainly in kind, it also included cash dues such as taxes on plows, the *bagh-bashi* and the *kharaj* (see below).

4. *Mal-o-jehat* (*mal va jehat*, *mal-u-jehat*): The khan was entitled to ten percent from the grain harvest and five percent from the silk and cotton harvest. This tax was generally paid in kind (wheat, barley, millet, rice, cotton, or silk). In some cases the local official would receive a third from the ten percent.[47]

5. *Bagh-bashi*: A tax collected in cash from the orchards and vegetable gardens. Although the survey does not indicate the type of fruit or vegetables, information from neighboring khanates indicate that apples, grapes, pears, pomegranates, grapes, peas, lentils onions, garlic, carrots, cucumbers, sesame seeds, walnuts, and melons were common in the region.[48]

   This tax was collected solely from villagers. According to the survey, the 187 Tatar villages paid a total of 185.20 rubles, while the 28 Armenian villages paid 73 rubles. The total *bagh-bashi* collected in 1820 was 258.20 rubles. This clearly indicates that the Armenians paid almost seven times more in *bagh-bashi* dues

[44] The gold rubles were converted to silver rubles (1 gold ruble to 3 silver rubles) to facilitate the division

[45] See Register 3.

[46] See *Akty*, VI/1, doc. 1211.

[47] The survey, however, only lists the percentage collected for the treasury.

[48] See *The 1823 Russian Survey of Karabagh*.

(9.21 rubles per Armenian village versus 1.38 rubles per Tatar village). The numbers also indicate that Armenians were more adept in cultivating fruit orchards and vineyards than the Tatars.

6. *Kharaj*: A tribute or poll tax[49] collected in cash solely from the Armenians. The survey indicates that the Armenians paid 1,037 rubles for the *kharaj*.[50]

7. *Darughegy*: A tax collected in kind for the upkeep of the *darugheh* of each *mahal*.[51]

8. *At-arpasi*: A tax collected in barley for the khan's or the *darugheh*'s horses.[52]

9. *Qullugh-puli*: Dues collected for the salary of the tax collectors. According to the survey, two Armenian villages in the Khazarud *Mahal* had born this burden in the previous year, but were exempted by the khan in the 1820 tax-rolls.[53]

10. *Toujih*: A levy collected in cash. In Shirvan and Sheki this tax was part of the *sursat*. Only one Tatar village in Shirvan, the Muradxan, paid *toujih* dues, while all villages, except one, paid the *toujih* in Sheki.[54]

11. The villagers, as well as settled nomads, had to pay a tax of one ruble for each wooden plow.[55] The Tatar villages paid 583 rubles in taxes for their plows, while the Armenian villages paid 180 rubles in taxes for their plows. Once again the Armenians paid more than the Tatars (6.42 rubles per Armenian village versus 3.11 rubles per Tatar village). The settled nomads paid the largest amount (1,448 rubles for their 1,448 plows). Although the survey does not indicate if the plows belonged to the nomads, the large number of plows makes it likely that the khan or landowners rented out these plows for one ruble each.

12. The peasants and nomads were required to send firewood and charcoal to the khan. Unfortunately unlike the Russian survey of Karabagh, the survey of Shirvan does not list the amount or the price per load.

13. The peasants and nomads were required to perform various services such as tilling, sowing, and harvesting the fields belonging to the khan, landowner or official. The total days and the monetary value are not mentioned.

14. The peasants had to supply carts and beasts of burden to transport the taxes collected in kind. The total numbers and the monetary value are not mentioned.

15. The peasants also had to provide laborers to work on roads or construction. This

---

[49] This tax was known as *jizya* in earlier times.

[50] See pp. 17, 37.

[51] See p. 35.

[52] See p. 39.

[53] See pp. 19–24.

[54] See p. 128.

[55] This tax was called the *juft-bashi* in Iran and some other khanates.

tax fell under the general term of *meji*, which was similar to the *bigar* in other khanates or the *corvée* in Europe. Once again, the total number of days and the monetary value is absent. In rare cases the larger villages had to host envoys at their own expense.

16. Some Tatar villages and nomad pastures had to pay a part of the salaries (*mirzayani*) of the khan's *mirzas* (secretaries/book-keepers).[56]

It is important to note that the number and variety of taxes were less than those collected in the khanates of Karabagh, Yerevan and Nakhichevan.

The khan collected a total of 8,607 gold rubles from the peasants and nomads. The Tatar villages paid 4,128 gold rubles (48%); the nomads paid 3,762 gold rubles (43.70%), while the Armenians paid 717 gold rubles (8.30%).

The total revenues paid in cash and kind by Tatar villages: 56,529 rubles in Russian currency, or 70.64%.

Total revenue paid in cash and kind by the nomads: 18,118 rubles in Russian currency, or 22.64%.

Total revenues paid in cash and kind by the Armenians: 4,374 rubles in Russian currency, or 6.72%.

The Tatars paid an average of 14.83 rubles in cash and kind per family; the Armenians paid 5.74 rubles per family, while the nomads paid only 3.75 rubles per family in kind and cash. However if we consider that Armenian had only 28 villages, they paid 156.21 rubles on average per village, whereas the Tatars paid 302 rubles and the nomads117.65 rubles per settlement. Once again the Armenians paid more than the nomads.

The Armenians were not involved in the production of silk, rice, millet or cotton. The nomads were the sole producers of small rugs, floor mats and cords. They also provided butter, cheese and meat to the khan's *divan*, as well as serving as horse herders for the khan.

The khan's greatest private source of income was that from the city of Fitdagh and especially from the leased or farmed out reve-nues in the Salyan *Mahal*. Such revenues were collected from soap making, weighing machines in the bazaar, slaughter rights, dye works, fishing rights, ferry rights, and so forth. His income in 1820 from all of the above was 48,259 gold rubles,[57] which was six times the number of gold rubles collected from the entire province for the annual tribute paid to Russia. Madatov and Mogilevskii note this fact, by repeatedly stating that the tax-farmed revenues had to be carefully examined; they would probably be increased considerably in the future.[58]

It is interesting to note that in 1822, the last Khan of Karabagh, Mahdi Qoli, collected only 7,955 gold rubles and the equivalent of 58,883 Russian silver rubles in cash, while

[56] These were the Lahich, Qobustan and Qarachoban.

[57] See registers 1 and 3.

[58] See pp. 25–28 and registers 1–3.

Mostafa Khan, collected 8,607 gold rubles and the equivalent of 89,715 Russian silver rubles, despite the drought and invasion of locusts. It seems, therefore, that either Shirvan enjoyed far better economic conditions, due to their rice, cotton and silk production, or that the khan, who had kept control of the khanate for more than two decades, managed to squeeze more from his population.[59]

Ironically, the rather large number of taxes in cash and kind did not bother the compilers of the survey. In fact, they felt not only that the above taxes (including the farmed out dues) should continue to be paid to the new Russian administration in Shirvan, but that the tax-exempt status of some families, Christians and Muslims, should be verified. If proven false, they should be included in the future tax-rolls.

Although the survey indicates that the Russians planned to honor valid documents regarding tax-exemption and property rights, we do not how many were eventually accepted and for how long. It is very probable that the majority of the taxes paid by the local population continued to be collected in order to maintain the Russian troops and administrators who, except when they were fighting the Chechens and other mountainous tribes of the Caucasus, enjoyed a comfortable existence for which they repaid Yermolov with expressions of their great love and loyalty.

Since the figures for the taxes collected for certain years after 1820 (see below and nos. 7–8 in appendix) were recorded, we can safely state that the taxes were not reduced under the Russian administration. In fact, the Russians tried to collect more taxes and began to question the unsubstantiated claims of the *molkdars*, *toyuldars* and the *mo`af*. The policy of russification continued, off and on, with Yermolov's successors and, in 1840, the Russian government ordered that all local laws and customs be set aside, all business be conducted in Russian, and most administrative offices be held by Russians. Although this new system was partially successful in some cities, it lacked the organization needed to replace the rather large local bureaucracy that continued to use Persian, and caused great resentment. It was only during the vice-regency of Prince Michael Vorontsov (1844–1854) that the region finally achieved some success in blending the indigenous system with that of the imperial administration.[60]

---

[59] A comparison with the 1819 Russian survey of Sheki should be interesting.

[60] The Russian colonial policy in the Muslim regions of South Caucasus is detailed in the two parts of the *Kolonial'naia politika*.

Prices of Commodities in Shirvan Prior to the Russian Annexation

The survey is a major source of information on the various commodities produced in Shirvan in the first quarter of the nineteenth century, as well as their prices in local currency:

A *taghar* of wheat:	20 rubles
A *batman* of wheat:	40 kopeks
A *taghar* of barley:	8 rubles
A *batman* of barley:	20 kopeks
A *taghar* of millet:	8 rubles
A *batman* of millet:	20 kopeks
A *taghar* of un-husked rice:	8 rubles
A *taghar* of husked rice:	24 rubles
A *batman* of un-husked rice:	20 kopeks
A *batman* of butter:	4 rubles and 8 kopeks
A *batman* of cheese:	60 kopeks
A *batman* of cotton:	5 rubles and 4 kopeks
A *batman* of silk:	70 rubles
A floor mat:	2 rubles and 40 kopeks
A small rug/horse blanket:	4 rubles
Straw:	80 kopeks per load
Cords:	80 kopeks each
Sheep:	1 ruble and 60 kopeks each

Although, unlike the Russian survey of Karabagh, there are no prices for wool, coarse calico cloth, sheep, bulls, furs, caftans, pantaloons and silk covers, a comparison of prices for various grains among the three khanates of Sheki, Shirvan and Karabagh may prove valuable.

The peasants and nomads paid a total of the following produce as taxes in kind:

Butter:	2,500 lbs.
Cheese:	1,000 lbs.
Silk:	2,000 lbs.
Rice:	150,000 lbs.
Wheat:	500,000 lbs.
Barley:	125,000 lbs.
Cotton:	12,000 lbs.
Millet:	35,000 lbs.
Straw:	352 loads
Small rugs (Horsecloth, horse blanket, or coarse kilims):	88

Floor mats or *palas*:	95	
Ropes/cords:	15	
Free labor and other unpaid services:		Unknown
Meat:	Unknown	
Charcoal:	Unknown	
Firewood:	Unknown	

The Administration of Shirvan prior to the Russian Annexation

The Khan: Although Fath `Ali Shah appointed his sons and grandsons as governors of the various Iranian provinces, the Russian encroachment into the South Caucasus forced him to accept the khan of the major local tribe as the governor of a province in exchange for his nominal submission. It is not surprising, therefore, that these khans would frequently change sides. Mostafa Khan, as other khans in the South Caucasus, was in charge of the *`urf* or customary law in his domain. He dispensed swift and arbitrary rulings in his *divan* (chancery, tribunal, court). There is no mention of a *shari`a* (religious) court in the survey, but there is no doubt that it must have existed.

The Begs: These were notables composed of Mostafa Khan's brothers, sons, close relatives, courtiers, and top officials who served in the civilian administration or as military officers. A great number of them served as the *darughehs* of the *mahals*. The survey clearly indicates that they, their families and retainers were tax-exempt and either received a portion of the harvest from the district under their control, or were given a local village as their private property and collected the entire harvest, without having to give a percentage to Mostafa Khan's treasury. On January 7 (19) 1822, General Yermolov ordered the commandants of Shirvan and Sheki to make a list of all the *begs*, indigenous and those appointed by the khans to administer the *mahals*, in order to determine their true status. Documentary evidence or the statement of 12 men was required.[61]

The Mirzas: The *mirzas* were scribe-bureaucrats, who supervised the *monshi* (secretaries and accountants) in Mostafa Khan's *divan*. The survey mentions two such chief bureaucrats, Mirza Hoseyn and Mirza Hasan, with the former being the more important.

Darugheh: This office, which was originally that of a police official in charge of a town or ward, underwent some changes. In the nineteenth-century Shirvan the office of the *darugheh* was that of a prefect of a *mahal*, or one or more villages in that *mahal*. He acted as an overseer or superintendent of that location. The office, as indicated in the survey, was generally held by a *beg* or a *soltan* (a military officer, not to be confused with sultan). These officials were tax-exempt and received a portion of the harvest as their salary (*darughegy*).

---

[61] *Kolonial'naia politika*, II, 199.

Nazer: The *nazer* served as a steward of the khan.

Nayeb: The Khan's deputy in the main income-producing district of Salyan.

Sarkar: He held the post of chief overseer of Mostafa Khan in the main income-producing district of Salyan.

Yüzbaşi: In Shirvan they served as the police of the *mahals* or local military officers with the rank of captain. They and their families were tax-exempt.

Nokar: The *nokars* were servitors or retainers of Mostafa Khan, the *begs* and the *darughehs*. They and their families were tax-exempt.

Kadkhoda/Kevkha: They were, respectively, the Muslim and Armenian village elders, whose job was to resolve minor arguments among the peasants. They were allowed to carry out light punishments or impose minor fines. They and their families were tax-exempt. The 28 Armenian villages had 12 *kevkhas*.

Clergy: The Armenians had 7 priests for the 28 villages; a rate of 4 to 1. The Muslims had 275 religious figures. The Armenians, therefore, had one priest for every 108 families, while the Muslims had one religious figure for every 35 families. Even if we deduct the *sayyeds*, *akhunds* and sheikhs, the Muslims had one mullah for every 43 families.

There is no information on the *kalantars*, *mirabs*, *mizandars*, *rahdars*, *qaravuls* and other officials described in the Russian surveys of Karabagh, Yerevan and Nakhichevan.

It has to be noted that at the time of compiling the survey, most of the various properties, with the exception of properties belonging to the last khan and those who fled with him to Iran, were still held by their private owners or fief-holders. The present tense is therefore used when describing ownership of such villages or nomad pastures. Whether the ownership changed later is unknown, but it can be safely assumed that many former officials eventually lost their fiefs following the complete Russian conquest of the Caucasus. The revenues paid to the khan's *divan* were for the fiscal year ending in March 1821.

Shirvan under the Russian Administration

The survey clearly indicates that Mogilevskii and Madatov recommended a total reassessment of the revenues to include those who had escaped paying their fair share or were exempt, thereby increasing the revenue collected by Russia. They add:

> *We have recorded the revenues from the private holdings of Mostafa Khan or members of his family, which were collected in wheat, barley or silk, prior to his flight, forgiven, or gifted to those near him. We cannot be certain, however, what*

was collected and what remains to be gathered. We cannot ascertain the truth about the exact amount of grain, due to the drought and invasion of locusts this year, as well as the flight of Mostafa Khan, which has left the khanate in chaos.[62]

The first group to be examined was the tax-exempt (*mo`af*) retainers (*yüzbaşis* and *nokars*) of the khan and the *begs*, who were now required to serve in the Russian forces.

The following report written in January 1839 states:

The ma`af (mo`af) belong to a particular group of people, who reside at present in the four Muslim provinces of Shirvan, Sheki, Karabagh and Talesh. In addition, there are also a number of such individuals in the Tatar districts of Georgia and in the Armenian Province, who, in exchange for serving in the army's Muslim cavalry corps, have been granted this privilege from the highest authorities.

The term mo`af refers to a person, who, regardless of rank, is exempt from paying taxes and performing services... During the rule of the khans the mo`afs were, for a designated period, free from all taxes and services. However, the moment they were summoned for battle, they had to present themselves with their own horses and weapons. The mo`af status was given by the khan in exchange for some service, or through the petition of a beg, or was directly purchased from the khan. Although after the end of the khanate the above duties were terminated, the mo`afs continue to enjoy their tax-exempt status, which has gradually become hereditary from father to son.

There are currently 1,968 families in the Karabagh, Shirvan, Sheki and Talesh provinces; some 4,400 men between the ages of 20 and 60, who claim to be mo`af. Not all of them have a ta`liqeh. Some are mo`af because they were the nokars of the previous khans; others claim they were mo`af prior to the Russian annexation as attested by their community. Many, especially in the Sheki Province, falsely and without any proof, claimed that status and were recorded as such in the survey conducted by Russia.

The well-to-do mo`afs are only found in the Shirvan province, and even there not all. In the other three provinces, the mo`afs are poor. Their poverty, according to local officials, is due to laziness, for, since they are exempt from taxes, they do not make any effort to earn something through their own labor...

In the Sheki province the mo`afs have not performed any services until the current year. This year 94 men guarded (qaravul) the ravines bordering Daghestan...

In 1829, when we organized Muslim regiments to fight against the Turks, more than 200 mo`af horsemen came from Shirvan and Karabagh. The well to do came equipped at their own expense, while the public [treasury] paid for the horses, weapons and clothing of the poor. The cost was 15,000 rubles from the Shirvan and

[62] See page 15.

7,000 rubles from the Karabagh public funds...The Muslim horsemen preferred to join during wartime in order to gain booty. They shirked their duty in peacetime or asked for public funds for their horses and equipment. For example in 1834, 123 mo`af horsemen serving in Warsaw cost their mahals 6,714 rubles and 78 kopeks. In 1837 the Muslim horsemen were gathered from volunteers, both mo`af and peasants, costing from 200 to 400 rubles each.[63]

Ironically, the privilege of the *begs* and the former Muslim officials remained intact as long as they served the Russian administration. The following report, written in April 15 (27) 1839 states:

...The peasants send all the revenues in cash and kind to the treasury, just as they did during the reign of the khan. However on lands called khalese, the administrators [begs, darughehs, etc.] collect the percentage due to the treasury.

The villagers, who are under the administrative care of the begs, at present, as in the past, give the following to the begs: 1) Mal-o-jehat...2) At-arpasi...3) Sixty kopeks for each plow...4) Three rubles for each wedding. 5) Bagh-bashi in cash, depending on the size of the orchard. 6) Darughegy...7) Tilling, sowing and harvesting the land belonging to the begs 8) One cartload of firewood from each household 9) Providing ranjbars 10) Hosting special guests, dues for silk workshops and weaving machines, as well as rugs and other minor items.

The nayebs, who supervise the mahals, some hereditary, others appointed by the government, had, during the rule of the khans, judicial powers and enjoyed a large income. Their power has been reduced considerably by the Russian State and they receive some of their former dues as salary. The nayebs of the 12 mahals collect some 16,000 rubles, while their scribes/accountants receive 1,800 rubles.[64]

A report written by Minister of Finance E. F. Kankrin to Senator Baron E. F. Gan' (Hahn), on November 12 (24), 1834 states:

The 9,262 tax-paying households in Shirvan paid 33,000 silver rubles in cash dues, or 3 rubles and 57 kopeks (in round numbers) per household. However, according to the new census—excluding the begs, the clergy, the ranjbars belonging to the treasury, the canal-water distributer (mirabs), and the orchard keepers (baghbans)—there are 20,677 households in the Shirvan Province. The census tables do not include the households in the cities/towns who are exempt from paying taxes. This has to change, for, the citizens of other cities in Transcaucasia

[63] The report is from General Golovin, the Commander-in-Chief of the Caucasus to the Minister of War, Count Chernyshev. The document then goes on to suggest 16 points on how to reform the *mo`af* system, Central Historical Archives in Leningrad, Archive of the Caucasus Committee, no. 116 (1840), folios 2–17, *Kolonial'naia politika*, I, 83–91.

[64] *Ibid.* 110.

> *[South Caucasus] pay taxes. Thus, if we collect 3 silver rubles from every household, the revenues will increase to 62,021 [62,031].*[65] *We should eliminate all the minor dues and just collect the silver rubles per household... The Shirvan Province has also households belonging to the begs—they have to be assessed at half the amount, that is, 1 ruble and 50 kopeks per household (in fact this has already been done in the Karabagh Province)... If in Georgia, each household pays 3 rubles, Shirvan, which considerably richer in resources, can without any difficulty pay the same.*[66]

A report written by Senator Hahn to Tsar Nicholas I, dated September 29 (October 10), 1837, states that:

> *The peasants are forced to transport their dues in wheat, barley, rice and other agricultural produce to the provincial central treasury. They have to abandon their fields and work and to travel sometimes 100 or more versts, without any compensation. In addition, the lack of a strict and accurate control gives the commandants the opportunity to record the amount of dues from the land in an arbitrary fashion.*[67]

The information on the revenues paid to the khan's *divan* were for the fiscal year ending in December of 1820. There are no records for the revenues of Shirvan collected after the Russian takeover until 1829 (see appendix). By 1823 the seven khanates of the South Caucasus, became part of the Georgian, the Muslim and the Caspian provinces of the Russian Empire and were no longer viewed as separate entities.

Following the Second Russo-Iranian War, when the entire South Caucasus became part of the Russian Empire, Russian officials viewed South Caucasus as a large colony, which supplied cash, grain, horses, and some local cavalrymen. In fact the aforementioned surveys conducted in 1819, 1820, 1823 and 1829–1832 all recommended a through examination of the assessments in order to increase the revenues collected by the local and central governments.

Between 1827 and 1868 local officials made every effort to comply with the above recommendations. First, they questioned the legal land ownership and tax-exempt status of individuals and families. Second, they inquired about the actual yield from the land. Third, they reinstated some of the indirect taxes, which had been abolished following the Russian annexation. The documentary evidence of the results was gathered from the archives of Moscow and especially from the Central Historical Archives in Leningrad (St. Petersburg) and appeared in two volumes.[68] Some of those relating to Shirvan appear in the appendix.

---

[65] The text includes a note that the amount should be 3 rubles and 57 kopeks and not 3 rubles.

[66] *Kolonial'naia politika*, I, 254–255.

[67] *Ibid.* I, 308.

[68] *Kolonialnaia politika rossiiskogo tsarizma v Azerbaidzhane v 20-60-kh gg. XIX v.*, 2 vols. (Moscow and Leningrad, 1936–1937). The main editors were N. G. Bogdanova and Ya. M. Pritykin who compiled them under the direction of the famed Orientalist I. P. Petrushevskii, who as I have noted (see page xv) use the term Azerbaijan, which does not appear anywhere in the five Russian surveys or any other Russian document or publication prior to the 20th century.

There is no doubt that Russia viewed much of the South Caucasus as a colony, which, in addition to cash, provided grain, silk, cotton. Despite the claim of imperial Russian historians and administrators, who stated that the region escaped backwardness and hardship and was transformed under the guidance of the enlightened Russian people, the abovementioned data, as well as the material in the appendix clearly demonstrate that the burden on the peasants continued and was, in fact, increased for the next five decades.

It is obvious that the Russian survey of the Shirvan khanate is less precise than a present-day census. In fact, even a modern day census cannot be 100% accurate. Nevertheless, the 1820 Russian survey, the second of its kind to be conducted in a former Iranian province (the first was conducted a year earlier in Sheki) provides valuable information on the demography and economy of Shirvan. In addition, the information on land tenure and the administration, although limited, is also important for those interested in the sociopolitical conditions in the South Caucasus in the last decades of Iranian and the early years of Russian rule.

Appendix

1

The Treaty Between Russia and Mostafa Khan of Shirvan December 25, 1805 [January 6, 1806]

We, that is, Mostafa Khan of Shirvan and Prince Paul Tsitsianov, General of the Infantry of the Russian Army and Inspector of the Caucasian Line, Commander-in-Chief of Georgia, and Astrakhan and the Military Governor of the Caucasus, Governor of all the provinces under his control and the Commander of the Caspian Flotilla, having been awarded the medals of Alexander Nevskii, Order of St. Vladimir, First class, and three classes of the order of St. George, and having been given full authority by His Imperial Majesty, the Sovereign Emperor Alexander Pavlovich, have, with God's help, made the following agreement by which Mostafa Khan of Shirvan and his entire family have sworn allegiance to the Russian Empire, to the Great Sovereign Emperor Alexander Pavlovich and to His Highness, the designated heir to the throne. We have agreed to the following articles:

Article I

I, Mostafa Khan of Shirvan, in my name and that of my heirs, remove myself forever from the vassalage or honors of Persia (Iran) or any other state. I declare before the entire world that I do not recognize anyone as my liege, except His Imperial Majesty, the Emperor of All the Russias and His heirs to the throne. I promise to be a loyal slave to that throne. I swear this by the Holy Qur'an.

Article II

His Imperial Majesty, the Emperor, on His part promises and affirms by His Imperial pledge and that of His heirs that they shall continue to favor and protect Mostafa Khan of Shirvan and his heirs from his coreligionists. His Imperial Majesty and His Heirs guarantee the integrity of the said domain, its ruler [khan] and his heirs.

Article III

His Excellency Mostafa Khan of Shirvan recognizes the suzerainty of His Imperial Majesty, the Emperor of All the Russias and His Heirs. It is agreed that the aforementioned khan and after him his eldest son and so forth, will rule the khanate and will receive the Imperial confirmation from the Commander-in-Chief of Georgia, with the Seal of the State. Upon receiving his copy, the khan will take a solemn oath of his loyalty to the Russian Empire and will recognize that he and his heirs are subjects of the Emperor of All the Russias. Mostafa Khan of Shirvan takes the formal oath in the presence and by the agreement of the Commander-in-Chief of Georgia.

Article IV

I, Mostafa Khan of Shirvan, as proof that my heirs and I are loyal subjects of the Russian Empire and recognizing the supremacy of that Empire, promise that, without the permission of the Commander-in-Chief of Georgia, we shall not communicate with any neighboring rulers. If any envoy or letters arrive from them containing important or unimportant matters, I shall forward them to the Commander-in-Chief of Georgia and seek his permission to respond. We shall not accept any letters from across the Arax (Aras)[1] River, from the *sardars* (commanders) of Baba Khan [Fath `Ali Shah], from Baba Khan himself, or from anyone else.All such letters and envoy will be sent to the commander of the Russian garrison in the fortress of Aresh in Nukha (Sheki).

Article V

His Imperial Majesty, in recognition that Mostafa Khan of Shirvan has become His subject, promises in His name and that of His heirs that: 1) He shall treat the people [of the khanate] in the same manner as other loyal subjects of the Russian Empire. 2) His Excellency Mostafa Khan and his progeny will continue to act as the khans of Shirvan. 3) The internal rule, the courts and administration, as well as the collection of the taxes will remain under the khan's jurisdiction. 4) The town of Salyan will remain part of Shirvan, since at the time of the signing of this treaty it is under Shirvan's control. In case of aggression from outside to seize it, Russia promises to assist Shirvan militarily.

Article VI

I, Mostafa Khan of Shirvan, as a sign of my loyalty promise: 1) To return to Ebrahim Khan of Karabagh all the Karabaghi families who have immigrated to Shirvan, but not those who had formerly lived in Shirvan, went to Karabagh and have then returned to

[1] Arax is in the original.

Shirvan. 2) To hand the town of Javad to Ebrahim Khan of Karabagh after he establishes his claim. 3) To safeguard the caravans traveling through Shirvan from Astrakhan to Georgia by providing an official escort and a convoy. 4) Since I control the part of the Kur River by Javad, it would be beneficial to fortify it. The Commander-in-Chief of Georgia will provide the necessary laborers.

Article VII

His Imperial Majesty, the Emperor, as a sign of His affection and benevolence toward His Excellency, Mostafa Khan of Shirvan, is presenting him and his heirs with medals containing the insignia of the Russian Empire, which they are obliged to keep as a sign of their authority. If they are called to join Russia in a war, no one except the khan can leave [the khanate].

Article VIII

I, Mostafa Khan of Shirvan, who, in the name of His Imperial Majesty, am authorized to collect the revenues [of Shirvan], promise to pay the treasury of His Imperial Majesty in Tiflis the sum of 8,000 *chervonets* [gold rubles] a year. The payment is to be in two installments, that is, half to be paid on February 1st (Ziqa'deh) and half on the first of September (Jamadi I) of each year. The first installment, that is, 4,000 *chervonets*, will be paid immediately after His Imperial Majesty confirms the treaty. In addition, following the Asiatic custom, I, as a sign of loyalty, promise to send hostages [to Tiflis]. Since I have no children and one of my brothers is blind and the other one is ill, I shall send Ahmad Aqa, Aqa Beg, Mukhay Beg, and Esma`il Beg for the first three months. At the conclusion of that period, in place of these four, I shall send the sons of the following high-ranking *begs*: Sheikh-`Ali Beg, `Omar-Soltan, and Mostafa Beg.

Article IX

His Imperial Majesty, as a sign of His kindness and as a favor, agrees to allocate ten silver Russian rubles a day for the livelihood of the four hostages.

Article X

This treaty is everlasting and is not subject to any alteration.

Article XI

His Imperial Majesty and His Excellency shall ratify this treaty by placing their seals on this document within six months, or sooner, if possible.

As a sign of trust, the above articles were signed and sealed in the camp of the ruler of Shirvan on Mount Chartmu in the year 1805 (corresponding to the Muslim year 1220) on December 25.

Affixed with the seal of Effendi Yahya of Shirvan.[2]

[2] The text of the treaty is included in report no. 51 from General Tsitsianov to Emperor Alexander I, dated December 27, 1805 [January 8, 1806); see A. Berzhe, ed. *Akty sobrannye Kavkazkoiu Arkheograficheskoiu Kommissieiu*, II (Tiflis, 1868), doc. no. 1366.

2

The Officials and Attendants that are required to Administer the Shirvan Province and their Salaries

18 [30] November 1819

For the City Court

The Commandant or Chairman of the City Court: 500 rubles, plus 500 rubles for food allowance and 200 rubles for office supplies, sealing wax and general expenses of the chancery, for a total of 1,200 rubles; 250 rubles each to the two Begs, who served as assessors/jury members, for a total of 500 rubles; 150 rubles each for the representatives of the people, one Tatar and one Armenian, for a total of 300 rubles; 30 rubles each for the night watchman and two guards, for a total of 90 rubles; 75 rubles to heat and light the court and paper.

Total: 2,165 rubles.

Staff Attached to the Commandant

For a clerk, who will also serve in the City Court, 200 rubles; for two translators: 150 rubles to the one who does written translations, 120 rubles to the one who does verbal translations; 10 couriers, who have to supply their own horses and their own expenses, 50 rubles each and exemption from taxes, for a total of 500 rubles; for 3 foot messengers to be dispatched around the city, 30 rubles each and exemption from taxes, for a total of 90 rubles; 350 rubles to the treasurer; and 150 rubles to his assistant.

Total: 1,560 rubles.

Grand Total: 3,725 rubles.[3]

[3] *Akty*, VI/1 (Tiflis, 1874), doc. no. 1209.

3

Lt.-Colonel Vadarskii to General Yermolov

23 August [September 4] 1820
Nukha [Sheki]

Today, I received two notes in the Tatar dialect [Persian], from Malek Aqa and Mostafa Beg of Aghdash [Sheki] (who were sent to the Khanate of Shirvan to inquire about the rumors of Mostafa Khan's flight). The first states: "Mostafa Khan has fled and left on Friday [September 1] after the noonday meal. His suite by the village of Mullah-kendi [on the bank of the Kur River crossing into the Mughan Steppe] consisted of some 300 individuals, 200 of whom were notables and the rest his *nokars*. They plan to seek refuge in Persia [Iran] with Ata Khan of Mishkin (Meshgin). Mostafa Khan did not have time to take his property or his herds."…[4]

[4] Ibid., doc. 1215.

4

List of the Family Members and Relatives of the Traitor Mostafa Khan Who Did Not Follow Him [to Iran] and Have Remained in Shirvan

The khan's wives

1. Fatemeh Begum, daughter of the blind Mohammad Hasan Khan of Sheki. Although she has been divorced from the khan for some 12 years, she has been treated with respect and has been given an income from two villages and a dye shop.
2. Pari-Jahan, the Daughter of Mohammad Sala Khan of Mughan. She quarreled with the khan and for the last two years has been living in Mughan.
3. Zembak, a commoner, who lives in Fitdagh. The two sons she bore for the khan were taken to Persia (Iran).
4. Zeynab, the daughter of Allahverdi, also a commoner, who lives in New Shamakhi.

Note: These last three wives of the khan are left without any subsistence.

The khan's daughters

Bibi Khanum, born last year to Nakhay, the daughter of Sorkhay. During the hurried flight of Mostafa Khan, she was abandoned in Sulut. She was taken by Captain Prince Makaev and was sent to be educated here.

Another daughter of the khan, also from the daughter of Sorkhay Khan, was born recently and has no name as yet. She was found in Sulut among the trampled and crushed equipage.

First cousins of the khan on his mother's side

1. Eskandar Beg; 2. Hajji `Ali Beg; 3. Mardan Beg (all of these men are loyal to the Russian State); 4. Hajji Ahmad Soltan; he did not take part in any of the khan's plans,

feigned sickness, and even before the khan's flight, he sent his sons to Captain Prince Makaev; 5. Mostafa Beg, a man loyal to Russia, the same person who, before the khan's flight, visited Your Excellency in Tiflis.

First cousins of the khan on his father's side

1. Aqa Reza Beg, who is married to the khan's sister Balash Khanum. Twelve years ago, Mostafa Khan took his sister away and drove this man away from his presence. Prior to his flight the khan showered him with kindness and returned his wife to him hoping that he would flee with him. But Aqa Reza refused to take her back. Mostafa Khan became enraged and took Balash Khanum and Aqa Reza's son Pasha Beg and his daughter, whose name is unknown, with him to Persia (Iran). 2. `Ali Naqi Beg, the blood brother of the above mentioned Aqa Reza Beg, who is also loyal to us; 3. Hoseyn Beg; 4. Shahbaz Beg; 5. Nuh Beg. Since these three brothers were the children of the sister of Qasem Khan, Mostafa Khan treated them badly. Prior to his flight he kept them with him under house arrest, with the intention of taking them to Persia (Iran) or to kill them if they refused. But on the day of his flight they managed to hide and present themselves to Captain Prince Makaev; 6. Ebrahim Khan Aqa, who had been an enemy of Mostafa Khan, for the latter treated him harshly. He was in constant contact with Captain Prince Makaev and informed him of the khan's actions. He is a very well intentioned person.

The khan's brother-in-law

Nowruz `Ali Beg, who is the brother of Kichkin, the khan's wife; Learning of the khan's flight, he armed the people of Alvand and did not permit the khan to cross the Kur River. He also repulsed the wife of his own brother, `Abdollah Beg, who was fleeing with the khan. He is a trustworthy person.

Those who fled with the khan abroad [to Iran]

The khan's legal wives

1. Nakhay, the daughter of the traitor Sorkhay Khan; 2. Kichkin, the daughter of Malek Mahmud of Alvand; 3. Golandam, an Armenian taken captive as a young girl from Georgia.

The khan's sons

1. Teymur Beg, born from Pari Jahan Khanum, the daughter of Mohammad Sala Khan of Mughan; 2. Ja`far Qoli Aqa; 3. Javad Beg; 4. Umma Khan, born to Golandam Khanum;

5. Aghasi Khan, a 3-year old, born to Narkhay, the daughter of Sorkhay Khan; 6. Allah Qoli; and 7. `Ali Qoli, both born from Armenian concubines, the first from Mineh, born in Karabagh, the second from Yasaman, born in Sheki.

The khan's daughters

1. Sara Begum, born from Kichkin; 2. Ummi-Selemeh; 3. Ma`sumeh, born from Golandam; 4. Badre-Jaha; and 5. Khiusii-Jahan, born from Golandam.

Note: All the khan's daughters are maidens.

The khan's brother

Esma`il Beg, who fled with his two sons: Zolfaqar Beg and Ahmad Beg.

The khan's sisters

1. Zeyveh Khanum (maiden); 2. Nisa Khanum (widow), who fled with her son Qader Beg; 3. Sazdet Khanum; 4. Balash Khanum.

The khan's brothers-in-law

1. Qasem Beg, who fled with his son Ismi Bala Soltan; 2. Aqa Kishi Beg, who fled with his entire family.

The khan's first cousins on his mother's side

1. `Ali Beg who fled with his entire family; 2. Khanjan Beg, who fled with his entire family; and his nephew, Mehdi Beg, who also took his entire family.

The grandchildren of the khan's aunt

1. Salim Soltan, who also took his entire family; 2. Lotf `Ali Beg; 3. Mirza `Ali Beg; 4. Ata Kishi Beg. These last three are not married.

Note: Their mother, her daughter and their sisters refused to follow the khan and remained here.

In addition, 31 *begs* and 51 officials fled with the khan to Persia (Iran). Ten of the *begs* and 15 of the officials took their entire families with them.[5]

[5] *Ibid.*, doc. no. 1221.

5

Madatov and Mogilevskii to Yermolov

No 24, September 21 [October 3], 1820
Fitdagh

…According to the information from Lieutenant Kuznetsov, there are 12,224 rams, sheep, and lambs belonging to the khan and the Begs who fled with him. We have summoned interested buyers from Kuba, Nukha (Sheki) and Karabagh. Tomorrow we begin the first sale and if the prices are profitable for the treasury we will sell all but 2,545 animals, which belong to Malek Umud Beg. We ask you to determine whether we should sell this last group, as well as the cattle and horses belonging to the *beg*, or whether they should go to his relatives. This is because Umud Beg was forced by the khan to flee and wishes to return and his relatives, which include Kombai, his brother-in-law and nephew, who have remained here, are known for their loyalty to the Russian State.[6]

[6] *Ibid.*, doc. no. 1225.

6

Report of Prince Madatov and Councilor Mogilevskii to Yermolov

No. 34, October 16, 1820
Fitdagh

We have sent the remaining wives of the traitor Mostafa Khan and those of his relatives, as well as the wives of the *begs* and *yüzbaşis* who fled with him, to Persia (Iran). We have the honor to submit the list to Your Excellency for your consideration.

List

Mostafa Khan's wife: Pari Jahan, the daughter of Mohammad Sala Khan of Mughan.

Yasaman and Mineh, both commoners, whom the khan had left some time ago; they have boys who were taken by Mostafa Khan to Persia (Iran).

Mostafa Khan's daughter, Hajji Bike; she was born to Nakhay, the daughter of Sorkhay Khan. She has a child who is a year and a half and was sent with a nanny, who has to return.

Mostafa Khan's sister, Khadija Khanum, who is Qasem Beg's wife, with her five daughters and a 3-year-old son. Since she is the aunt of the underage daughter of Mostafa Khan, Hajji Beke, the child is under her care during the journey.

Zohra Khanum, the mother of the children of `Omar Soltan and her daughter.

The wife of `Ali Beg, the first cousin of Mostafa Khan on his mother's side, together with her daughter and a three-year-old son.

Baghesh Beg, their 6-month-old son.

`Abdollah Beg's common wife, with her 6-month-old son and her 5-year-old daughter.

The wives of `Abdollah Beg's two brothers, the first has two daughters, the second, one daughter.

The mother and sister of Shukur, the brother-in-law of Mostafa Khan, who also fled with him.

The wife of Hajji Baba Beg and her 1-year old son.

The wife of the *yüzbaşi* of Khanchoban, Shai` Ogli `Abdollah, with an undetermined number of her children.

The wife of the *yüzbaşi* of Khanchoban, Mohammad Amin Arab, with an undetermined number of her children.

The wife of the *yüzbaşi* Gerrus Vali.

The *nazer* of Shukur, Qasem, was allowed to leave because his wife was taken to Persia (Iran).

The *nokar* of Tari-verdi, Mohammad Beg, was also sent because his wife was taken to Persia (Iran).

Soltan Kurd, the *nazer* of the khan's sister, Zeyveh Khanum, the son of Soleyman who had also fled to Persia (Iran) and two wives were also sent to Persia (Iran).

Altogether: 36 persons.[7]

[7] *Ibid.*, doc. no. 1229.

7

Register of the Villages in the Sedenrud Mahal in 1828, which had belonged to Qasem Beg and were confiscated by the Provincial Treasury after his Flight to Iran in 1820

1. Qazyan

Tax-paying families: 60. Tax-exempt families: 18.
Tribute: 28 gold rubles, as well as 2 rubles and 60 kopeks in local money.[8]
Silk workshops: 12 rubles in local money.
For the 100 oxen: 18 rubles in local money.
Total in Russian currency: 103 rubles and 50 kopeks.

Sursat: 27 *batmans* of wheat.
Darughegy: 20 *taghars* of rice and 24 *stils* of silk.
Mal-o-jehat: 10 *taghars* and 15 *batmans* of rice, 5 *batmans*[9] and 7 *stils* of silk.

The tax-exempt are *ranjbars* belonging to the treasury, who work in the silk orchards and rice paddies.

2. Bığır

Tax-paying families: 42. Tax-exempt families: 4.
Tribute: 75 gold rubles and 3 rubles in local money.
Silk workshops: 12 rubles in local money.
For the 100 oxen: 12 rubles and 60 kopeks in local money.
Total in Russian currency: 241 rubles and 56 kopeks.

Sursat: 1 *taghar* of wheat.

---

[8] It seems that either the local money was still in use or that they were assessed by the old exchange rate of 1 ruble and 60 kopeks of local money for 1 ruble in Russian currency.

[9] Text reads *taghars* in error, for the total appears in *batmans*.

Darughegy: 3 *taghars* of rice and 24 *stils* of silk.
Mal-o-jehat: 4 *taghars* and 1½ *batmans* of rice and 22 *batmans* and 7¼ *stils* of silk.

3. Êlikənd

Tax-paying families: 10. Tax-exempt families: 2.
Tribute: 12 gold rubles and 3 rubles in local money.
For the 100 oxen: 3 rubles in local money.
Total in Russian currency: 37 rubles and 80 kopeks.

Sursat: 8 *batmans* of wheat.
Darughegy: 1 *taghar* of rice and 5 *stils* of silk.
Mal-o-jehat: 11 *stils* of silk.

4. Shefi-Bek (The 1820 survey reads Shikhi-Bek (Şıxbəy)

Tax-paying families: 7. Tax-exempt families: 2.
Tribute: 6 gold rubles and 1 ruble and 60 kopeks in local money.
For the 100 oxen: 2 rubles and 10 kopeks in local money.
Total in Russian currency: 20 rubles and 22 kopeks.

Sursat: 4½ *batmans* of wheat.
Darughegy: 15 *batmans* of rice and 2 *stils* of silk.
Mal-o-jehat: 13 *batmans* of rice and 10 *stils* of silk.

5. Mollahacılı

Tax-paying families: 13. Tax-exempt families: 2

Darughegy: 2 *batmans* of rice.
Mal-o-jehat: 26 *batmans* of rice.

The village has 11 *ranjbars* belonging to the treasury.

6. Qaraxıdır

Tax-paying families: 10. Tax-exempt families: 3.

Tribute: 8 gold rubles and 2 rubles in local money.
Silk workshops: 2 rubles in local money.
For the 100 oxen: 3 rubles in local money.
Total in Russian currency: 28 rubles and 20 kopeks.
Sursat: 7 *batmans* of wheat.
Darughegy: 1 *taghar* of rice and 5 *stils* of silk.
Mal-o-jehat: 12½ *batmans* of rice and 5½ *stils* of silk.

7. Danabasan [survey reads Danibasan]-Turkedzhi

Tax-paying families: 10. Tax-exempt families: 3.
Tribute: 12 gold rubles and 3 rubles in local money.
For the 100 oxen: 3 rubles in local money.
Total in Russian currency: 39 rubles and 60 kopeks.

Sursat: 9 *batmans* of wheat.
Darughegy: 20 *batmans* of rice and 2 *stils* of silk.
Mal-o-jehat: 2 *taghars* and 16 *batmans* of rice and 19¼ *stils* of silk.

8. Məlikkənd and Alpı

Tax-paying families: 4. Tax-exempt families: 35.
Tribute: 6 gold rubles, as well as 1 ruble and 60 kopeks in local money.
For the 100 oxen: 1 ruble and 20 kopeks in local money.
Total in Russian currency: 19 rubles and 68 kopeks

Sursat: 4½ *batmans* of wheat.
Darughegy: 10 *batmans* of rice and 2 *stils* of silk.
Mal-o-jehat: 4½ *stils* of silk.

9. Kelbend

Tax-paying families: 24. Tax-exempt families: 0.
Dues in cash (in place of *kharaj*): 36 Russian rubles.
For the 100 oxen: 7 rubles and 20 kopeks in local money.
Total in Russian currency: 40 rubles and 32 kopeks.

Sursat: 33 *batmans* of wheat.
Darughegy: 1 *taghar* and 30 *batmans* of wheat, 1 *taghar* and 24 *batmans* of barley.
Mal-o-jehat: 5 *taghars* of wheat, 19 *batmans* of barley, 12 *batmans* of millet.

10. Kürd

Tax-paying families: 20. Tax-exempt families: 0.

Note: The inhabitants of this village, due to poverty, paid no taxes to Qasem Beg. It was decided that if they remained in Shirvan they had to be assessed or be moved to the Sheki Province, their original place of residence. However, since in 1821 they all fled back to the Sheki Province, they are not listed in Shirvan's tax-rolls.

11. Xalillı

Tax-paying families: 45. Tax-exempt families: 0.
Dues in cash: 90 Russian rubles.
For the 100 oxen: 13 rubles and 50 kopeks in local money.
Total in Russian currency: 98 rubles and 10 kopeks.

Sursat: 1 *taghar* of wheat.

12. Küçeçedy

Tax-paying families: 0. Tax-exempt families: 12.

13. Mırtı

Tax-paying families: 30. Tax-exempt families: 0.
Dues in cash: 75 Russian rubles.
For the 100 oxen: 9 rubles and 20 in local money.
Total in Russian currency: 80 rubles and 40 kopeks.

Sursat: 45 *batmans* of wheat.

14. Çiyni

Tax-paying families: 19. Tax-exempt families: 9.
They are *ranjbars* working on silk farms.
Darughegy: 5 *taghars* of rice and 19 *stils* of silk.

15. Şah-arxi

Tax-paying families: 24. Tax-exempt families: 1.
They are *ranjbars* working on silk farms.

Darughegy: 9½ *stils* of silk.

Translator's Note: The village of Çaxırlı, which also belonged to Qasem Beg, is not listed. This village, together with the rest, was given as the toyul of a Muslim cleric (see below).

Totals:

Tax-paying families: 314.
Tax-exempt families: 91.
Tribute: 147 gold rubles and 13 rubles and 70 kopeks in local money.
Silk workshops: 26 rubles in local money.
Additional dues in Russian rubles: 201.
Annual dues for the oxen: 72 rubles and 60 kopeks in local money.
Total in cash dues in Russian currency: 709 rubles and 38 kopeks.

Sursat: 4 *taghars* and 38 *batmans* of wheat.
Darughegy: 1 *taghar* and 30 *batmans* of wheat; 1 *taghar* and 24 *batmans* of barley; 33 *taghars* and 15 *batmans* of rice; and 1 *batman* and 44½ *stils* of silk.
Mal-o-jehat: 5 *taghars* of wheat, 19 *batmans* of barley, 18 *taghars* and 24 *batmans* of rice, 12 *batmans* of millet, and 8 *batmans* and 36½ *stils* of silk.

The above villages gave 11 *taghars* and 18 *batmans* of wheat; 2 *taghars* and 3 *batmans* of barley; 12 *batmans* of millet; 52 *taghars* and 9 *batmans* of rice; and 10 *batmans* and 33 *stils* of silk.

Note: There are 70 silk orchards in the above villages, which belonged to the fugitive

Qasem Beg. They produce 23 *batmans* and 36 *stils*, 26 *zolotniks*[10] and 17½ *nokhod*[11] of silk annually, which equals 14 *puds*, 28 *funts* and 11 *zolotniks* in Russian weight. There are also 2½ mills, which bring an income of 8 *taghars* of wheat, 31 vineyards and fruit orchards, bringing an income of 610 Russian rubles and rice paddies producing 680 *taghars* of rice for the treasury. The total when converted to cash is 4,040 rubles and 6 kopeks in Russian currency. After combining it with the cash dues, the total collected by the treasury is 5,359 rubles and 44 kopeks in Russian currency.

The original document is signed by Colonel Miklashevskii and attested by Court Councilor Sluchevskii.[12]

Translator's Note: It is interesting to note that a decade after the Russian annexation, the number of tax-paying and tax-exempt families remained basically the same. The Russian administration continued to collect the tribute, sursat, mal-o-jehat and darughegy. In fact, as can be seen from the table below, the province collected 86,593 rubles and 83 kopeks in Russian currency in 1829, some 6,572 rubles more than the total revenues in 1820 (80,021 rubles and 86½ kopeks). The Russian annexation, therefore, not only did not decrease the burden on the population, but, following Madatov's and Mogilevskii's advice, the tax-rolls were examined and the revenues increased.

[10] Refers to the Iranian *mesqal* (1 troy ounce).

[11] Refers to the Iranian weight of approximately 1 gram.

[12] I. P. Petrushevskii, N. G. Bogdanova, and Ya. M. Pritykin, eds. *Kolonial'naia politika Rossiiskogo Tsarizma v Azerbaidzhane v 20–60-kh gg. XIX v.* (Moscow and Leningrad, 1936), I, 434–435. By the order of Tsar Nicholas I, dated August 13 (25), 1831 the income from the above villages was given to the *mojtahed* Aqa Mir-Fattah, for his services to Russia during the Second Russo-Iranian War on General Paskevich's request, *ibid.*, II 313. This Muslim cleric, who was responsible for the surrender of Tabriz to the Russians, also received the order of St. Anne, first class. The *mojtahed* established himself in the village of Çaxırlı (which had also belonged to Qasem Beg) and set the following rules over the villagers: 1) No Shi'i could marry the daughter of a Sunni and no Sunni could marry the daughter of a Shi'i. 2) No girl could marry an outsider, unless the man settled in her village. 3) The parents cannot marry their daughters without my permission. 4) It is forbidden to seduce girls. 5) It is forbidden to entice girls. 6) Unless a person has written permission, he cannot stay more than 7 days in the village. 8) Stealing is forbidden in the villages. 9) Trade is strictly forbidden in the villages; it should be conducted in the central bazaar. If anyone breaks any of the above regulations they shall be fined 500 Shirvani coins and 500 strikes. If the local *yüzbaşis* does not follow these statues he should be subject to the same punishment, *ibid.*, 314.

8
The Revenues of the Shirvan province for the year 1829

a) Revenues in cash:

1. Tribute: 8,854 gold rubles.

The above is the tribute to be paid by Mostafa Khan to Russia, according to the treaty signed by the Russian State and Mostafa Khan. After his flight and the Russian annexation, the tribute was collected from the population.[13] In recent times, some villages, which did not pay the tribute, were assessed anew. From this sum, 24,000 silver rubles go to the treasury.

2. Special taxes from the two villages populated by gypsies: 370 rubles in local money.

3. Newly established taxes: 1,302 rubles and 14 kopeks in Russian currency.

4. From the orchards: 468 rubles and 14 kopeks in local money.

From the nomads the following dues in cash are collected in place of the produce and merchandize, which they gave the khan.

5. Butter: 674 rubles and 50 kopeks.

6. Cheese: 44 rubles and 77½ kopeks.

7. Rugs: 266 rubles and 40 kopeks.

8. Horsecloths: 125 rubles and 40 kopeks.

9. Straw: 140 rubles and 80 kopeks (see no. 14).

10. Silk farms: 244 rubles.

Total [not counting nos. 1, 3, 9 and 10] 1,964 rubles and 16 kopeks in local money.[14]

---

[13] The tribute, as noted, was 8,000 gold rubles, or 24,000 silver rubles. Russia thus not only continued to collect the tribute, but also collected more than the agreed sum.

[14] The total, some 1,950 local rubles, does not agree with the above.

The assessment and collection of taxes is as follows: Each year officials go to the *mahals* and villages and determine the number of households with the help of the *yüzbaşi* or *kadkhoda* (village elder). They collect the revenue at the appropriate time and then the *kadkhoda* and other elders take it to the provincial court and receive a receipt (signed by the finance office describing, in detail, the amount) as indicated in the table. At present, only 9,262 households pay an average of 3 Russian rubles and 4 kopeks each in cash in round numbers. However, some in the *mahals* pay from 2 to 5 rubles and 25 kopeks per household. As for taxes in produce, each household pays 4 rubles and 80 kopeks in round numbers.

11. Silk workshops: 56 rubles in local money.
12. The taxes for plows: 264 rubles.

These two dues in cash are collected in place of the revenues collected for the *darughehs*, who were appointed by the khan to supervise the villages.

13. Firewood and charcoal: 49 rubles.
14. In addition to the above dues for straw, 15 rubles in cash.

Total: 541 rubles and 12 kopeks in local money.

15. Cash dues: 162 rubles and 175 rubles and 78 kopeks in local money.

The above dues were collected for the khan's *mirzas*. That is from 60 kopeks to 1 ruble for each plow and each *taghar* of grain.

16. *Juft-bashi* (a plow with two oxen): 1,671 rubles and 25 kopeks.
17. *Taghar-bashi* (tax for each *taghar* of grain) 334 rubles and 14 kopeks.
18. For the 100 oxen: 2,503 rubles and 17⅓ kopeks. The khan collected this tax from the entire province.

Total: 4,508 rubles and 36⅓ kopeks in local money.

The total direct taxes in cash: 32,926 rubles and 97.11/23 kopeks.

According to the report submitted to the Minister of Finance on November 30 (December 12), 1833, the total cash revenues including the *juft-bashi* came to 31,187 rubles and 29 kopeks in Russian currency, minus 1,739 rubles and 68½ ⅓ kopeks (in the original).

b) Revenues in kind:

1. *Sursat*: 130 *taghars* and 18 *batmans* of wheat; 5 *taghars* and 22 *batmans* of barley.

The treasury collected this from all the villages.

2. *Darughegy*: 4 *batmans* and 40 *stils* of silk; 80 *taghars* and 10 *batmans* of rice; 39 *taghars* and 38 *batmans* of wheat; 62 *taghars* and 34¾ *batmans* of barley.

The *darughehs* took the above as their salary. At present some 56 villages pay this to various individuals who have no right to collect it.

3. *Mal-o-jehat*: 46 *batmans* and 8½ *stils* of silk; 38 *batmans* and 22 *stils* of cotton; 476 *taghars* and 43 *batmans* of wheat; 62 *taghars* and 12 *batmans* of rice; 177 *taghars* and 29½ *batmans* of barley; 25 *taghars* and 37½ *batmans* of millet.

The inhabitants (not all) gave from one-fifth to one-tenth of the harvest. Except for the inhabitants of the Rudbar, Mughan and Khanchoban *mahals*, all others paid the *mal-o-jehat*. Sixty-nine villages give the *mal-o-jehat* to certain individuals. Everyone who is subject to taxation has to give the *mal-o-jehat* to the treasury; however, there are villages, which do not pay it.

Total revenues in kind:

Silk: 51 *batmans* and ½ a *stil* (31 *puds* and 9 *funts*), worth 34 rubles and 20 kopeks per *batman*: 1,744 rubles and 55¾ kopeks.
Cotton: 38 *batmans* and 22 *stils* (19 *puds* and a ¼ *funt*), worth 3 rubles per *batman*: 116 rubles and 75 kopeks.
Wheat: 646 *taghars* and 49 *batmans* (16,175 *puds*), worth 12 rubles per *taghar*: 7,440 rubles and 24 kopeks.
Rice: 142 *taghars* and 22 *batmans* (2,141 *puds*), worth 3 rubles per *taghar*: 428 rubles and 20 kopeks.
Barley: 246 *taghars* and 61¼ *batmans* (4,923 *puds* and 10 *funts*), worth 6 rubles per *taghar*: 1,475 rubles and 95 kopeks.
Millet: 25 *taghars* and 37½ *batmans* (393 *puds* and 30 *funts*), worth 10 rubles and 30 kopeks per *taghar*: 267 rubles and 15¾ kopeks.

Total: 11,473 rubles and 85½ kopeks.

The dues in kind are collected in the following manner: At the beginning of the harvest, 3 or 4 men are sent to each *mahal*, who, together with the *nayeb*, check the total harvest and determine the *mal-o-jehat*. They also record the number of plows. After that, the *qesmdars* (men responsible for each sector/portion) submit the required amount of the *mal-o-jehat* to the commandant's office with their signature. After that the cash dues for the *juft-bashi* and the *taghar-bashi* are collected.

Thus, the tax assessment for the above is not examined further and depends totally on the *gesmdars*. In fact, the *mal-o-jehat* collected in 1829 was around 477 *taghars* of wheat, 178 *taghars* of barley, 62 *taghars* of rice, 39 *batmans* of cotton and 46 *batmans* of silk, which is very low. Actually, the Shirvan Province annually produces 77,000 *taghars* of wheat, 16,000 *taghars* of rice, 7,500 *batmans* of cotton, 2,500 *taghars* of millet, 18,000 *taghars* of barley and 3,900 *puds* of silk. Even if we assume that one-fourth of the population has to pay taxes (which is very low indeed), then the revenues should be 1,925 *taghars* of wheat, 450 *taghars* of barley, 750 *taghars* of rice, 62½ *taghars* of millet, 375 *batmans* of cotton, and some 168 *puds* of silk. The number of plows is also inaccurate. The whole system is impossible to examine. The *mal-o-jehat*, *juft-bashi* and *taghar-bashi* should be eliminated. The inhabitants have asked that a permanent tax be established. If we do this, the revenues will be considerably more.

According to the new survey, the Shirvan Province, excluding the *begs*, clergy, residents in the cities and towns (who do not pay taxes), state *ranjbars*, *mirabs* and *baghbans*, has 18,444 households, of which only 9,262 households pay taxes of 3 rubles and 4 kopeks each in cash and 4 rubles and 80 kopeks in kind. If we collect dues from the other 8,582 households, the treasury will gain 26,099 rubles and 28 kopeks in cash, for a total of 42,193 kopeks. Thus when we add the 44,400 rubles and 83½ kopeks in cash and kind taxes in the table, the total received by the treasury will be 86, 593 rubles and 83 kopeks.

Collegiate Councilor Kalinovskii[15]

---

[15] *Kolonial'naia politika*, I, 451–457.

Select Bibliography

Abe, N. "Preserving a Qajar Estate: Analysis of Fath `Ali Khan Donboli's 'Property Retention Tactics'," *Studia Iranica*, 43, 2014.

Akty sobrannye Kavkazskoiu Arkheograficheskoiu Kommissieiu [Official Documents of the Viceroyalty of the Caucasus]. 12 vols. Tiflis, 1868–1912.

Allen, W. E D. & P. Muratoff, *Caucasian Battlefields*. Cambridge,1953.

Asnadi az ravabet-e Iran ba mantaqe-ye qafqaz [Documents of Iran's Relations with the Caucasus]. Tehran, 1993.

Atkin, M. *Russia and Iran, 1780–1828*. Minneapolis, 1980.

Avery, P. "An Enquiry into the Outbreak of the Second Russo-Persian War, 1826–1829." In *Iran and Islam*. Edinburgh, 1971.

Baddeley, John. *The Russian Conquest of the Caucasus*. New York, 1969.

Bakikhanov, `Abbas Qoli Aqa. *Golestan-e Eram: based on the critical text by A. Alizade*. Baku, 1970 (reprinted in Tehran 1383/2004).

Bamdad, M. *Sharh-e hal-e rejal-e Iran dar qarn-e 12, 13, va 14 hejri* [A List of Iranian Notables in the 12–14th Centuries of the Hejri Calendar]. 6 vols. Tehran, 1968.

Bosworth, C. E. "Arran." *Encyclopedia Iranica*, II (1986), 520–522.

Bournoutian, George A. *The Khanate of Erevan under Qajar Rule, 1795–1828*. New York, 1992.

______. *Russia and the Armenians of Transcaucasia, 1797–1889: A Documentary Record*. Costa Mesa, CA, 1998.

______. *Armenians and Russia, 1626–1796: A Documentary Record*. Costa Mesa, CA, 2001.

______. *The Journal of Zak`aria of Agulis*. Costa Mesa, CA, 2003.

______. *Two Chronicles on the History of Karabagh*. Costa Mesa, CA, 2004.

______. *The 1823 Russian Survey of the Karabagh Province: A Primary Source on the Demography and Economy of Karabagh in the Early 19th Century*. Costa Mesa, CA, 2012.

______. *From Tabriz to St. Petersburg: Iran's Mission of Apology to Russia in 1829*. Costa Mesa, CA, 2014.

______. *The 1819 Russian Survey of the Khanate of Sheki [Shakki]: A Primary Source on the Demography and Economy of an Iranian Province prior to its Annexation by Russia*. Costa Mesa, CA, 2016.

______. *The 1829-1832 Russian Surveys of the Khanate of Nakhichevan [Nakhjavan]: A Primary Source on the Demography and Economy of an Iranian Province prior to its Annexation by Russia*. Costa Mesa, CA, 2016.

Butkov, P. G. *Materialy dlia novoi istorii Kavkaza, s' 1722 po 1803* [Sources for a New History of the Caucasus from 1722 to 1803]. 3 vols. St. Petersburg, 1869.

Cambridge History of Iran. Vol. VII. Cambridge, 1991.

Donboli, *`Abd or-Razzaq Beg Maftun ibn Najaf Qoli Khan, Ma'ser-e Soltaniyeh*. Tehran, 1972.

Dubrovin, N. F. *Zakavkaz'e ot 1803–1806 goda* [Transcaucasia from 1803 to 1806]. St. Petersburg, 1866.

______. *Georgii XII poslednii tsar Gruzii i prisoedinenie eia k Rossii* [Giorgi XII, the Last King of Georgia and its Unification with Russia]. St. Petersburg, 1867.

______. *Istoriia voiny i vladychestva russkikh na Kavkaze* [History of the Wars and Russian Rule in the Caucasus]. 6 vols. St. Petersburg, 1871–1888.

Evetskii, O. *Statisticheskoe opisanie Zakavkazskogo kraia*. St. Petersbrug, 1835.

Farasti, R. *Farmanha va raqamha-ye dowreh-ye Qajar* [The Decrees of the Qajar Era]. Vol. I. Tehran, 1993.

Geograficheskii Atlas Azerbaidzhanskoi SSR [Geographical Atlas of Soviet Azerbaijan]. Moscow, 1990.

Grigor'ev, V. *Statisticheskoe opisanie Nakhichevanskoi provintsii* [A Statistical Survey of the Nakhichevan Province]. St. Petersburg, 1833.

Hedayat, Reza Qoli Khan. *Tarikh-e Rouzat ol-Safa-ye Naseri*. Vol. IX. Tehran, 1961.

Hurewitz, J. C. *Diplomacy in the Near and Middle East: A Documentary Record: 1535–1914*. 2 vols. Princeton, 1956.

Ibragimbeili, Kh. M. *Rossiia i Azerbaidzhan v pervoi treti XIX veka* [Russia and Azerbaijan in the First Third of the 19th Century]. Moscow, 1969.

Ismail-Zade, D. I. *Naselenie gorodov Zakavkazskogo kraia v XIX–nachale XX v.* (The Population of the Transcaucasian Cities in the XIX and early-XX Centuries). Moscow, 1991.

Jahangir Mirza. *Tarikh-e Nou* [New History]. Tehran, 1948.

Kazemzadeh, F. "Russian Penetration of the Caucasus." T. Hunczak ed., *Russian Imperialism from Ivan the Great to the Revolution*. New Brunswick, 1974.

Kotzebue, M. von. *Narrative of a Journey into Persia in the Suite of the Imperial Russian Embassy in the Year 1817*. London, 1819.

Krymskii, A. E. "Stranitsy iz istorii severnogo ili Kavkazskogo Azerbeidzhana (klassicheskoi Albanii)," *Sbornik statei k piatidesiatiletiiu nauchno-obshchestvennoi deiatel'nosti Sergeio Fedorovichu Ol'denburgu* [Pages from the History of Northern or Caucasian Azerbaijan (Classical Albania)]. Leningrad, 1934.

Lambton, A. K. S. *Landlord and Peasant in Persia*. Oxford, 1953.

Lang, D. M. *The Last Years of the Georgian Monarchy, 1658–1832*. New York, 1957.

Lornejad, S. & Doostzadeh, A. *On the Modern Politicization of the Persian Poet Nezami Ganjavi*. Yerevan, 2012.

Meredith, C. "The Qajar Response to Russia's Military Challenge, 1804–1828." Ph.D. diss. Princeton University, 1973.

Minorsky, V. Tadhkirat Al-Muluk. *A Manual of Safavid Administration*. London, 1943.

______. *Studies in Caucasian History*. London, 1953.

______. *A History of Sharvan and Darband in the 10th–11th Centuries*. Cambridge, 1958.

______. "Caucasica IV: Sahl ibn Sunbat of Shakki and Arran. The Caucasian Vassals of Marzuban in 344/955," in *The Turks, Iran and the Caucasus in the Middle Ages* (London, 1978), 504–529.

Mirza Mohammad Taqi (Lesan ol-Molk/Sepehr). *Nasekh ot-Tavarikh*. 2 vols. Tehran, 1966.

Mohammad Hasan Khan (E`temad os-Saltaneh). *Tarikh-e Montazam-e Naseri*. 3 vols. Tehran, 1985–1988.

Opisanie Shekinskoi Provintsii, sostavlennoe v' 1819 godu [The Survey of the Sheki Province Conducted in 1819]. Tiflis, 1866.

Opisanie Shirvanskoi Provintsii, sostavlennoe v' 1820 godu [The Survey of the Shirvan Province Conducted in 1820]. Tiflis, 1867.

Opisanie Karabagskoi Provintsii sostavlennoe v' 1823 godu [The Survey of the Karabagh Province Conducted in 1823]. Tiflis, 1866.

Pagirev', D. D. *Alfavitnyi ukazatel' k' piativerstnoi karte Kavkazskago kraia, izdaniia Kavkazskago Voenno-Topograficheskago Otdela* [Alphabetical Index of the Caucasus]. Tiflis, 1913.

Petrushevskii, I. P, N. G. Bogdanova and Ya. M. Pritykin, eds. *Kolonial'naia politika rossiiskogo tsarizma v Azerbaidzhane v 20–60-kh gg. XIX v.* [The Colonial Policy of Tsarist Russia in Azerbaijan in the 1820s–1860s]. 2 parts. Moscow-Leningrad, 1936–1937.

Petrushevskii, I. P. *Ocherki po istorii feodalnykh otnoshenii v Azerbaidzhane i Armenii v xvi–nachale xix vv* [Studies on the History of the Feudal Conditions in Azerbaijan and Armenia from the 16th to the beginning of the 19th Centuries]. Leningrad, 1949.

Pogodin, M. "Aleksei Petrovich Ermolov: Materialy dlia ego biografii." *Russkii Vestnik*, XI, 1863.

Potto, V. *Kavkazskaia voina v otdel'nykh ocherkakh, epizodakh, legendakh, i biografiiakh* [The Caucasian War in Separate Accounts, Legends and Biographies]. 4 vols. St. Petersburg and Tiflis, 1885–1888.

Quzanlu, J. *Tarikh-e nezami-ye Iran* [Iran's Military History]. 2 vols. Tehran, 1934.

Rhinelander, L. H. 'The Incorporation of the Caucasus into the Russian Empire: The Case of Georgia, 1801–1854." Ph.D. diss., Columbia University, 1972.

Shopen (Chopin), I. *Istoricheskii pamiatnik sostoianiia Armianskoi Oblasti v epokhu eia prisoedineniia k Rossiiskoi imperii* [A Historical Survey of the Conditions of the Armenian Province at the Time of Its Unification with the Russian Empire]. St. Petersburg, 1852.

Tajbakhsh, A. *Tarikh-e ravabet-e Iran va Rus dar nimeh-ye avval-e qarn-e nuzadahom* [The History of Russo-Iranian Relations in the first Half of the Nineteenth century]. Tabriz, 1958.

Troynitskii, N. A. ed. *Pervaia vseobshchaia perepis' naseleniia Rossiiskoi Imperii* [First General Survey of the Population of the Russian Empire]. St. Petersburg, 1905

Yilmaz, Harun. "A Family Quarrel: Azerbaijani Historians against Soviet Iranologists," *Journal of the International Society for Iranian Studies*, volume 48, no. 5, September 2015, 769–783.

Yuzefovich, T. *Dogovory Rossii s Vostokom: Politicheskie i Torgovye* [Russian Treaties with the East: Political and Commercial]. St. Petersburg, 1869.